Will Work
for
Food or $

Will Work for Food or $

A Memoir from the Roadside

Bruce Moody

Red Wheel
Boston, MA / York Beach, ME

First published in 2003 by
Red Wheel/Weiser, LLC
York Beach, ME
With offices at:
368 Congress Street
Boston, MA 02210
www.redwheelweiser.com

Cataloging-in-Publication Data available upon request from the Library of
Congress.

Typeset in Minion and Frutiger by Grace Peirce
Printed in the United States of America

Maple Vail

10 09 08 07 06 05 04 03
 8   7   6   5   4   3   2   1

The paper used in this publication meets the minimum requirements of the
American National Standard for Information Sciences—Permanence of Paper
for Printed Library Materials Z39.48-1992 (R1997).

To my dear sister and friend
Kathleen Mary Moody LaMarsh

You're not too fat.
You're not too old.
You're not too stupid.
Go for it!

—Arlene Huntington, age 89

Note to Readers

Except for family and close friends, all names, distinguishing characteristics, and locations have been changed.

New Year's Day, 5 P.M.

I walk down the street toward the freeway exit. On the left a tall embankment holds weeds and pale dirt. The sidewalk is unshaded by any tree, unbordered by grass. It is one of those public ways that is no one's direct responsibility, and no one cares for it.

I walk in the late sunshine in a town which I have chosen as far enough from my own that I won't be recognized. I am fortunate to do this in a place that has mild weather, Contra Costa County in the East Bay of San Francisco.

I feel a bruise. It is a bruise not from the outside, but from within, which I feel in the bones of my chest, in my head, and which has something to do with crying. Not that I need to cry, but that it is useless to cry. I would say my life hurts, at this moment, as I walk toward what I have resolved to do. It hurts like a fate. It hurts because I have had to resolve to do it. It hurts because wishing it could be otherwise is useless.

I don't want to be seen. I would be ashamed for anyone who knows me to see me. And I would be ashamed for anyone who doesn't know me to see me. But they have to see me in order for me to do it.

I come to the end of the pavement. I am standing where the off-ramp traffic stops. I push the crossing button. I am holding my breath in the top of my lungs. Once I cross I will be committed. So as not to be seen by the cars, I keep my eyes lowered. The light changes. I cross, still not looking at the cars, now stopped. I don't want to be part of them until I am a part of them.

Once across, I walk halfway down the off-ramp toward the freeway. I stop and swing off my backpack. I put it on the ground. I take out two cardboard signs. In the backpack I had put the signs and two bungees and an old white towel, nothing else. I had bought a fresh magic-marker especially to letter these signs. I do all this as a ritual. I feel that all this is degrading if it is not sacred, at least it ought to be treated as maybe sacred, not a disgrace, although it is a disgrace, but still, even as a disgrace, sacred.

I set the backpack so it stands upright. I strap one sign against it with a bungee to keep the wind from taking it.

I walk halfway back up toward the street, Appian Way. I fold the towel and spread it on the dirt. I sit on it cross-legged, the other sign on my knees. Then I raise my eyes to the traffic that is coming.

The sign says:

WILL WORK

FOR

FOOD OR $

Eight months ago, I was fired.

How could that be? I was the rock of the business. I was its best salesman. I'd worked there upwards of nine years. I'd taken for granted I could work there as long as I wanted, that I'd never be fired.

As soon as it happened, I knew the injustice of my being fired was not going to be profitable to dwell upon. But I couldn't bear to stay in the building. My knees wobbled, I thought I might faint. I had to get out of there, into the fresh air—not just to leave the past but in order not to imagine: how would I feed myself, house myself?

I wandered across the street. Sitting on the pavement were two Berkeley panhandlers. As I approached they asked me for dole. I was their age, almost sixty. Why should I come upon them now? I hunkered down to learn.

They hadn't started drinking that day. The loquacious one played Honest John to the other's Gideon. He was good-looking, showered, clean-shaven, save for a trim, white, doctor's moustache. His clothes were spanking clean. When I told them I had just been fired, he spoke of begging and the money he made every day at it. Holding forth with broad proprietorial savvy of Mystical Things, he sought to nail me. I extricated myself.

Might I come to that?

I went back to the office and told my fellow workers I'd been fired. They were stunned but did not speak up for me.

I wanted to get away from there. I left at once, got in my car, and drove to Annie Hallatt's mask factory, Masque Arrayed. I needed to stand next to someone I could tell this to, someone my own age.

I opened her outer gate. Her front yard is furnished with salvage. I am greeted by her springer spaniel Blacktop who gallumphs off a sofa and paves my hand with his tongue. He returns to the sofa and collapses on the sofa like a sofa.

Inside the factory, masks hang from the walls like trophies: Zebras, wolves, the spangled faces of mermaids, brows of lace, beards of pearl, crimson schnozzolas. On worktables: hot glue, knives, heaps of tender minute cable, contraptions for baking, molding, drying. Pots of paint—orange, blue, pink—carousel without stop. At the tables her workers sit, dutiful. None of them spoke. The vacant mouths of the masks look up at them as they paint them. They did not speak either.

Annie appeared, her small sinewy body was staunch and at the ready. She had the cracked voice of an experienced tar but she neither smoked nor drank. Her ash-blond hair, flattened by a rakish hat, gave her a hunched appearance. Her pretty face wizened from years in Sausalito sea light, she looked up with a prankster grin and said, "To what do I owe the honor?"

"I've been fired."

"You mean it?"

"Just now."

She took the news impassively. "Ya wanna read the runes?"

I never had, so I would do the next indicated thing.

She took out the old stones, and I drew:

Hagalaz—Disruptive Natural Forces

Change, freedom, invention, and liberation are all attributes of this Rune. Drawing it indicates a pressing need within the psyche to break free from constricting identification with material reality and to experience the world of archetypical mind.

The Rune of elemental disruption, of events totally beyond your control, Hagalaz, has only an upright position, and yet it always operates through reversal. When you draw this Rune, expect disruption of your plans, for it is a great "Awakener," although the form the awakening takes may vary. Perhaps you will experience a gradual feeling of coming to your senses, as though you were emerging from a long sleep. There again, the onset of power may be such as to rip away the fabric of what you previously knew as your reality, your security, your understanding of yourself, your work, your relationships or beliefs.

Be aware, however, that what operates here is not ultimately an outside force, not a situation of you at-the-mercy-of-externals. Your own nature is creating what's happening and you are not without power in this situation. The inner strength you have funded until now in your life is your support and guide at a time when everything you've taken for granted is being challenged.

Receiving this Rune puts you on notice. You may sustain loss or damage— a tree falls on your home, a relationship fails, plans go wrong, a source of supply dries up. But do not be dismayed; you are forewarned, and therefore encouraged to understand and accept what occurs as necessary for your growth.

There is nothing trivial about this Rune: the more severe the disruption in your life, the more significant and timely the requirements for your growth. Another of the Cycle Runes, the term "radical discontinuity" best describes the action of Hagalaz at its most forceful. The universe and your own soul are demanding that you do, indeed, grow.

It was more than I could digest.

When I came in, Annie had been sticking feathers on masks for a rich woman's party. I put myself to work next to her, pasting labels inside, packed them into plastic bags, saying nothing—which is what I wanted to do, work. I am a worker.

I had been a contract employee, so I had no unemployment insurance, but I had four thousand dollars saved, so, figuring that I could live frugally, I decided to write a play—about Christopher Columbus—which would bring me fame and fortune! After it was written and until fame and fortune arrived, I'd grab a job. I was hardworking; I'd kept jobs for years; it'd be a cinch.

I'd lived this way since I was thirty-five. Before that I'd worked in advertising. But writing Cheerios Kid commercials with one hand and stories for the *New Yorker* with the other went against the grain: I had a classically tuned instrument, which made me not very good at advertising, and this was dishonest to advertising, because I could never give myself to it fully, which is what it deserved. So when I left advertising I decided never to take a job that involved writing and never to take a job that required the devotion of a career. I'd work only to write. Writing was my calling.

Writing was my calling and my craft, and I cannot say I sacrificed anything for it that I could ever have had. I'd been writing since I was fourteen when my father brought home a used upright Royal for me. Devotion to writing was not a choice; I was always devoted to it. One can only choose the inevitable.

However, I had also been an actor. And acting remained the touchstone of my life.

My interest in acting and the theatre led me to write plays, and now one about Columbus. One of my father's books, Samuel Eliott Morison's *Admiral of the Ocean Sea,* sat on my shelves for years, waiting. Now I read it and eight other books about Columbus and wrote the play and sent it out. By now it was September and since money was growing low, I began a job hunt.

But I couldn't get one. I couldn't figure it out. I was pushing sixty. Maybe I looked too old to be out of a job. Maybe people hiring wanted people younger than they were themselves. Maybe I looked like everybody's father and they didn't want him working under them. I went out on a lot of interviews, I went to reemployment classes, and worked up ten résumés for different fields. No takers.

In the old days you could always get a temp job, so I signed up with the agencies. But nine years had gone by since I was in the job market, and temp work now required elaborate computer skills. The agencies provided some training and I took it and I called fifteen temp agencies a day but got little work. Times had changed. The papers said there were 40,000 families homeless in the Bay Area.

By October I had too little money from temp work coming in to meet expenses so I looked into Food Stamps. It turned out you had to have a kitchen to qualify for Food Stamps, but also to be poor enough not to be able to afford the rent of a place with a kitchen. I looked into Public Assistance. I learned it paid $300 a month—but they made you work for free two weeks out of four for it which, because the work occupied job-interview time, I could not do and look for work as well. So food stamps and public assistance were out. They were good for people with undeclared income who lived with others.

I worked for nothing stuffing envelopes at an employment agency for media organizations so I could use their listings free. Every Friday I scoured a publication of jobs in the nonprofit area and pursued them actively. One time I was half-promised a job as a touring presenter for a charitable foundation; it fell through. Another time I was ordered to dress up in a three-piece suit to be interviewed for a temp job as a file clerk; I didn't get the job.

October waned into November. It was clear by now that the entire nation had turned against Columbus; he was considered a villain, an imperialist, a racist exploiter. So I had no hope for my personal Santa Maria. My play, like his ship, was not a ship that came in. This made me nervous. My expenses were not great but they were mandatory: $450 for rent, then food, phone, electricity, gas, and auto insurance and registration. I bought no clothes; I hung my laundry on the line. My nut came to around $750 a month and I had not enough income from the temp jobs to meet it.

I was not disposed to turn to anyone for help, and in any case I had no one to turn to. My family of origin were estranged from me—except for my sister Kathy in Rochester, whom I talked to once or twice a year and whom I loved. My daughter Amanda, who had worked for a living since she was a teenager, would have been generous, as would Kathy, but she didn't need to be burdened with an indigent father. Besides I had my pride. As to my friends—I'd told them all I was looking for work; that was enough. I feared no one would give me a job if they knew I was this badly off. I had no one but myself.

Daily I fell into a well of horror, Horror was a maelstrom, moving slowly, carrying me down. Only two things could extricate me from it: destitution, starvation, and death with their practical, earthy conditions—or digging a nail hold out of horror's well that day: make the rounds, answer the ads, tell people you need work—even in the common certainty such actions were not working. Action, even futile action, was better than horror.

Was the horror shame at having fallen so far from Expectation's shelf? Was the horror that, having been cut off from work, I was cut off from humanity? Was it the horror of no one wanting me? God's cursing me this way, was that the horror? I could not be sure; horror does not think too well.

But this I did know: whatever it was, I knew there must be something wrong with my life, such as had made my whole life wrong. Oh, I was healthy, tall, reasonably good-looking, fairly bright, a God-given foundation, but there was something else, something in my temperament maybe, or, or something that influenced my life that made its whole course wrong, made it, for troops of friends, for love, for work, slowly fail and steer downhill. I stood like an ox who has been smashed on his brow by a sledgehammer and doesn't know what hit him. What was I to do?—sell my old Plymouth to pay the rent? Without it I couldn't get to a job, there being no public transportation out of my town. Selling stuff was a stopgap, not an employment, and I'd eventually run out of stuff and still have the rent to pay. There seemed no window, no effort, no idea that prospered. I was baffled. I said to myself, The worst that could happen to you, Bruce, is that, in nothing but the clothes on your back, you die of exposure—but as millions of people before you have done that on this earth, unlike paying the rent, at least you know it can be done.

For without the rent, I might soon be living under a bridge, my possessions taken, nothing but the clothes on my back and a copy of Keats. . . .

But, rather than have homelessness thrust upon me, if I saw it really about to happen, I might embrace it, actually walk toward it! And yet, homelessness is very difficult for people to extricate themselves from, since the homeless have no base an employer can phone, nowhere to store work clothes, or to keep themselves clean. It would not be a good idea to court it.

I searched and I searched. Am I actually going to wed homelessness? Is homelessness actually going to happen to me? Yet, search as I might, I could not visualize that God actually had this in mind. On the other hand, I might be wrong about that, for I could no longer trust myself—and I was willing not to trust myself, to let God do God's will in the matter. However, surrender to God did not mean giving up. No, I would hand myself over to God and at the same time work to keep a roof over my head. I would listen for God's word standing.

It was now deep into December, Christmas was coming. At least for this month, I had a roof, and, figuring someone might be less fortunate than I, I bought a roasting chicken. If I was alone on Christmas Day, I would put it in the oven and find someone who really didn't have a roof over his head, and invite him home for Christmas dinner.

I did find myself alone Christmas day so I put the chicken in the oven, and drove down the I-80 to scope the on-ramps for a hitchhiker.

I drove twenty miles and there were no hitchhikers, but as I drove off the last ramp, I saw a man seated by the roadside holding a sign saying "Will Work for Food or $." I parked the car around the block and walked back.

Above middle height, heavyset, with black hair and a narrow jaw-beard, he had the look of a proficient pirate fresh off the high seas. As he might think I was up to no good, I didn't beat around the bush.

"Hi. I saw you standing there, and I wondered if you would care to come to my place for Christmas dinner?"

"No, thanks, I've already eaten."

I was surprised. I would have thought he would be broken down and starving. "I may be in your shoes before long," I said. He asked what I meant—and I told him—looking for work and not finding it, the various shifts I tried to stay solvent and housed—and he picked up his backpack and drew himself away from the roadside where he was being given money by drivers-by. We talked.

Something urgent in him to impart, a mission, a moral kindness, motivated him. He had this treasure. He talked to me as though I were someone who might benefit from it too. His name was Brendan Moon. He had a wife and four-year-old son living upstate and when he had lost his job he had come down to the Bay Area to find work and couldn't so he'd staked himself out here. He supported them with this work.

"This work is the greatest work I have ever done. My whole life has been changed because of it. I was helped by someone to get started, who told me the rules of it."

"Rules?"

"Principles of the trade."

"I don't understand."

"Because you're here to serve."

"Serve?"

"Serve anyone who passes by."

"In what way?"

"You offer yourself to people. You do anything you can do for them."

"Such as?"

"Any job they have. One of the rules is: take any job that comes along."

"Really?"

"Take the job and don't ask in advance how much you are to be paid for it."

"What's another one?"

"Say 'God bless you.'"

"I couldn't do that. I'm Episcopalian."

"I hadn't said it either when I started."

"But I would be embarrassed."

"That's what I thought too. But you get used to it."

"I mean, there's the crux: isn't one ashamed?"

"It's natural to feel ashamed," he said. "People assume you are only a bum, but if you know differently . . ."

"But you'd be begging."

"No. You'd be offering your services. I used to be a shy person. I had a low opinion of people, didn't want to be around them, didn't trust them, but since doing this work all that has changed. I have a relationship with everyone who goes by," he said. "They know me. I help them. So don't feel guilty. That's not what you're here for. Behave so as to be proud of yourself. Your sign says, 'Will work for food or dollars' and people will reach out money to you just to pay you to stand here and hold that sign. You think you're a panhandler? But you don't really know. Standing here on the roadside isn't my story. So, whenever anyone gives you money, offer your service. Make that your story."

"How?"

"I say to them, 'Is there anything I can do for you?' Cars break down, run out of gas: offer to help them—don't ask for money—just help."

"I see."

"Don't worry about *earning* the money: you'll do jobs you won't be paid for, and you'll also be paid for doing so-called nothing. It's not about the money. I give money back to people if I feel they need it more than I do."

"Really?"

"It's not about the money. I've had people load me up with food and give me more money than they would pay a regular person to do the work. I offered to take less, but they refused. It's about something else."

"Still all this is a lot to swallow. I mean, don't people ever attack you?"

"People treat you well for the most part. It's different from what they can do for the cashier on the checkout line at the supermarket. They don't know that person's situation, but here they do: a stranger whose situation they can read. 'Cause I wouldn't be here if it weren't for a situation, and being here itself is a situation. They can see it and so they give. But that's not all I do for them. There are people who pass by here who look forward to talking to me. I know their stories. I hear them out. It's a service."

And so it was he stood before me, giving me the ethics of his trade, principles that had been passed on to him and that he felt honor-bound to pass on in turn. He was looking for a convert.

As I did not suppose that I would be one, I just listened, and as I did, we got to know one another better. I remarked that the first letters of our names were the same, a coincidence that didn't touch him. He had gray in his beard and I took him to be in his early forties, but he was in his early thirties. He said he camped out of sight nearby (he was mysterious about where), did not bank his money but buried it (he was mysterious about where). To prove that he was not a bum, he showed me mounted glossies of a beautiful wooden airplane tricycle he had made for his son, and of a varnished toy chest. He was going to become a manufacturer of toys for children—and was aiming for a huge order from F.A.O. Schwartz by the end of next year. Some passing millionaire might foster their production.

I gave him my number and told him of a lady in my town who makes children's furniture she sells to department stores. I said I'd tell her about him. He showed me how to tack a message for him to the telephone pole where he stood.

How did he live? He kept all his valuables with him in his backpack. He lived on little. He liked the hardihood of the out-of-doors. He moved in the world of the homeless. He told me of others who did this work, and the off-ramps that were profitable. I wondered how he got up and down the road without a car. Public transportation, he said, and I guess he had a good deal of time on his hands to use it. Still I was suspicious. There was an Eden promised here and I am wary of promised Edens.

For instance, he told about a panhandler who had given out a newspaper interview that he had bought a house on his roadside proceeds. I thought, since the man must have known the interview would kill the goose, the bird must have stopped laying golden eggs already. I always suspect panhandlers of being alcoholic scam artists; I suspected Brendan of being an alcoholic, too, but he said he didn't drink particularly. It wasn't an Eden of money.

And yet in part it was. I had been curious all along about how much he actually collected and would it be enough for me to get by on, but I felt it was vulgar to ask, but of course finally I did. He said he made three hundred and eighty five dollars last night on Christmas Eve, and was probably going to make even more today. I was surprised it was so much. But his focus was on principles.

"There's good money to be made on the road," he said. Good Money is a relative term; I did not press him as to what he meant by it.

"One thing you learn as you do this work is, no matter what happens, you can survive. There's money out there, and you can always come out and get it if you need to. I've told other homeless people about this and how to do it, but none of them could bring themselves to come."

As I drove away from Brendan Moon, what had impressed me about him was that what he emphasized was not the money to be made, but the code behind it, and his generosity in entrusting the mysteries of his trade to a stranger—and that, although not an educated man, he was not a bum. Also Brendan's words, like those of a guru, were directed into me personally. It was a sale's pitch, yes, because he was looking for someone to pass on a salvation to, but he did not intrude; he was reserved behind it, and, because of that, it had the cadence of the sacred.

I pondered the curious chance of our meeting. I had gone out seeking to do a good deed on Christmas day—but had I gotten a present instead? If so, how strange: for God to wish me this—was I really supposed to go out on the roadside and beg? I accepted the gift, though, and drove home to eat my chicken alone.

27 December

December 25 goes and is replaced by December 26, December 27. Time is eating up time. Nothing is getting better. I have the rent but the rice will run out. I don't know where to turn. I journey into a shamanic divination.

I see my spirit guide, John Keats, from the back, seated, covered in a blanket. When I come around, his face is chalk-white, and then it dissolves into powder. I am dismayed.

The animals speak. White Wolf says: "Go out on the road and be like Ice Fox who takes his food where he may. You are at survival, so you are right to do it." He says to make a Compact with the work. The proceeds of the work have to go to maintenance and training. "Don't get hooked on the money. Don't play it for pity. Don't play it for anything. Just do it."

"Should I keep it secret?"

"No."

Strange: I should have thought I would have to.

"Don't make such a fuss about it," he says. "Go out and get laid."

28 December

I can't face going on the roadside. I spend half the morning whining, and the other half writing an essay on whining. I don't want to have to make this decision. Besides it's pouring outside.

I go to an interview at a local theatre company: the business manager describes the atrocious work prospects of theatre folk. I lose my umbrella. I buy another. I eat bad Chinese food which I don't need, and buy a Florentine cookie, which I can't afford. I want to be unconscious. I go home. I eat pea soup, which I don't need. All this postpones meditation. Postpones the issue. I perform another shamanic journey. A bald eagle tears at my entrails. Dry heaves retch up debris. The eagle is disentangling my innards.

29 December

The rent deadline gets closer.

I question what the theatre manager said, that art will not produce income. Will anything that means anything produce income? All my life I made literature, and for me a force of literature was that it would free me financially. That was always a set figure in me. Was that an ego-draft? No. I made my pots, I wanted a high price in the bazaar for them, there's nothing wrong with that. Should I give up writing? Is that the message of this poverty and of Keats' face dissolving?

As to starting on the roadside—do it. Take fear as the next door. Go to it, open that door.

I don't go to that door.

31 December, New Year's Eve

It is evening now.

What I have done in my life has failed. I am faced with the failure of my ambition, the failure of myself to support myself. I eat a cookie. Is that life now? Cookie to cookie to grave?

I am angry.

I eat a lot of cherries.

I watch some scientist on TV and don't understand what he is saying.

I am in my sixtieth year. I don't want to know this stuff at the end of day. I eat more cookies.

I watch a program on Edison. They say he hired wage slaves and took the credit for what they invented. He used to be an American hero and now like Columbus he's déclassé.

What is this life?

A check came through for January rent, and I have $40 left over from it, and that's it. The temp people are nice to me but they say the job market has shriveled up and blown away. I foresee no income in January and no steps available to generate any. I have no positive fuel to move me, no hope, no courage. But I have to go ahead even so. For the February rent I must take steps now.

Tomorrow I will go out with a sign to stand by the road. Today I bought the magic marker for the ceremony of making it—at the stationer, a favorite haunt of writers.

I will stand by the roadside, and take what work is offered.

And I'll also write. I'll also pursue the temp jobs. I'll also try new jobs to see where I belong.

Maybe all will be well. Maybe some unaccountable good will come.

There's something important in me. An importance. Maybe it's my story that's important. But I don't know what my story is. Unless, it's the story of failure. Or maybe I should give it all up and work to save the trees; maybe it's some message about the trees:

> I am not here to make you feel terrible about the trees. I am not here to
> tell you that fifty million trees lost their lives last year to the manufacture of

mail-order catalogues. I am not here to tell you that those catalogues are taking the breath out of your lungs and that if we don't stop them we will not breathe. No. I am telling you only one thing. I love the trees. If you love them too, save them. Stop killing them. Give money to organizations that prevent their murder. Pray for them, pay for them, plant them. I say love trees near and far. I say love them and make them live. I say, let them live in preabundant abandon.

When I was little, I hugged an old oak in the back of my garden, and then, though I could not get my arms around that tree and could not get them around it now, I knew that that tree was a god. God was more in that tree than in the church I went to. I knew God was in trees, in their silence, in their mystery, in their embrace of tall air. God is in them in their ordinariness. Undistinguished trees, yet God is in them, and what God is saying is: love is stronger than a single life. Love is stronger and older than life. This is the solid message of trees.

Don't worry. Some trees have bad tempers, and some trees are petty. But let us have them all. Because they bring an eternal message to our hearts, and if we lose that message, we lose the reminder that love is more important than what we can do in the span of our single life. What the trees are saying is that what is important is what we do *not* do. Do not do that, say the trees. Do not do what? Consider not doing it, if it outlasts your life.

If we cut down the trees we lose this message. No other being on earth brings it to us with such memorable finality. Not the mountains, nor the stones, nor the bones of planets turning in the air—nothing brings this message but the trees. Life that is older and lasts longer than our lives must be allowed to outlive us.

1 January, morning

I stand doing the dishes, and I must make a plan, but my planning machine is jammed with threatening degradation.

Going on the road may buy me time to plan.

I make a list of things to do around the house. Clean the apartment. Clear the papers off the dining room table.

All I feel is reluctance. To stand at the roadside begging? I'll never learn anything. Begging may be bad for my character. I may be worse off than before. I may end up cheating.

I meditated this morning. Yes, I meditate, but I meditate less frivolously when, as now, I am in difficulty. I ask God for the answers. I am in the dark. Meditation stares fixedly at it.

I remain skeptical about Brendan Moon's teaching. But it is not wise to spurn such messages. So this morning I return to him for further counsel.

"Brendan, is this right? I am not homeless. I still have a roof over my head."

"No one says you have to be homeless to do this work."

"The thing is I'll be homeless if I don't do it. But it feels terrible, as though I'm going to faint, and I'm not a fainter."

"Do it for one day for half an hour, then increase it, to get used to it. I set myself up at 10 A.M. after all those disgruntled workers going to their jobs have gone on by. Southbound exits are more profitable—nobody knows why. Stop signs are no good, because traffic doesn't stop long enough for people to get to their money; it has to be a stoplight. Sit on the ground so as not to be intimidating. Make quick eye contact with the driver but don't hold anyone with your eyes. And if you can stand it, you can make good money in the rain."

"Do you get offers of work, really?"

"Sure."

"So you ever refuse any?"

"Only once and that was from a man who wanted me to move eighty-pound batteries all day for twenty dollars and promised no ride back when I asked him."

When I ask about jobs that were illegal, he said he had an offer from a man who wanted him to pose in the nude but he didn't do it. He said most people are on the up-and-up—even the nude photographer was since he asked Brendan outright.

The only real problem, he said, is that he might find it hard to leave the work because it pays so well. "Expect a miracle," he said, as I left. "Let me know how you're doing."

I go home.

I dig in my heels. I don't want to go.

But I'll feel worse if I coward out.

I make the signs with the marker. I exhume an old never-used blue canvas backpack from the basement, and choose the shoes.

New Year's Day, 5:15 P.M.

The dirt is damp under the towel I sit on. With my sign propped on my knees, my stomach is cramped, so I stretch my legs out and hold the sign on my lap. My toes sticking up are silly, but sitting on the ground is what I was told to do.

The cars come up to the light. It is too painful to look at them. They'll have to see me instead. But maybe they can't see me with the low light of the five o'clock sun in their eyes. Red evening is coming down.

The very first car that stops reaches out a bill. I get to my feet. I take the bill, but I don't look at it, I put it in my parka pocket. Instead I look at her.

"Try to have a happy new year," she says in a tragical voice.

She's a well-to-do black woman with rich red lipstick. For her to give me money is simple. For me to take it is simple. I am not ashamed but grateful. And surprised to be grateful. It has happened. I go back and sit down. I feel like a child. I don't feel like a bad child or a helpless child—but an obedient child. When I took the money from the woman, I sat down again, dutifully.

After a time my back aches bending over to hold the sign. It's getting colder because dark is coming.

I vowed to remain for exactly half an hour. I vowed to say, "Bless you" silently to every car that passes. I also resolved to bless out loud those people who give. For I must repay people somehow.

Bless you over there, bless you truck, bless that car and that and that, and the one just turning the corner. And bless you stopping, and that one behind you, and I'm missing that one, bless you, and bless you too, and bless that black car, that yellow car, that white convertible. And bless you all the cars on the freeway, and bless that van coming up, bless you, bless you limo, what was that, a bug, to hell with it, bless it.

Someone stops to give—the car's not in good shape—coins.

"Thank you," I say. "Bless you."

I said it out loud!

I sit down again. It's fun. What's fun? The contact is fun. This exchange. Blessing people. I jump at the chance, I search for it.

Another car offers a bill—young black girls and boys in church clothes. I jump up to take it.

"Thank you. Bless you." I am surprised. Their car was not so hot either. I forgot to offer the money back.

And I forgot to ask for work!

I sit again.

Such an odd position, legs straight out sitting on dirt. But I'm okay. The sky is gray with evening. The air is cold on my cheeks. But I feel all right. Bless you, bless you. Bless you pink van, bless you old lady in a turquoise whatsit, bless you roadster, bless you man on a motorbike may you never have an accident, bless you young lady dressed for Sunday dinner, bless you station wagon with a battery of children, bless you grandma in your hat with all you know, may you find fame and fortune on national television. Bless you bless you bless you.

Two things I observe.

One, that poor people give.

The other, the big generosity of black folks, an imagination of the heart beyond the call of duty. It has a flavor all its own; I taste it and remember it of old.

Clint Eastwood enters my mind. I don't even like him, what's he doing here?

The biggest money making actor in the world. Beat it, I don't need the degradation of stark comparisons. He goes.

I get up for a moment to shake out my legs. I look about at the hills. On the ridge of the highest, the farthest, there on the north horizon, stands a single odd tree, asymmetrical as a cloud. Probably a live oak such as they have here in California with small holly-shaped, holly-hard leaves. From this distance, black. It has no occasion to it, does not supersede a statistic, is not tall or notable. But to this tree, silhouetted by the sky, I say, "You is my mascot—okay? Every day I'll say to you, 'Hello, tree. You is my friend.'"

In the cold out-of-doors at sunset I am not miserable as I thought I would be, and the pain I felt at the start has gone. I am not deceitful or degraded sitting here, I am free of that, I don't know why. I feel elated—not ashamed. Not wrong, but shy and happy. I sit here in an unusual kingdom. People see me and I don't mind. Why is that? Part of me belongs in this adventure.

At the end of half an hour I drive to the dollar video store and rent pictures with Geraldine Page and Maggie Smith—actresses are more daring than actors. What am I doing, taking money from poor black people and renting videos with it?

When I get home I write out my rules.

SOME OF THE INGREDIENTS OF A COMPACT
- Ask for work every time you can get the words out.
- Take all work offered.
- Don't ask what they're paying beforehand.
- Bless all drivers-by.
- Be there to be there, and watch a desire for money arise over a desire for work, since you know this will happen.
- Arrange for company in the evening. What you are doing is not punishable by Solitary Confinement; humans are sociable at the end of the day.
- Distribute funds in separate envelopes.
  - Charitable contributions
  - Rent
  - Schooling
  - Publication of writing
  - Food
  - Pleasure, records, films
  - Auto maintenance
  - Office equipment and upkeep
  - Daily awareness of funds

- Look for marriage:
  - To god
  - To the mate
  - To the friend
  - To the passerby
  - To Nature
- Record responses and earnings in a journal.
- Run it like a business.
- Never leave early.

Immediately I add:

- Never look at the money as you take it.

I look in my pocket to see what the money is. The three black people gave me $6.30. That first woman said, "Try to have a happy new year" in a tragical voice— but she has given me a five-dollar bill!

2 January, Saturday

I return to the same spot, at the southbound Appian exit. But where to park? The Doctor's Hospital lot is crowded and for sick people. On the other hand, among so many cars it's easier to hide mine, lest people think, since I still own a car, that I am here under false pretenses. People might attack me if I own more than the clothes on my back. They might assume I'm not poor enough to hold this sign; I think it myself. I park in the shopping center across the freeway.

The air is damp and chill. Night is coming on, night without sunset, and as I walk to the off-ramp, I do not want to be here. I don't have the stomach for this. There are people worse off than me. I am not cheating, but I feel I am cheating. I feel I am taking more than my share. My body aches with wrongdoing. I feel I am going against my fiber. On the other hand maybe the pain is just my body facing something different. I also feel I am snobbish: I Was Meant For Better Things. And yet I wasn't, for here I am.

I settle the backpack and sit. I forgot to dry my towel last night, so it's damp.

I'm scared the police will drive me off or arrest me.

I'll stay for a half hour again.

I look up. I want to give blessings to the cars but the pain in my body is intolerable. It's visible in my face. It isn't fair to people to have to deal with me like this.

Clint Eastwood comes again. Get outa here. Twenty years ago I saw one of his pictures and didn't like him and never saw another. I love acting too much to like him.

He goes. I sit down.

Back to the broad light of day.

When I was young I used to act. I gave it up when I was twenty-five. Over the years I've played a part or two. People see me as an actor; I don't know why that is; perhaps it's something in the way I talk. I don't like people thinking I'm dramatic or unreal in real life and so belong in the freak show of a theatre.

Actually I have scheduled an audition soon with a quite large theatre for *Catherine of Aragon*, for the part of Cardinal Wolsey. It's kind of silly to go ahead with it. What conviction could I bring to creating the richest man in England, a grandee in laces, in my secondhand parka on the roadside begging?

A man jumps out of his car from the middle lane to give me money. I am energized by his effort.

An East Asian man sits in his car for a good while. East Asian people won't give. Then he opens his window and gives. Where did I get the idea that East Asian people are close with money? I don't even know any East Asian people. And even if I did, how could a conclusion about the tightfistedness of an entire race be gathered?

Four black women roll down their window as they pass and hand me a bill. I say thank you and ask if I can do anything for them. "Just have a Happy New Year," one says. I wish them the same back—a lovely moment.

A man in a car in the far lane hails me—the traffic starts but I can't get to him; he tries to pull into my lane but can't. "I'll catch you on the way back," he calls. And he may, but it's all right if he doesn't. His positive intention is a felt good. How much would he have given, though—a hundred-dollar bill? Darn. I sit down again.

From some cars I feel a stony indifference. Perhaps my being here is hard for them. Well, I can endure it.

I leave at 5:30 exactly and trudge like a down-and-outer over the freeway to the shopping center parking lot. I go into a chain restaurant to pee. The supper rush hasn't begun. Crystal chandeliers hang low over booths. In my canvas backpack and old clothes I feel out of place. I count the money in a toilet stall. Boy, it's a lot—$7.00!—I believe another black women gave me another five-dollar bill! I put the money back in my pocket.

I consider having a spot of food, but no, I leave the restaurant like a prince. Outside the night air is high, black, and cold. It feels good on my skin. I have been preserved. I am enclosed in a jar of happiness. I am safe. Through the night, cold headlights, like stars, abound. Of them I am not a part.

Once home, I record all this . . . "the pain in my body was intolerable," I write, but was it intolerable? My whole body hates to beg for money—but it tolerated it.

3 January, Sunday

For seven years my sister Kathy has been afflicted with lymphoma in partial remission. Today is her birthday. I call her in Rochester.

"Happy Birthday. How does it feel to be—what are you anyhow?"

"Fifty-one. It feels great."

I want to know about her illness, but I also fear knowing about it as though there were something contagious in its mention. "How are the girls?"

She has a good sense of her daughters' characters and talks about them cogently and about her husband Gerry. And then she asks after me. I am tempted to tell her. I have told no one and while it might be good to tell someone who loved me, Kathy's got enough to think about with cancer and her children and her life. Besides, I don't want to face her commiseration; she might send me money, which I don't want her to do—she's earned her money, she deserves to keep it. Besides I feel bad to have done so poorly, and I don't want it entered into family gossip—although I suppose she would keep it confidential if I ask her. I am ashamed, as only a show-off can be.

"How's your health, Kathy?" I say gingerly.

"I'm doing just fine."

I hope it's true. Kathy is considerate to a fault of the feelings of others, and she may not want me to worry. I believe her because I want to believe her.

Afterward I drag toward the roadside. It's rainy and cold, but I've said I will go. I put on the jacket, the sweater. I have secured the signs and backpack behind the front door—they are not to be despised because I despise this work. I can't believe I have to do this.

Throughout history, people have been pressed into terrible work: work they didn't want; work that was inhumane, onerous, poverty-making; work that arose out of careless, unjust, unimaginative greed, their bones thrown any-where. But I lived in better times —I worked to write, and there used to be work so I could do that. Now I am a beggar. I don't blame anyone. And yet I can't believe it has come to this. I began life with such high hopes.

I hate getting money this way. My chest hates it. My arms hate it. My back hates it. But inside a piece refuses anything else. The Inner Brat with its heels dug in *demands* to be taken care of. Not getting the care it needed as a child made it mis-erable and now getting the care makes it miserable. This brat wants money without working for it. It feels like theft, I hate it, and my body seethes with hatred as I go forward to do it anyhow because there is nothing else to do.

I place the backpack in the trunk of the car like a salesman's case. I drive out of my neighborhood where no one knows.

Though it goes against the grain, I park in the hospital lot again. I trudge down to the freeway. I feel wicked and lowborn. I feel I am getting more from people than I am giving. I'm doing something I don't want to do in order to survive to do something I do want to do, which is write. I've been doing that all my life—advertising, teaching, magazines, office jobs, waitering, taking care of invalids—too many years.

I have written all my life. I wrote in high school; in boarding school my first short story was published; I wrote in England where I was an exchange student, and at Yale, and I wrote stories in Korea during the war. At Columbia I wrote a story that came out in *Botteghe Oscure*—which was then the preeminent literary magazine of the world. After I got married a story appeared in the *New Yorker* and a novel was published, a university founded a collection of my work, I won a literary prize. So I had some reason to believe I should write. I was devoted to it; the jobs I took were to support myself, my wife, and daughter while I wrote. And I made money at it. Then I became involved with gigantic projects and a novel which I rewrote for thirteen years. I published only theatre criticism and poems, when I mustered myself to send them out. I wrote every day, always aspiring to make my living at it. And now? Day by day has added up, and what they add up to is that I am pushing sixty and walking to this freeway exit in the rain, and coming to realize I would be wise to doubt what I had never doubted—the ambition to earn my living by writing and therefore that writing is my calling at all. My hands are empty. The rain on my cheeks has more solidity than I.

I arrive at 3 P.M. I will stay an hour and a half.

As I prop up the sign, I feel myself greedily hoping for money even before I have started. I push that out of my mind until I am ready.

In the fine soft spangle of the mist I sit. Again I have not hung the towel up to dry, and it is still damp from the day before. The cars whiz by, big, above, and near me. But I bless every one bar none: bless you, bless you, and blessing washes out the fear. It's hard to raise up on this hospital bed to do this. Sitting straight-legged on the dirt hurts my lower back. But maybe I'll develop the muscle. With my legs extended, I have to bend over my sign uncomfortably to sit upright, so I bend my knees up again and prop the sign on my instep.

"How long ya been there?" I look up. A Hispanic man looks down at me.

Does he mean: how long today or how long in my life, what does he want to know for? He knows that his function is to give me money not vocational counselling.

"I just got here," I explain.

"It's too late in the day," he admonishes.

What does he know about this business anyway? "Why is it too late in the day?"

The traffic takes him away before he can answer. The exchange is wounding, baffling.

There are long periods of nothing doing. Except to bless.

A man in the middle lane calls, "What sort of work do you do?"

"Anything." Is he curious or does he really have a job? Should I say, "I taught college English"? Or "I wrote columns for *Look* and the *National Lampoon*. Do you have a job on a national magazine for me?"

I must work out a civil answer. I could say: "I do various things. What sort of work do you need done?"

He hands me an old bill.

"Are you here often?"

"Yes. Sometimes."

"I have work for you."

Does he mean it? He drives on. Will I ever see him again? I am lost in the loss of a career with him as in the loss of the dearest love of my life. The sea is junked with jetsam, and from it I scavenge a calling—a contradiction in terms—for a calling calls, it doesn't float around like shipwrecked luggage.

I get up to take away the damp towel. Eastwood comes again. What are you back for? Don't answer me. Just scram.

Why does he keep bothering me here?

He threatens me.

Because I'm not at all like him—he's the sort of male that everyone wants to survive—that's what such men are for—because people wish they themselves could survive like that—gunshots, weather, slim cigars. I have to survive by some other standard entirely, I don't know what yet, and it is a miracle I am alive at all. If I have survived it is by the grace of God solely—and the grace of God doesn't pay the rent.

Or does it?

I'm breathing.

That's the rent.

Sitting here with the cars above me zooming by, I feel helpless. At least the police haven't hassled me, that's something. Is there a law about what I do? The police sometimes make up the law, they might move me off or arrest me, and what redress could I have? I've always had good relations with the police but I shrink at them moving me on.

Instantly, a California Highway Patrol car drives up and stops.

"You have to move off the exit road," he says evenhandedly, but he means it.

I get up. "Oh, can't I stay, I'm not doing any harm?"

"You could cause accidents," he says still evenhandedly, but he means it.

"But people only give when they're already stopped." I feel ashamed, though he hasn't shamed me.

"It's against the law," he says still evenhandedly, but he means it.

"Can I be on the sidewalk?"

"You just can't sit here," he says. He drives off and he'll probably drive back to check.

I walk down toward the freeway to retrieve my second sign. It was my Burma Shave: Ten Miles To Bruce's Tin Cup! My spirits sink. Up by Appian Way I'll only have access to the first drivers stopped.

But, who knows, maybe this means I'll do even better.

So I make my way up to the Appian sidewalk where it meets the exit. I lean the backpack against the *Do Not Enter* pole and I bungee the second sign to it. I put the damp towel down on the sidewalk. Few people walk here, I won't be in their way. Evidently, there's no law against being on the sidewalk at the top of the off-ramp, only against being on the off-ramp itself. Sitting here I feel safer. Also I feel good about the cop; he was a harbinger of better times. Across the road rises the concrete abutment; the sight of real dirt on the hillside behind it refreshes me.

Concrete's hard on my rear, though, and extending my feet feels silly. But putting them in the gutter might get them run over. A car might want to hit me. People offer me money, but no one offers me work, maybe because people are turned off by someone sitting on the pavement. I would be. Sitting on the concrete, I keep adjusting my legs, propping my knees up or keeping them flat, holding the sign up this way or that to stay comfortable. The towel is damp and my ass is cold. Sitting feels stupid and unnecessary. It's awkward scrambling to get up to take the money. Sitting down is a drag in fact. In fact I'm not going to do it any more. Brendan sits, but I don't have to, I'm not a pirate-looking person, my hair is gray.

I stand up, shake my legs out, dust myself off, stretch back my shoulders, and, hey, I feel fine about standing. Standing is where I should be!

Strange that cop coming immediately after my thinking of him—yet somehow I was not surprised. It was more than a coincidence. It was a fast-food miracle.

The three lanes of the exit go right or straight or left, and mine is the left. It is my territory, my land, my office.

A well-to-do girl in a van in the middle lane calls, "What sort of work do you do?"

"Anything."

"All I have is some popcorn."

I cross to her lane and thank her with a joke. Entering the stopped traffic is a risk, the bad-tempered horns of the drivers, people would as soon kill me as look at me—but the fun of getting popcorn from her is worth it, and fun makes one nimble.

Immediately a black couple in a black car with a young child in back give me a bag; the man says it has ham in it and Triscuits, and there's a candy cane. Someone else hands me a box of Cheese Ritz. A woman reaches out and her hand is spread with dollar bills as the traffic starts. I put all the three food items down where I stand, for they have come all in a row, and then other bills come, I don't remember all of them.

A pain comes into my chest, the pain of gratitude mixed with the surprise of good fortune. And since this food is unexpected and was chosen by others, the gifts are even funny.

The late afternoon sunlight is in people's eyes. But they see me. I am not hateful to them. I am allowed to be here, I am welcome.

My face is in the mist and mist is on my hair but I don't mind. I would think I would mind, that I would whine, would pity myself to suffer exposure, but the air is decent to me. And being in this lowly place does not dishearten me, in fact just the opposite. I am happy. I am a child who needs to be taken care of and is being taken care of and so is wide-eyed. Because finally he is getting what is proper—his life being tolerated. No one who passes wants the child to die.

Suddenly a wild woman, laughing with reckless goodwill, screeches around the corner in a big old dinged brown Olds and onto Appian waving madly. Maybe she's a drunkard and thinks I'm one too. I wave back in acknowledgment.

BMWs don't give.

East Asian people probably won't give.

Black people probably won't give.

Poor people probably won't give.

People with families probably won't give.

People will give after dark. Because they'll pity me for having to be here.

People will give in the rain for the same reason.

I see that I make up these opinions even before I have proof. And even after I'm proven wrong, they adhere to me. Irrational.

Where does it come from—the notion that black people would be too poor to give—when, of course, black people already have given? It's just nuts. And these opinions have nothing to do with getting work but only with getting money. I have melodic ideals, with this greed-obligato. Also it's Sunday and people don't hire people for work on Sunday, so at this late hour, "Do you have any work I can do?" is baloney. I should take a day off, and keep honest about the sign. Add to the

COMPACT

- Take a day off—Sunday.
- Be on the roadside during ordinary working hours.
- Stay here exactly the hours I say I will, to the minute, just like a regular job.

Interesting how people give to me despite my unworthy thoughts. They don't know what I'm thinking. Yes they do, my face is so obvious.

Still, "Bless you," I think to every car. It makes me smile. Maybe my face looks too happy to be given to. But I can't help it, I am in a blessèd state. Bestowing blessings is a free fall, exhilarating, adventuresome, and new. I am deliriously industrious. I want to cry out for joy.

God bless you RV, God bless you Chevy over there. Hey, coming from below, God bless you, and you in the semi, bless you though you may think I'm a jerk for saying so, and you, scowling old man in a beater bless you. Bless you unknown car, bless you who are you? Bless you turning the corner, bless you and you and you. Bless you all in the world.

My hands are cold.

Bless you.

I step forward to take a bill from a moving car.

To moving cars I notice I am not able to say, "Is there any work I can do for you?" because they get away too fast.

When I am ready to go, do not say: "I will stay until I get just one more dollar." No, do not work a minute longer than you say you will. Or a minute less.

COMPACT

- Don't wait for that one more dollar.

I stay until exactly 4:30.

Closed For The Day, I sling the backpack on and start across the street. Halfway, I hear a whistle, turn, a hand is reaching out of a dark red moving car two five-dollar bills my eyes pop I can't see the driver the glass is smoked the car turns the corner and is gone.

It's unlikely a person would give money to someone with no sign. "Expect a miracle," Brendan Moon had said.

With the miracle digesting I continue across. As I walk by the bare embankment, I feel content. I have kept my word. If I'd stayed until 6:00, I might have more money or I might not. You cannot force God's luck. It's not about greed—greed has no practical function—it's about doing it right.

I go to the hospital rest room and lock the door—to pee and count the money. $19 in 1½ hours: $13 an hour, more than I could earn at temporary work. When I leave the restroom and walk down the hospital corridor, I notice I seem to be remaining moderate in response to the roadside. What is happening to me is that nothing is happening dramatically. Something is balancing out in my nature. I'm changing.

When I get home I divvy the money into the yellow envelopes. Then I sit down to record what I can remember. These people, they must not be forgotten, —every one of them is precious. Thomas Wolfe felt this same omnivorous devotion to everyone being remembered.

Two people threw money at me from moving cars—one woman threw down two dollars.

A white truck stood pat at the light and from the woman inside I expected nothing, but suddenly the passenger door opened and a man came back around the bed of the truck and handed me a dollar and hopped back in. The woman made an "Oh, you!" face at him because what he did was risky.

I saw many faces, many sorts of human—the big lady in the truck, the sixty-year-old man with a white beard and handsome way, smoking, who wouldn't look at me.

I realize that I am not neutral, that I draw conclusions, hold views. I find passersby interesting. Perhaps I'm too interested. It's not my job. My job is just to be there and to allow work to come to me, or money.

But I remember the young man with the handsome jaw, his mother in the back from whom he got the jaw. Although he has an aristocratic face, the car he drives is a beat-up sedan. Reading his visage I say to myself, he will give me something. But he didn't even look at me.

4 January, Monday

Tonight I'm supposed to audition for *Catherine of Aragon.* Should I go? I don't like the play, but the job pays. Will I have even gas money to get to rehearsals? I'd have to stay on the roadside to do it—and suppose they found out.

In the morning I do a temp job at Dr. Winkin's office—half a day's work at seven dollars an hour, work which takes $5 to get to and back!

I sit in the office and answer the phone, learn the computer, make appointments. I've worked jobs like this many times in my life and I can apply myself, put on a pleasant face, and learn a thing or two, but I feel the poison of an unsuitable task and yearn to get away.

Since the paycheck for this half-day's work will not come for a week, in the afternoon I go out on the roadside.

The rain has let up some, but I am thinly wet all over. I stand and smile and bless. And I think about the audition.

I've borrowed the play from the library; I've borrowed the video; I know the part's requirements and I can do it. But isn't this whole idea of acting beside the point of finding a way of surviving? Still, the company pays $350 for 3 months work, and it would be good to get my foot in the door there so I could have a source of parts. Parts.

Here I am with the rain trickling down my back, and I'm thinking about parts and whether I should go to that audition.

The wet hills stand here with me too. How free they are. The sky with its mist and gray is free. The trees and the coming green are also free. Space is free. Air is free. And I am free.

I have no responsibilities to anyone. I have no mate. My daughter is grown and long since on her own. I have no job. Nothing anchors me. I don't have to stay in this part of the country. I could go in any direction I want. Because I don't have work, I don't have to be anywhere or deal with anyone. I don't have to make the mortgage or the car payment. I owe no one money and I have no debts of time.

I feel this as a desert of empty calm. A vista inside. A breadth and ease of landscape. Plain. Simple. Undramatic. Open.

I have nothing that calls me, one way or another. No ambition. Nothing that tells me: you should be a stockbroker, Bruce, or a psychiatrist, or a lawyer. The jobs in my life that I came to an end of—journalism, teaching, waiting on tables—I have no regrets about; I've let them go. I realize now the roadside provides me with this wonderful freedom, the freedom to see that I am free. Free from things and free to go in any direction I want, or in none at all.

Clint Eastwood comes again.

I don't know why he comes. He wasn't my sort of actor.

In my life, acting has held me as religion holds the devout, and Marlon Brando was my standard.

Going to the movies was where it started.

I couldn't play ball as a kid. Due to a defect of vision, I couldn't see a ball coming, and I threw like a girl. I was called a sissy, and as I didn't fight back, I was exiled from the male community, which was wholly a ball-playing community in that town. Oh, I was a live wire, I was active. I could roller-skate while the boys were playing stickball in the schoolyard or play jump rope with the girls. I could ride my bike or play with toy cars or read. But those were solitary occupations. Males mount their survival energy by being around other males in whose presence they imbibe it. They imbibe it from themselves, but they do this in the presence of other males. So for this survival I had no equipment ready and none being readied. I was exiled from the male community, and I did not share in the common male energy on which later life survival for the male depends and in which it takes place. When I got to be twelve I saw the future: after the teen-age years, at seventeen, I'd be on my own and have to make my own living and I wasn't going to be able to do it. What was going to become of me? I sensed the handwriting on the wall and I didn't want to read it. So I hid in the dark of empty matinees.

They changed the double feature three times a week at the Bayside on Bell Boulevard, Queens, in those pre-TV days. I'd take my books home after school, bike downtown, hide the bike around the corner, and boldly skulk in. When I slid my 27 cents up to the cashier's booth I would feel ashamed at her seeing me here again—Young fellow, where do you get the money for this? (I stole it from my mother's purse.) I would go in and be hidden by the dark of the lobby, where I would buy as much candy as the money I had stolen for it would go, and with sweets mask the crimes of eating between meals, illicit movie attendance, not being out playing in the sunshine, and theft. I'd hunker down with my knees up on the seat in front, eat Good & Plenty, spit the licorice on the floor, and, in oblivion, indulge in the greatest crime of all: I became a user; I'd watch someone else survive.

I liked all kinds of pictures, but what I liked most were musicals because of the female stars they were built around, particularly Betty Grable. Betty Grable was, like me, energetic, but put-upon. Two-timed by handsome cads, she was open, talented enough, hardworking, and she survived—by gosh, more than survived: she survived in spangles. She *prevailed* in fact because in the end she was centered in and surrounded by the protecting and inviolable exaltation of The Spotlight. Raised above everyone in her good humor, big heart, and gullibility, the spotlight justified and made clear to one and all her vulnerability and her destiny. That spotlight was a halo of steel. It made those less vulnerable eat crow. Once in it, you couldn't be laughed at or touched—they couldn't getcha if ya wuz in a spotlight.

I was a big-hearted kid. What I identified with was the Survival of Those Who You Wouldn't Think Would Survive. Maybe my life could be a movie. Maybe my life could be a production number!

I knew and did not know this. So much of my survival energy was connected to escaping from fear about my survival energy that I could not see that the dark of a motion picture house was not the broad light of day. Or rather that the broad light of day was not a motion picture house. Anyhow, a need to perform, already in me, grew. I wanted to sing, I wanted to dance, I wanted to *behave*. For if I needed to survive through Attention, that is, through the spotlight, I had to be doing something while I was in it. As I was already inclined from early childhood to act up, I now in real life imagined myself Up There On The Silver Screen and in the privileged decor of film. And if people hurt my feelings, then that would be my solace and my revenge: I'll show them, they'll be sorry, one day they'll see, one day I'd be a star. In fact I'd be one right now. So I would dance in my bedroom, not for but in front of my disgusted brother; I would dance in the street surrounded by the cheering, astonished Cub Scouts. But the cheers of the scouts were worse than my brother's disgust. I wasn't even dancing like Betty Grable, I was dancing like Maria Montez, who survived through veils and divans. I was immediately ashamed to have been seen surviving as a female.

Because I liked being a male, even if at age 10 a not very masculine one.

As role models, male movie stars were as useless to me as sports stars. Bogart, Cagney, Cooper—none of them were really at survival as I was; their roles were just foils for their masculinity, which guaranteed their characters success simply because it existed with such force and made them stars to begin with. Gable, Tracy, and McCrae were in the masculinity business. I enjoyed them but I didn't identify with them. There were a lot of guns going off, but if there hadn't been they'd have just done fine in real estate. But the women?—no; their real lives were at stake. Like me, the female stars were sitting ducks.

At home I endured violent physical and verbal abuse. At school I was a poor athlete and a mediocre student, exiled from the great male world of aggression and competition by which male energy ripens into itself. So I adopted female energy to survive—phony since I didn't learn it from myself but from the girls around me. My favorite films began with a plane crash in a jungle. The mist settles. The monkeys resume their screeching. And twelve motley survivors climb out. After that the film lost interest because it was the males who breasted through. The craft and litheness and stamina of women heroed it nothing. My life was a plane crash in a jungle. But I looked at someone else's crash to avoid my own. Addicted, I went as often as they changed the bill. The smoke-dusted aura of a movie house was the closest thing to a bar but booze.

I'd emerge in a daze. Staggering out under the marquee, my eyes would be met by a crude and dazzling sun having nothing to do with the moving entrancement of the dark. For half a block I would walk in the shoes of the picture and the light of the star. Then the story, the star, and the picture would fade into skedaddling back to my mother's liver and onions and my homework, the movies a shame forgotten.

But one time was different.

In Flushing, where Northern Boulevard met Main Street, stood the splendors of RKO Keith's, a Byzantine picture palace with minarets *inside*. When you looked up, clouds and stars moved across an indigo desert sky. When I was fifteen I took a bus and went to see *The Jazz Singer* with Peggy Lee and Danny Thomas, and I walked out of that picture in a different daze.

The actor playing Danny Thomas's mother was even-handed, firm, loving. She fostered the survival of her children on their own terms, yet saw them clearly. This character was revolutionary. She was everything in the reverse of my own mother; she was a mother I had never conceived possible. I didn't know the actress's name, it wasn't important; she had entered me.

Because of her there was a standard now in me for maternal behavior. That actress was playing a role, yes, but also and more important she was a foundation of love and tenacity. Love and tenacity were grounds for survival. But where were my grounds? And where were my role models for it?

All my life I had grown up with great men and women. How did we know they were great? They were people of great character: everyone knew it: Marian Anderson, Sibelius, Churchill, Rachmaninoff, Clarence Darrow, Frank Lloyd Wright, Toscanini, Harry Bridges, Helen Keller, Stokowski, Arthur Rubinstein, F.D.R. and Mrs. Roosevelt, Myra Hess, Jim Thorpe, Schweitzer, Einstein, Babe Ruth, Shostakovich, Rommel, General Marshall, Thomas Mann, Lindbergh, O'Neill, G.B.S., Jesse Owens, DiMaggio, Sister Kenny, Joe Louis, Fritz Kreisler, Hank Greenberg, Madame Chiang Kai-Shek, Paderweski, Hemingway, de Gaulle, Paul Robeson, Miro, Calder, Sea Biscuit, Matisse, Diego Rivera, Bertrand Russell. All these were my elder contemporaries. I had taken for granted there would always be such persons. It did not happen. By the 1950s they had either died or retired, and I did not know it then, but they would never be replaced. Today one can name the great with ease because they are so few: Nelson Mandela, the Dalai Llama, Mother Teresa. With Eisenhower, greatness ended.

By this time, I was a teenager and at prep school, and the blond was no longer Betty Grable, but rather (no, not Marilyn Monroe but a much bigger star) Doris Day. With her tense bleached style and clarion song, there was nothing vulnerable to get behind. For Doris Day, like the Eisenhower years, survival was a fait accompli. However, what rose up exactly concurrent and inconsonant with Doris Day was Marlon Brando. Suddenly in the early '50s, Marlon Brando appeared, and in a single blow, Emotional Truth supplanted Character as a standard of greatness, another room entirely. Emotional Truth was instantly my instrument of survival.

The fame of having great character was not Brando's necessarily. Indeed one never thinks of Actors as being great apart from what they do, as, say, one thinks of Tolstoy, whose personal greatness one can vouch for through his work. One never knew great people; one knew *of* them. Greatness is the decantation of good repute. Acting, however, is guzzled from the bottle. Brando, one swigged directly.

For here there appeared for the first time a force of authenticity so supreme as to make me able to recognize in myself localities and potentialities which the Tupperware soul of the '50s had no certain space for. Brando was the American nightmare—and was exactly what the doctor ordered. With the appearance of Brando, acting became for me where greatness lodged.

In Acting. Not in me acting. But in Acting.

Aside from a Christmas pageant where I impersonated Frankincense, my first acting was in a grammar school play where I said my line, "I am the dunce!" with such boldness that I was at once lauded and dismissed, as who should say, "Oh, now we know where to pigeon-hole you, social derelict as we have always known you to be, you should be on the stage." It sounded to me like a life sentence, another dismissal. I didn't like being thought of as castrated because I was a clown, but what other part could I play that was true to my difficulty? And how could I admit my difficulty by playing it? I didn't want to act at all if that was the case.

If I had had the courage to face my life at age 13, I would have seen that, yes, I could be an actor. But—to take acting lessons, to commit myself professionally?—it never occurred to me. I could not imagine myself being an actor or anything else. I was too frightened to. And I needed to imagine something. Imagination is the first tool of survival.

Nor did Brando inspire me to act. Acting was what *Brando* did. And it seemed so real that I felt real life should be like that, too. Indeed, I never understood it as acting. For what Brando did was to go to a depth that corresponded to a truth in me I had had no prior permission certainly to voice or even to know. To see him was a *spiritual* excitement. Acting was something someone else did, but it was an altar. With Brando, my allegiance to movie-going became supplanted by devotion to acting itself.

The last thing I did before I went to Korea in '53 was to see *Viva Zapata* in San Francisco. On the front, the only film shown was *Member of the Wedding* with Julie Harris. As I waited for a plane to take me to Japan on an R & R, I slipped into an empty quonset to catch a bit of *On the Waterfront.* The first thing I did when I got back to New York was to go to *East of Eden.*

With *East of Eden,* and never so intensely again, I was in that daze once more. For in James Dean I had met myself. His story in that movie was mine. His older brother was like mine, my parents like his, his relations to them like mine, his romance with Julie Harris my dream romance. He was seductive with his pain such that his pain, not just the role, told my truth, lived it out, released, expressive, lovely. All this in the infiltrating dark of a movie house. I never dressed like him, I simply desired him as—with a need that did not distinguish between us—the friend I loved with, and better than, my soul. James Dean was a female star. I was suddenly possible.

That fall, I went to Columbia.

In the '50s, New York City was the mecca of the art of acting in the world. *A Streetcar Named Desire* had been done. *Death of a Salesman* had been done. I had gone to *Cat on a Hot Tin Roof* the week it opened, the week I got out of the army. And all this was emerging from the Actors Studio and from the director Elia Kazan, who released the great gifts of the actors, and they knew it. My yearning for a gutsy truth led me to seek out his work and the work of all of them. Also, and it's probably been forgotten, in the '50s, live television was The Museum Of The Modern Art Of Acting and was where one got to see its great young practitioners, especially the women—Julie Harris, Geraldine Page, Kim Stanley. At Columbia College I majored in English Drama—at one remove from actual acting and the theatre, which in those days was happening more on-Broadway than off. I went to plays a lot, which you could do cheaply. I hung around the Columbia Players, participating distantly.

Across the street was Barnard; my friends talked about a teacher of scene study; she was Big Mama in *Cat on a Hot Tin Roof;* she was Mildred Dunnock. I didn't like the name Mildred, so I didn't audit the class. But reluctantly, eventually I went.

I sat in the back of the little Minor Latham Theatre. Down front, I could see the back of a head of curly auburn hair. When the scene was done, she said, in a melodious and beautifully modulated voice—even-handed, firm, loving— "Thank you. What were you after?" Then she got on the stage to illustrate a point, and I saw she was the mother in *The Jazz Singer.* I'd seen her as scrawny, scrapple-voiced Big Mama in *Cat* and not recognized her. I'd seen her in *Kiss of Death, The Corn Is Green, Viva Zapata* and not recognized her. When the class was over I went to her at once and accused her of this deception. She had a delicate, strong, wise, open face; big eyes; flexible mouth. I was drawn to her. I loved her at once. I walked her to the subway. I hung out, danced attendance upon her.

Through Mildred Dunnock the world of acting became the most exciting thing alive for me. The truth of the actor's world dazzled me, and I longed for it and looked forward to it. And that world was immediately before me: Millie moved in it, was of it, created it. During that time at Columbia she played Aunt Rose Comfort in Kazan's film of Tennessee Williams's *Baby Doll* for which she was nominated for an Oscar, and *Love Me Tender,* Elvis's first film—so she was both in the vanguard and highly commercial! She had acted with Tallulah Bankhead, Katherine Cornell, Mary Martin, Helen Hayes, Ruth Gordon, Ethel

Barrymore—and the greatest actor of the twentieth century, Laurette Taylor—so she had participated in the big tradition of the New York Stage. She was also a founding member of the Actors Studio. She was Kazan's character woman. She was the first Linda Loman in *Death of a Salesman*. She was to be the greatest Mary Tyrone of the twentieth century.

I took her scene study class. And during my three years at Columbia I began to act on the New York stage.

The morality of Method Acting was grounded not on personality, but on authenticity of feeling in situation—that was its strength and limitation—for it was a value that could not be applied everywhere and in all plays, as I was presently to learn. But at the time, I knew The Method not by experience but through the performances of others. Watching it, it seemed to cut through the bunk in which I had been raised, but I couldn't distinguish between the truth of it as I saw actors body it forth and the appropriateness of myself as a participant in it. I wasn't trained in it, all I had was scene study with Millie, I'd just do it on instinct. On Broadway I held a spear in Siobhan McKenna's *Saint Joan*. Off-Broadway I played leads.

All the reasons for envisioning myself as an actor found consonance with the time, for a new sort of actor was emerging, the female/male star. Montgomery Clift was a female/male star—a male men could actually kind of fall in love with in a pre-sexual way, because the feminine side of the male was, for the first time in American films, visible and because he was so beautiful. Dean was the second of these and confirmed the trend that goes through Christopher Jones, Leonardo di Caprio, Eric Roberts, Brad Pitt, Brad Davis, Billy Crudup, and on to the next. With Dean and Clift, a tolerance had been started for a male like me. I had a place to survive. The thing in favor of it was that I thought to prevail by force of truth. The thing against it was that I did not consider myself sexy, and that I did not realize at the time that these actors were all jeune premiers. Jeune premier, sometime called "the juvenile," means the second and more youthful romantic lead; he plays opposite the ingenue, while the leading man plays opposite the leading lady. And because they have to be shorter than the leading man, jeune premiers are usually short. In *Much Ado About Nothing*, John Gielgud is tall and is the leading man and plays Benedict; Michael York is shorter, is the jeune premiere and plays Claudio. Suddenly, however, and for the first time, with James Dean jeune premiers had become leading actors.

But I was not destined to be a jeune premier leading actor. I was six two.

I didn't get this until summer stock, which I did after graduation. In stock, I wanted to play the romantic swain who gets the girl. I was cast instead in large parts but ones that called for me at twenty-four to play forty-five-year-old men: Patrick in *The Loud Red Patrick* who had marriageable daughters, Doolittle in

Pygmalion. Some authority I had on the stage must have dictated such casting, but I longed to kiss the girl, or to be thought of that way.

I was not happy with that, and I was not happy with my work that summer, which was not up to a standard I could envision but not reach. I feared not being true, feared not having every moment connect with the one before—a demand unreal to be placed on Shaw, who doesn't write for actors that way— and a standard unnecessary in commercial comedy, which requires for its humor the comeuppance of fixed personalities. My standards interfered with my learning the craft. I was also a slow study. I was miserable, didn't know why, and wasn't easy to work with.

As soon as I got back to New York City, I made a date with Millie for lunch so that I could kvetch. After all, she was a master. She would have the answer to all this.

We met on Times Square—but she had an errand to run first, which was to go to Elia Kazan's office to turn down the part of Aunt Nonie in *Sweet Bird of Youth*, which he was mounting on Broadway with Paul Newman and Geraldine Page. As we walked, I began but did not finish my lament, for before I was done we reached the Astor/Victoria Theatre; Kazan's offices were above it. As we began climbing the stairs, I realized I was maybe going to meet The Great Kazan. I was nervous and excited, but because the meeting wasn't about me I became quiet, respectful.

Kazan's office was a dark dingy suite, and when he came out of his inner office he hugged Millie encompassingly. Millie's back was to me and Kazan was facing me, and as he hugged her, she said, "Gadge, I want you to meet Mr. Moody."

"To hell with Mr. Moody," he said to me and went on relishing the hug.

I watched as they went into his inner office and said to myself, The greatest director of actors in the world has just said to me on sight, To hell with you. I am going to give up acting.

And at that instant I did. I decided to write instead.

I gave up acting. But I never gave up my devotion to it. Indeed, it holds a spell for me. I remained close to Mildred Dunnock, who held that spell also. We palled around, she and her husband were witnesses at my wedding, my wife and I stayed at her house, went to see her in her plays, her many films and TV shows. I met well-known people because she was friends with them. I loved Millie. She wasn't easy, because she was a master, but I rejoiced in her mastery and her nature and her femininity and her gift. She was always exciting to me, and I thought the excitement of my relations to her were sufficient to my relations to acting because she desired my criticism of her work from the first day I met her. Criticism was the sphere of mastery in which I operated, and her own mastery was so great she was worth the attention. How great an actress was she? One story must suffice. She once starred in a play the young director of which I asked how it was to direct her. I sensed his experience had been difficult because she read his inexperience and went her own way, but what he said to me about her was, "She knew so much about acting it had become innocent again."

I was a moon to the art of acting. It was the magnet of my soul. I stood as close to it as I could. As though I never wanted to do anything else but stand close to it. Its light. Its force. Its truth.

For what I loved about acting was the authenticity of the actor. Authenticity is rare in humans, Millie had it and I was fascinated by it because authenticity wasn't a virtue I myself much possessed.

And now I stand here wondering.

Acting was a calling I spurned.

A calling calls to awaken one's authentic self. It is the whisper of an angel. And it will never go away.

What if this lure of acting all these years—what if that really meant I myself was supposed to be an actor? What if it meant that my own authenticity was to be discovered there? What if being an actor had nothing to do with being famous? Or even good at it?

A calling means you press though every difficulty, even the difficulty of being bad. And the result is the realization of the soul.

And I didn't even press through the first barrier—Kazan's remark.

No. Not Kazan's remark. That wasn't the first barrier. The first barrier was my difficulties in summer stock. Kazan was just kidding—I used his remark to quit. I could have persevered, I could have trained. Instead I made a momentous petty decision, I copped out.

Should I go to this audition? Should I go back into acting? And if I do, would I have to give up writing, which is also a calling?

For there is a certain fatality in a calling, a death, a grave of all other lives. The life will be realized if the calling is met. But other lives must remain outside the path of its sovereign and daimon force. And even if one does honor the calling, one does not know in advance how exactly the calling will be met.

And could I make a living at it? Millie once said that she had known many actors of great talent who had not made it, and many of small talent who had, and that there was no accounting for it; being a working actor is a question of Destiny.

But a living is perhaps not the question.

For now I am free. The landscape around me has no obstacles. The roadside is a tabula rasa on which my life could write anything. Antarctica to the south, the North Pole to the North, to the west the Pacific, and to the east who knows what. I could go in any direction. I am free to do what God intends me to do—if the chance is once presented, the sign given, if God makes the gate plain enough for me to see.

As I look about, there are no gates.

Save one. This audition.

And if I go back into acting, would I really invest myself in it? Would I really do what has to be done?

An old woman, Arlene Huntington, said something to me recently. She was talking about me in relation to acting, although how she knew there was such a relation I have no idea. "Bruce," she said in her rasping voice, "I've learned one thing in life: you're not too old, you're not too fat, you're not too stupid. *Go* for it!"

Taking her at her word, how serious then could I be about acting if I went into it again; would I *go* for it? My moral views about art are still there, it's still the friggin' holy of holies, I'm still a pain in the neck, it still is hard, I'm still vulnerable to ridicule. And would I really pursue it? With a passion! Consistently! On its own terms! I don't know.

There's a death of all other lives if you pursue your calling, and there's a death of your own life if you don't. And there's an even meaner death if you don't try to find out. I don't know if acting is my calling. I don't want to go to this audition tonight. There is every sort of reason not to. And I don't know if this audition will show me one way or another. But I have only one life to live. All my life acting has been a template for my soul. Now I have to find out if my soul itself is meant for it as a practice. If I don't, on my deathbed I'll look back and say, Bruce, you had your chance on the roadside to find out, and you didn't take it. From where I stand begging in the rain, this audition is an unlikely move, but right now it's the only move I have. I'll never forgive myself if I cop out again.

I am going to that audition.

I go home and change. I set out. It's dark, but the night is mine. I know exactly how to get there. I drive over the rain-black hills and I land in the empty mall where the theater is.

Only two cars parked—means I'm the last audition of the evening; they'll sigh a sigh of relief that they have found me at last.

The stage door is locked. No answer. I search for another entrance. Knock. Nothing.

I walk to the front of theater itself.

Nothing. Have they forgotten me?

I go around back and try again.

I'm downcrest. And baffled. I drive home over the doomed hills. How could they treat me that way?

Wait a minute—was that the right theater?—oh my God, I went to the wrong theater! Oh my God, what a fool.

As soon as I get home, I call my actor friend Maddy Fluhr.

She says to call, tell them truth, and ask for another audition.

Tell the truth?

The idea is inconceivable.

5 January, Tuesday

Inconceivable, yes. Why should I tell the truth? I don't like telling the truth. They'll just laugh at me. I probably already have a reputation from last night; they're bound to say the auditions are over. If I call, I have a ninety-nine percent chance of not being given another audition.

On the other hand, if I don't call: zero chance.

A half day's morning's work at Winkin's again. I call.

The woman at the theater says to bring out the head shot. It's a long way, it's raining, what hope do I have? Besides I'm afraid. Besides I'm too important. I say I'll mail it. But when I hang up, I realize I have turned down an invitation for personal contact at a theater. I call back and say, yes, I'll drive it out after work.

As I drive there, I realize that the first thing I must do is come clean about the missed audition.

It's to the receptionist I do that. She laughs: the disgrace is over.

The director isn't there, so I leave a note to him saying he needs me, a senior actor who can speak the lines.

When I get home, a message is already on my answering machine asking me to call immediately for an audition. I call Maddy to thank her. I drive back to the theater.

The director, Saul Camber is six foot seven, thin as a snake, nervous as fire, and grateful to see me—not enough senior actors have turned up for this play crammed with parts for them.

I read really well.

Then he tours me around the theater complex which is modern and fancy, and shows me the model of the set. "It's a cross," he says, "with a crown hanging over it, because it's a conflict between church and state."

Catherine of Aragon is about a woman in a bad marriage to Henry VIII. The king throws away church, state, and queen for two minutes of love with a seventeen-year-old minx, Anne Boleyn. Between Henry, Catherine, and Anne moves the greatest political figure in Europe, Cardinal Wolsey. This is the part I am reading for. The play itself is a boulevard tragedy written when the playwright had a drop taken, I think. At any rate, he is entirely out of his shallows, which were for the light commercial comedies of his day. But he wrote a number of these over-upholstered historical pieces, all of them successful, none of them done any more. *Catherine of Aragon* was a hit on broadway fifty years ago, and Saul Camber saw it when he was young. Cornell played it—an over-upholstered actress if there ever was one. The play is no more about the conflict of church and state than it is about the price of cabbages. I forebear to correct him in the matter.

"You're exactly what I'm looking for," he says as we part. "It looks promising. I'll call in the next few days."

It's still pouring as I drive home. Missing the first audition got me a private one, and it was so easy it's bound to be right. And I told the truth! I'm on my way. A burden has lifted.

Should I go on the roadside? Nah, It's raining, I've had a career lift, take a holiday.

But I don't actually have the part, so go.

On the other hand there isn't much time before nightfall.

Never mind, make the effort. I go home, have tea, dress. At 4:30 I am there.

I stand disregarded. But inwardly in my stomach I am warm.

I stay until my appointed hour.

$6.75. Going there kept me honest.

I get in the tub with the play. I'm raving with fame and fortune, it's the most luxurious theatre in the Bay Area, I am in the catbird seat. No, Bruce, be humble, just work hard, read up on the character, and keep it simple. All the great actors who ever lived are rooting for me! No, what I have to do is honor the art—surprise the art. No, until I have the part all I have to do is commit to it. No, all I have to do is wait for the phone to ring.

8 January, Friday

He said he'd call in a few days, and this is three days, and no message.

11 January, Monday

I stare at the answering machine as at a mountain yielding gold.

13 January, Wednesday

No word. So that's that, I guess. Not kind. Not efficient. Not truthful.

Brendan Moon calls. I'm his first convert and he has a mentorly concern to find out how I'm doing. He's outside in the rain, a phone booth somewhere, at night. He says he works in the rain without a hat. He doesn't want to make things too comfortable for himself, which I understand.

I ask if he called the woman who makes the children's furniture. I can tell he's not going to. He prefers the bank withdrawal of the road. And so might I.

14 January, Friday

Nine days. No call.

I drag my feet to the roadside. We've had a month of rain. I am depressed—but not by the rain—by the deflation of my dreams. Here I stand in the downpour. Yes, I've entertained aspirations of high accomplishment. I once had lunch with Elizabeth Taylor, she and I were young, but it wasn't because of my accomplishments that we were together but because of hers and Millie's who was in the movie with her. It's name-dropping to say I went to Yale and Columbia, had columns in national magazines—all people and institutions more renowned than myself. I wanted and I still do want to do beautiful and liberating work and be famous for it. I still want my glory. I want it so badly I filch someone else's.

The good-looking young man in a black pickup painted with fire waves back to me as he passes! He's waved before.

The first car to stop gives—a good sign—a new dark red sedan driven by a white haired man and wife in their seventies, a well-to-do middle class couple in plaid—Republicans—they sure won't give. But they do.

I stand making like an orphan—Poor Me.

I hate Poor Me. I don't have a sob story, I never had bad luck. Luck, good or bad, wasn't my sphere. I'm strong, I'm healthy, reasonably good-looking, but all that came in the mail, it wasn't good luck, it was good fortune. Besides, none of this orphan-drama has anything to do with standing here. I don't have to milk it, look grievous, I'm not here to "get" people to give me money with looking winsome. It's pouring but I don't care, I won't wear a hat, I won't put up the umbrella. I'm not made of sugar, the rain is the rain. I am here as I am. To be in it is bearable, and possessing its own sufficient qualities. In the rain I have no past, no future. I am the history of the rain. I am just this standing with these cars, this water, this day.

A boy stops and holds out folded bills, change from a bridge toll. His face is the common face of the country, you wouldn't think he would give, but he does.

A woman with frizzy blond hair stops. I smile, but turn away so as not to alarm her. Presently she opens her window and gives.

A young woman, although I was near enough to go to her, jumps out and runs to me and gives—all before the light changes.

I say, "Bless you." But "Bless you" sounds off, as though I am doing the blessing, whereas it's God who does it. But the word "God" seems presumptuous. Maybe I'll come to it. I'll try. *God* bless you.

When people give I feel such joy! God is drenching me with it. When, after an hour and a half, I leave, though the shoulders of my fir green parka are soaked through, the wool sweater underneath is not. Inside my body I am warm, I am safe.

It's 4:30 when I get home. I check the answering machine anyhow. Nothing. I feel like giving up. Well, the theatre answering machine will announce the cast tonight; so as to get the bad news entirely over with, I dial it.

When Wolsey is announced, I hear my name unfold syllable by syllable and hang up. I can't believe it! I got the part! Whoopee!

I call Maddy, then my daughter Amanda; I call Annie Hallatt, and other friends; they're delighted!

We start rehearsal 11 February. The schedules and contracts will be sent. Moola!

Although I was given to by only five people, there is $17.00 —a lot! I'm so grateful. I try to record everyone, I want to remember everyone, but I'm tired and can't.

27 January, Wednesday

I feel energized by want. I'm full of the juice of ambition. To take every step I can, I get out four biographies of Wolsey from the library.

And also, to really go for it, to really convince myself I am committed, I'm going to go to acting school. I don't believe in schools of art, except to get to know like-minded people, but I must challenge that belief. I must challenge the intensity of my limitations.

School will cost $4000—a $65 application fee due on Monday. The audition is 6 March, 39 days away. I'll keep on the roadside to finance it. I'd have to save $40 a day extra to do it. Trouble is I have to make phone and utility and rent also—$515 by 1 February. I can eat off the roadside, but there's a leaking gas tank and new tires—slowing down it skidded 180 degrees in the rain on the freeway yesterday and came to a halt facing traffic. Well, I'll trust I can earn it, and that everything will work out.

I also make an appointment for the Theatre Bay Area acting auditions on 14 February, nineteen days away. Once a year, fifty-five local theatre companies send their casting directors to these auditions.

I also send my old theatre criticisms to the papers to get a job. My hunch is God doesn't want me to do that work any more—but I must leave no stone unturned.

I'm energized, yet I drag myself to the roadside. I'm lazy, I am, I am.; I balk at change. Thomas Moore's *The Care of the Soul* says the alchemical solution is the acceptance of all that lies within. This is the same as Keats' negative capability—

the capacity that rests unprejudiced beneath our malice, envy, hopelessness, sexual irregularity, laziness—and accepts them all. Acceptance is the alchemist's retort. I am laggard but I go. Because on the roadside I accept everything.

I also go because I need the rent.

I harden myself and park in the hospital lot—absurd when I don't have the sort of self that hardens. I also have to stand here longer hours, not just for the money but for the discipline, and to get serious, and because it's right.

The January sky is cold and happy, but as I walk down the hill toward the exit I feel the wrong of the roadside as an electric current I can't get my finger out of the socket of. To take money in this way!—I had noble ambitions, I was a high king, and here I am a mendicant! What has this degradation to do with the romance of my life? There is something in it that wrongs me—but does it wrong something that was ever right? Were all my noble ambitions just dreams of grandeur? Is my going to school just a scam?

I walk on toward the burning gate. Toward *Do Not Enter.*

A good-looking powerful young man hands out a bunch of bills, saying, "Sorry that's all I have"—the first car, a good sign as a rule.

Some other roadside rules: People with cell phones don't give because they don't have a hand free to get to their dough. The first two cars stopped to give more often than those behind because they have more time to pass through their resistance and get into their wallets. I relate to drivers not to passengers; the drivers are in the driver's seat: they have the power to stop, to influence the passengers, to drive away; they're nearer to me. If people are going to offer work, I probably won't see them reach for their money. It's harder for men to get to their money because they have to undo their seat belts to get to their back pockets; women just have to reach over into their purses.

Whether people give seems not a question of gender: males and females give equally. Giving is not a sexual issue either: whether being on the roadside I am sexually attractive or sexually despicable, or masculine or not. For people give irrespective of their view of my nature, which is perfectly obvious, for I am porous, known, read without eyes. So none of that need tempt me to assume one attitude or another to inspire them to give. The clean mountainside air of neutrality opens up inside me.

The sun is bright, the breeze blusters. I am exposed and poor but I am content to be here. Bless you car, bless you Spanish lady, bless you heap, bless you pickup, bless you. . . . Will people give to me because I am content—to those who have, more is given? Being happy maybe I will do well. Or maybe people feel I am too happy.

What am I doing—in one breath I say I need not be tempted and in the next moment I am plotting to make people give! I'm not here to plot. All I need do is stay. Plots come up, though.

Bless you bad tempered truck driver, bless you scared-of-me lady, bless you US Mail truck—US Mail trucks don't give, maybe it's against the law.

What am I saying?—"US Mail trucks don't give?" How to stop these money calculations? The sign says "Will Work," but I think only of "$."

The daylight is free around us all. I stand here free also, but my ability to stand here depends upon my spirit, and greed will keep me away from this place if I continue in it.

Greed is as palpable as porridge, the bowl of it right there in my stomach. If God wants Greed to go, it will go, if God wants it there, it will be there. God, please come into this bowl of Greed in me. I can feel God come into it; Greed thins into a vapor; Greed goes.

Greed is future-oriented—Wanting What's Coming—which is how it achieves dissatisfaction, which is how it regenerates itself.

But, as I glance for signs—the looked-for purse, the shift to a wallet—Greed comes back. For the main human communication I have is how drivers, having seen me, move (or do not move) in their seats. My being here says something: I am here; I am holding this sign; I am not a neutral situation for them.

Bless you old man, bless you boys going to the fast-food joint to work. Bless you, East Asian lady, East Asian people won't give, bless you. . . .

Wait a minute: East Asian people? The idea that East Asian people won't *hire* me never occurs to me. East Asian people have already given to me. Why do I keep saying they won't? Immediately, as the light turns yellow an elderly East Asian man stops.

I catch his eye and look away so as not to intrude. Eventually he opens up his window and hands me a bill.

"Thank you, God bless you, thank you. Is there any work I can do for you?"

He smiles modestly and shakes his head that it's all right, and another fast-food miracle drives away. Well then East Asian people *will* give! Will or will not, either way it's the same concern about money.

An old lady in a Buick sedan passes; bless you.

Rich old people don't give.

Immediately an elderly couple stop in a gray Chrysler. He in a brown and white checked Pendleton shirt, she in a fine wool sweater with red and yellow spruce trees on a white ground. Ah, I too have a charge account at Brooks' Brothers, though I don't use it. They're too old, too well-off to give. They hand me a bill. Another fast-food miracle. And others like them have given too. But prejudice high-hats its teacher and stalks back to the same dry water hole.

I didn't think of myself as a prejudiced person before the roadside.

Prejudice . . . what good is it here? It has nothing to do with work or dollars. Nothing to do with blessing. Nothing to do with standing here neutral. Prejudice demeans me—I feel worse for thinking myself better in thinking others worse. Yet here Prejudice is, as though it were an advantage. Why, with all this against it, does it persist?

And where is this Prejudice coming from all at once? Is Prejudice my pride scrambling for a finger-hold? Prejudice, that promotion of the self through the de-glorification of others. Prejudice—that avarice of survival: Ya don't kill them outright, ya just keep them down on the farm. And if peonization is too costly, well then: erasure! Mentally, I am no different from Hitler, with his extermination camps. Except Hitler would have eliminated even Prejudice itself—for once the Jews, homosexuals, gypsies, cripples had been eradicated, Prejudice must have withered, having nothing to feed on. Wrong. He would have gone to work on age groups, eye colors, sweater sizes. Prejudice needs groups to keep itself alive. If every BMW did give, I would concoct a prejudice against Fords. Prejudice is a survival technique which destroys Groups, but must first manufacture them. Prejudice whispers to me: "You are more worthy of survival than they. They might not give, which makes them miserly, unimaginative, unmannerly. They are morally inferior. They deserve to die, or at least be demoted." And what does Prejudice really want? Prejudice whispers its answer: "What everything wants: to survive, to keep going. Like Greed. Like Hope. Like Breathing."

Prejudice: the desire to eliminate Groups as equal before God. If I had the power, I might have the inclination. Except for when the cars actually stop. Oddly enough, when I look in the face of the East Asian man, whether he gives or not, Prejudice vanishes.

Bless you, bless you teenagers. Teenagers won't give.

Teenagers—that's billions of people. Very well, the larger the group the more people I may look down upon. See Bruce sneer. See Prejudice climb its ladder of Jell-O.

For here I stand on the highway, manufacturing belittlements; I can feel their force-field inside my body; I can analyze Prejudice, but so what, I cannot stop it. I stand here blessing others and I stand here cursing others as well.

I take a deep breath and look around. The day is fine. The skies define the universe as free. The clouds belong to all, the color green liberal to all. The sky curves over the Earth, and everything is in its cape. The beauty of that common embrace supersedes Prejudice. Prejudice is dispelled. I breathe it out. I breathe the sky in.

And this knowledge of this sky that I feel now is the exquisite privilege of begging. I had to come here to know this. To know it. Everyone in the world would come if they knew what at this moment I know now: to be subject to the unbigoted sky.

I want Prejudice to end but I must not be prejudiced against Prejudice either. For Prejudice is older than me and is in me—a shark's fin skirting through me with every right to swim here.

Bless you, bless you, bless you with the grocery bags on the seat next to you, bless you with the cigarette in your mouth, bless you businesswoman coming home from work in your more than perfect suit, bless you.

My calves ache. My regimen is to stand absolutely still, not shift or seek ease, so people may see I can endure my job steadily without complaint or coddling. And so as not to fish for pity. Not be shifty and shiftless. However, I take the liberty to move my legs, one foot then the other. That's all it takes. I stand still again.

A woman hails me from the second lane. I scope the traffic and skip over, she hands me a couple of bills. She's a fine looking woman in her early forties. When I say God bless you, she says, "You too." The free fall of the gift makes me happy. At that moment, nothing in it but the gift.

Hey, my mascot tree, you're calling me. Where are you, ah, there on your hilltop, working away just standing, I working here, just standing.

From four to five no one gives. Will I collect $40 for the acting school tuition? Never mind, Bruce, just be aware and say, Bless you.

The good-looking guy in the fiery black pickup waves back at me as he turns in the far lane. The fire on his truck is like the fire of his beauty, the chief ingredient of him as we notice him pass by in this world. What is it to be inside a life with so much male beauty broadcast around it? He can't help it, he knows he has it, checks it like a coat at the door—he has to, to survive it. I envy him, and yet this twenty-eight-year-old male, envied by not only me, throws me a greeting every time, like a fish rising up over a wave, free of his beauty entirely for a moment, while a part of it entirely, and then returning to it splashless entirely.

In all this, people are wonderful and I experience it keenly. I am in an ecstasy of sweetness not because of the money but because of something exchanged even when they give no money, no food, no work. People nod, wave at me, smile. Without giving, they give.

My joy is keener when they give, though, for there's something in a deed.

I take my eyes from the cars, I look about. The sun is out after some days, the hillside turned green as things do here in the winter. And the trees' green on the green hills. The air is even. I am happy. I am not ashamed. Why don't I feel bad? Maybe because this place is on a the top of a hill where there is light and because I find myself outdoors. I never suspected outdoor work would suit me, but I like it. Still I should feel bad, shouldn't I; where is my pride? Gone. Turned into something else.

Two boys in the second lane toss me a lollypop. Someone lobs a can of Green

Giant corn, and I catch it, pat. A beep from the road behind me, and a couple with a little child hand me the rest of their pizza.

After that, no one gives.

As it grows close to five, it gets colder and I put on my khaki wool mittens. My stomach is cold inside. I feel miserable. A beep from behind. I turn and go, lean down courteously. A woman parked leans over the passenger seat to speak up at me.

"Do you do yard work?"

"Why, yes."

"Would you work for a meal?"

"Yes."

"I have some yard work, if you'll take a meal for it."

"Oh, yes, I will."

"Can you do it now?"

"Yes." My first work! I am frightened. Also afeard of getting into a stranger's car, being carried off I know not where. But I must do it. "I have to get my things."

I gather my backpack and signs and get into her car, clutching them in my lap, afraid of leaving them behind in her car. "Where is it?"

"It's not far from here."

"How will I get back?"

"I'll drive you."

She drives to an unprepossessing ranch house backing on the freeway, probably a rental. The front yard has not been gardened. I get out. I feel helpless. She herself has to leave to shop. She goes in to get her husband, Barry, and drives off.

He shows me a pile of spruce clippings next to the front door to be bagged and taken to the back yard. I can do it. It's hardly worth a meal though. He watches his little daughter, Angela. He's been out of work since April when roof tar fell on him. How come he doesn't do the work himself, he doesn't look disabled? Maybe he is, though. Or maybe he's offered it me out of generosity. Or maybe it's one of those little jobs you have around your house and never get to. He goes inside.

I know exactly what the meal's going to be: franks and beans. But it'll be a change. Accept generosity generously, Bruce.

I do the job meticulously, to be sure I've earned my keep. When I'm done I knock. Canned soup and hot dogs. He serves me at the dining table. He does not sit down with me. I look about the room, up at a high shelf at china car models she has collected. You've promised not to intrude, Bruce, don't look—you're help. Eyes lowered, I eat in prim pain—to be here, to have done this.

She comes from shopping and drives me back to the roadside. I stand on the hilltop in the departing sun. The whole thing took an hour, and I missed the money there might have been on the roadside, but there might not have been any. But I went out and actually took a job for food or money, I went through with it, I did it, I kept my word.

After four hours at 6:15 I leave, and when I get home and count it it's $41— $17 an hour —one of those kind people gave a $20 bill—not enough extra for acting school, though. But even if it were enough that's not the transaction, that's not what's really happening. Because something has happened to me, something that is good for me. Being on the roadside has its painful parts, but they are turning into something else and not into something cynical. Something is over. Oh, there are problems of mind the whole time I am there, they are an agony and I face them because I must stay, but that's not what is happening. Agony is not the happening. What is happening is that something is burning. The burning isn't over. I am in the burning. What is over is the fear that what lies on the other side of the burning is worse than the burning.

28 January, Thursday

I've been on the roadside a month and not told a soul. Now I tell Ellen, my mentor. I fear she will think me low although she has never done so. I tell her because it is my policy to tell her everything, particularly things I don't want to tell her.

Her response is praise for my being proactive to remedy my situation. How unexpected! I never thought of myself as praiseworthy in this. I felt the roadside as a disgrace in my own and the world's eyes, but I feel now another truth walking alongside it, which is that I am still standing. For I have embraced the roadside in good time. It makes it possible for me to search for work, to call newspapers about the reviews I've sent, to attend seminars at the state employment agency, to call about jobs, to call the temp agencies. I couldn't do any of that without a roof over my head. Yes, things about the roadside suit my situation.

But each day I approach it with sorrow. I don't go every day, because I resist it, but for that very reason, the roadside is the ditch I must dig. And also, because there may be some unforeseen salvation in it, I, in fact, treat it reverently. Reverently will do no harm.

For instance, the clothes.

I knew they had to be robes of office. Beginning with a forest-green Timberline parka. Biking through Alberta ten years ago I found it in a free-box in a hostel. Such parkas came in kits and were hand-sewn, and I treasured it because someone's mother made it for some kid who left it behind. In the same box was an orange wool sweater. It turned out I needed both to bike in the snow that began to fall. Now I wear them with clean old jeans and some old leather walking shoes for standing.

I dress cleanly. I don't put on a costume of rags or appear at the office in a matted beard. Instead I shave, shower, and dress properly just as I would for any job. Drivers-by have a right that I look like a decent person. If I stand here as work, dressed for work, conducting myself decently in work, drivers-by may see how I do work and I may get work. And whether they do or not, this is the way I like to work.

I wear the same clothes every day so people can become familiar with me and suppose this wardrobe to be all I've got, for these clothes do represent my actual financial case and are the uniform of this occupation—clean, not fashionable with oil stains and rips. I wear clean socks and underwear and thrift-shop wool shirts. In the backpack are moth-holed khaki wool mittens I've had since Korea 40 years ago. The backpack, of heavy pale blue-gray canvas, must be fifty years old. Its metal frame made it uncomfortable but now that frame props it up against the Do Not Enter pole with the second sign bungeed to it. These robes and accoutrements I use only here, and hang them when I get home, as in a vestry, behind my door.

I arrive at 11:06 A.M., I'll stay until 5:06 P.M. As I set up I feel I'm out here to do a job. I like that feeling.

A young man hands me money on the first stop of cars. But his face leaves my brain at once, as though quick greed effaced it. All this money coming at me from people whose faces are immediately lost to memory—that is not right.

"Thank you. God bless you. Is there any work I can do for you?"

The person I just said that to—was it a woman or a man? Trouble is with moving cars it all happens in a flurry. A car drives by, I am caught up in coordinating my hand with theirs to take the money without hurting them or dropping it, keeping far enough from the moving car to receive it deftly and safely, which is what they wish me to do. I thank and bless them, look momentarily at them—but as soon as the car continues on, I forget them. The face flies by in the carousel moment of seizing a bill from a hand whose other hand is bent on turning a steering wheel left. How can I forget them? Is forgetfulness a greed, an ingratitude, a mental defect?

These people must be remembered. But by the time I record them at night I'm tired and sometimes do it the following morning, so some of them are lost. I've got to use a better system than memory.

I know, I'll number-memorize them. Let's see, who was number one? #1 was the first young man whose face I forgot. Well, he was a young man, that much I've got. #2 was the person whose gender I forgot.

A hand comes out a car window and my hand misses it and the bill blows about in the road. #3: the bill in the road.

Bless you yellow school bus, bless you truck driver smoking, bless you lady in the black van with the kids and bless your kids and bless your van.

Rich women with gray hair in fancy cars will not give.

Immediately a white-haired woman in a little white Cadillac pulls right off the road and onto the dirt to give. "I understand," she says, and she does. Another fast-food miracle. #1: First young man. #2: Unknown gender. #3: Bill in the road. #4: Rich old lady in Cadillac.

Bless you, bless you, bless you little girl next to your mother, bless you salesman in a sharkskin suit, bless you man out of shape.

Hispanic women are traditional and won't give.

Immediately stops a woman with black hair made more shiny by being bunned tight Spanish style and the rich hidalgo coloring of dark roses. I nod and turn away. A bit of time goes by but she opens her window and hands me money, for she is sweet. And all these people are sweet. #1: First young man. #2: Unknown gender. #3: Bill in the road. #4: Rich old in Cadillac. #5: Hispanic woman.

Later in the morning a good-looking young man deliberately drives his little pickup over into my lane to talk to me. "I don't have work, but are you accepting contributions?"

As I look into his eyes, there is a moment of connection to something so handsome in him, and not in me. What a distance I have always been from what I see behind his eyes. He drives away, and I feel the wound of an attraction to what I can never meet: the place in him where he had never been molested.

I have never been mistreated by anyone here.

At once, three men in a pickup—one shouts derisively, "Give you fifty dollars for your jacket!" I think that's what he yells.

"What?" I holler.

He doesn't answer, maybe he became ashamed.

Then two homely boys in a car, one with buckteeth, seem to find me funny. Fast-food miracles, one after another, over and over, keep happening: I'm afraid the police will harass me and, pat, the patrolman comes; Hispanic people won't give, and pat, the woman with the bun; I have never been mistreated, pat, the rude boys holler. If you read it in a book, you wouldn't believe it.

As to the rude boys yelling, I must be ready to put a shield up fast. But, if hurt, I will not die of it.

I leave for lunch at 2:06; I'll come back at exactly 3:06.

In the hospital cafeteria, I read a biography of Wolsey.

When I come back, a semi is stuck in the middle lane funnelling all the cars into my lane—aha!—more revenue!

Wrong: more unfounded opinion. Maybe more cars'll come, yes, but be so irritated at having to shift lanes they won't give anything at all. My opinions are crazy. Opinion itself is crazy. Opinion is the first recourse of the uninformed, and the last. No one has a right to their opinion, merely a wrong. For the purpose of being informed is not to form an opinion, but to not form an opinion. To form an opinion, information is irrelevant, indeed undesirable.

And so I form opinions based on nothing. Sacred spheres are irrational, physics itself requires the banishment of the mind, yet I try to put two and two together as I am juggled by this divinity, the roadside. Life is logical and random, but here I am, wanting guarantees. I am here, the drivers are there, a dollar bill joins us, that is all. Dramas go on in me and may go on in them, but dramas are not essential. What's essential is the transaction. But what is that? Sometimes I say, "How's it going?"—not to instigate them to give, for that's not the transaction. But what is the transaction?

A black man in a new ruby-red car: "How're ya doing?"

"Okay, how are you?" I'm glad to talk to him.

"Okay," he says.

"Good." I turn to face the other cars so as not to pressure him. But as he drives away he hands me $5 saying, "God bless you."

I shout after his departing car, "God bless *you!*"

I will try to say God bless you even when people just chat.

In the second car I see two kids canoodling, he eighteen, everyone's cute kid, and she everyone's cute girl. They're so luscious they're fragrant. He drives, and she feeds him from a little brown bag, he being the sultan as a young man will be. They don't see me. To give them their privacy I look away. Presently traffic starts. As they pass, they hand me that little brown bag—a literal fast-food miracle, their ambrosia: popcorn.

Bless you, bless you, and you rattletrap, and you Dodge van like my old roommate used to have, the rat, and bless you cars going by below I forgot about you. And bless you. And—there's nobody coming, ah, here comes someone, let them come, let them drift up, bless you, and someone else, bless you green car, bless you that one and that one and that one.

I stand here and the hours go by and the cars go by and there's something wrong that I want to make clear to those cars. My sign says I am asking for work, which would lead drivers-by to suppose I am looking for such work as manual labor and, sure, I would take it, but I really want it for school. I feel obliged to let everyone know this. Or maybe I don't have to. Maybe in acting I do my true calling, and every true calling benefits the community. Or is that just a bunch of horsefeathers?

Add to the invocation I say every day when I get here:

COMPACT
• May everyone find right work and do it rightly. Including me.

By four o'clock, I have been here five hours. I look forward to leaving. It's tiring to say Bless you to everyone, it's fun but it's frenetic. The semi has been towed away—its removal involved big tow trucks—and I didn't even notice! I stay until after five, then go home and I write down everyone. Because they should be remembered, and remembered forever.

What does it mean, "remembered forever"? It means not just to remember them because they were kind to me, but—more—that I should remember *them*, each in their living particularity and that this and only this can be sufficient thanks. Why should anyone ever stop being grateful for what is given? It is the beauty of gratitude that it can never be repaid, as Milton somewhere said. I, in my heart, want to remember them keenly. Yet at the time greed effaces gratitude and I turn to the next car coming.

After six hours, $81, eight $5 bills. Need $393 by Monday. Well, I made my $40, and into the school envelope it goes.

I take a sheet of paper and a pen, I go to the "Will Work For Food Or $" sign and clip them behind it—that way I can make notes on the spot. That way I can remember everyone.

29 January, Friday

Driving down the freeway I feel solid. Next to me, the backpack lolls in the seat like a passenger. It's mid-morning. I have done my prayers and meditation, read my spiritual books, I am on time and ready.

The story of my spiritual life is simple. Until I was fifty-five I thought I would never have one. The God of the Episcopalians is The Almighty, a very rich bully, a sort of celestial tycoon. From the time I was five I was obliged to go to church two times a week, and when I went to boarding school and as an exchange student in England, six times. I said to myself, after school, no more, so from the time when I went to Yale I never went to church again. It was the early '50s, and none of my friends were churchgoers or believers, and I assumed I would not have a spiritual life at all, although I read about others having such. To challenge this notion, I explored other Christian denominations: the Quakers, Unitarianism. When the smorgasbord of the Human Potential Movement set its table, I sampled the various spiritual dishes of the '70s. I read the Bible through, and other scriptures. Nothing took. I never became a devotee, but I hung out with Rajneeshers, listened to his tapes, and did chaotic meditation with the rest of them. Rajneesh provided a wonderful course in comparative religion, but I wasn't really a seeker, only a seeker to see if I was a seeker. I was without spiritual passion.

However, all during this time, I had a mortal illness that no psychological or medical agency could cure. Then around age fifty-five I found a group accustomed to treating my disease as susceptible to a spiritual cure and its literature spoke often of God. So I said to myself, damn it, if I have to believe in God to get well, I'll bloody well do it. I knew the God of the Bible or the church wouldn't help me, so I got down on my knees and said, "Would a God come that would suit me? Would a God come that would heal me?" And immediately one came and the illness was lifted at that moment and never returned.

The gift of that miracle is two-fold: the disease is gone, but more important, when I think the word "God" now a sweetness comes into me, just as it did the afternoon I made that prayer. So every morning I pray and meditate as best I can. I help others who suffer from my disease. And I read spiritual books, which I love to do: I read through the ecclesiastical English poets of the seventeenth and eighteenth century who don't speak to me much any more; but Kabir does, and Mirabai, and Thomas Traherne's *Centuries* the third time through seems brand new. I read my beloved Rumi. (Rumi is one of the five greatest poets who ever lived, or would be were he not beyond the category.) I read one poem every morning. He never runs out.

Driving up the Appian exit, I look over at where I always stand, a spot familiar and dear. As I slow down for the light I wonder if drivers recognize me and suspect my owning a car. People call this '64 red Plymouth convertible a classic, but a classic is an old car that's been fixed up, and this is just an old car. Looking for a better place than the hospital lot, I drive down the hill. The first street is a semicircle cul-de-sac of three houses. I park it under a tree to shade it. Will the people in the houses suspect me, will they call the cops? I hide my car to deceive people—deceive them lest they think I deceive them.

I put the sunscreen on my bald spot, shrug the backpack on, and walk up the hill. As I approach the exit ramp, I see that opposite from where I stand the square of dirt where the sidewalk was missing is ribbon-fenced, and orange traffic cones extend it into the roadway. The cementing of the sidewalk is being completed by a lone Hispanic man. I skirt him —he is alien both by extraction and by profession.

As I cross the exit and set myself up, I keep my back to the traffic and my energy off it, I make myself invisible. On the dirt and on the exit field on which I stand, fast-food cartons and plastic bags have come to ground. Because I want my workplace nice and because I don't want drivers-by associating me with rubbish, I pile up some to take away at lunch: tidying is the least I can do for the place for letting me use it. Then I say my opening prayers:

"May everyone and every car passing by here or down below on the freeway come to no injury in the entire course of their lives. May every person passing find their right work, and do it rightly—including me."

I turn to the cars, step to the edge of the sidewalk, and I am open for business. I said I'd start at 10 o'clock and it's 10:04, I'll lunch at 2:04, come back at 3:04, leave at 5:04. Six hours.

I notice that by now, I no longer feel foolish, pathetic, impoverished, inferior, out of place here. I face the cars openly. I know my business. The cars, the people in them, and the situation I am in are not my enemies. Being out-of-doors is not a demotion. In fact, it is a promotion. I stand here in the winter sunshine, which is not harsh. I am on top of a hill and see gold hills from where I stand. The view of the sky is large. The free air is all about and broad. To the south a mackerel sky is making up. I am content.

Across the freeway stand developments. (When I moved near here seven years ago each of those houses was a cow.) Also a big shopping center. On this side of the freeway is a smaller shopping center, out of sight. On the freeway below the stitches of the cars run, three lanes north, three lanes south, and are never seen on this earth again. Hundreds and hundreds of people going whither; how can it be, how can there be so much busyness, so much intention?

Beside the freeway stand five eucalyptus, stately as spinsters and with the same attar of poultice about them. These five Dames are not needed by the freeway and no one notices them. Guffawing genteelly into their crocheted hankies, the five eucalyptus trees love it, love being disregarded.

Their hill rises in low weeds to where I stand on the bare dirt, which contains the small forsaken stuff of the roadside: guano of ashtrays, the odd candy wrapper, a shrapnel of broken glass, the senseless pebbles. And a windshield wiper.

While other refuse disappears, this wiper remains—but—who kicks it every day into a different place? Every day I carry it back to the rim of the sidewalk, for, rather than stand on cement, I stand, my heels raised on the sidewalk and my toes on the dirt, the windshield wiper with gravel built up around it to support my arches. My job is to stand absolutely still for six hours, so the feet are important. I shift them from time to time for circulation but go right back to standing still. I never move, but every day something moves that wiper!

As I take my place my need for enough money for tuition, for rent, for tires, vanishes. In this place there seems to be no tension for me, just the task. As though this place were a sanctuary, which maybe it is. The most difficult thing I could possibly imagine doing has become a kind of paradise.

If the first car gives, the day will be prosperous. Where do I get that superstition? Because the first time I came here the first car gave. If it doesn't then the first hour will not yield much. Where do I get that superstition?

Yesterday, I changed my wool sweater from the orange to the light blue. I thought the blue would attract more money. And the money was greater in the blue sweater, which I also wear today. But do I ascribe prosperity to a blue sweater? Do I test that by wearing the orange again? I'm not really interested in persisting in this research; I will wear the orange from now on.

Shall I see whether the take goes down when I give no blessing? No, I won't. Blessing is another value entirely. And yet what is the relation between money and blessing, if any? I mean, blessing may be attached to money as to anything else. I give blessings for free and they give money for free. But what really is the transaction?

One thing I am faced with is feeling overwhelmed by the immense number of people going by. Blessing everyone helps antidote this, but I also see how recessed I have been since earliest days, how hard it is to cross over to others, especially to people who are "lower-class" because I was bullied by them when I was young and I still hang out in that cringe. Thus, since I believe only lower-class people will give because only they have imagination, heart, and experience enough to appreciate my fix, my survival is at the mercy of people I'm afraid of. So I feel separate from everyone, pulled back inside myself. Besides, I also chose being a writer; to enact a precedent choice: exile: writer's have the consolation of living later.

What audience had I in mind as a writer? An acquaintance, Caroline, wants to read a manuscript of mine—was it her I had as my ideal audience? In fact I had no one in mind. I wrote so that others would find it beautiful. I wrote so others would not have to know the suffering I knew. I wrote to right a wrong. I wrote for the whole world.

But there is no such thing as The Whole World. Books are read by individuals one by one, often as an act of sequestration. There is only Caroline. There are only the people driving by, one by one, each sequestered. I wrote because I was afraid to speak, to be seen, to be known. I wrote for that inner audience in everyone that would respond, applaud, rejoice, benefit, be healed. But of a sense of a common thread between me and others—this I am deficient in. I am frightened of people so I arranged not to be seen and chose writing because it was invisible.

Now I stand on this windy hill among these windy hills, exposed to the fate of the sun and the eyes of multitudes. I stand here and bless everyone and am afraid.

And yet I smile. How can that be? I stand here naked and afraid. What is that a quote from? It feels "tragical"—I am not tragic, I am not a hero. I'm not doing anything brave. Heros are not blessed while they live.

Down below, cars peel off the freeway and drive up. In the first hour only $3.50—I happened to catch sight of the money. No-money makes me nervous and hateful of wasting my time, I'll make nothing all day, not a penny.

Where does that superstition come from? From being used to being on salary. And even if I do get nothing, this is God's game: zero is one of his possible scores. Your job, Bruce, is just to stay. You'll make more money that way.

I calculate all this as though God did not hear.

Bruce, you are not here to get rich or stay forever. You are here to keep a roof over your head and learn your craft.

But no, it's not even that. I am not here awaiting something I can predict— even a career. Nor am I here to earn the rent. Nor do I have to do something to deserve the money. In fact, each time I try to *earn* the money God rejects the effort. The gift of life comes to me free every moment I draw breath, I don't earn it, I neither deserve nor do not deserve it. My continuing to be alive is at God's disposition every second.

But my mind keeps reverting to its old track—"I must be here for a purpose, I must earn my living." Living?—what a curious word for a thing to earn.

An orange cement mixer delivers cement to the sidewalk paver across the street. They have such business, these workmen on the roads, they have outdoor eyes. Is that the work I should do—laying cement? My body is perhaps too old, and I'd be afraid of the men. When the truck leaves, the man paves on, bent to his calling. He, wholly absorbed, truly has an occupation.

The cars drive into the off-ramp below, divvy up. Hey, come into my lane, I want you all to be *mine* so you'll give money to *me*. Idiotic. Hope is just placing cheap bets. Those who give, give. Hope will not make them give. Cars approach, hope rises in me, I hand it over to God, see it subside. If I could think of God at every moment of my life, my whole life would be taken care of. Besides I do not really expect people to give—it is always a surprise. Besides I am not for everyone. If I were, I would make thousands a day, traffic jams would line up, no off-ramp in the United States would be used but this. Bruce, you are not supposed to be loved by everyone.

"Bruce, you're not supposed to be loved by anyone" was a family curse I defied with, "Oh, yeah, just you wait, I'll be a big star one day," meaning loved by everyone! But popularity did not happen.

Well, one day I will be the king of unpopularity, then, popular for being unpopular. For popularity is rare, and is created by those who do not have it for the precious few who do. It is the people who do *not* have popularity who are the majority. I will graciously incline to be their hero.

The vapid stench of piety—does it arise about me now? Well, tough, I got some lung capacity, man, I breathe in every cloud, every car, every person, every hill, and then I exhale them all back again and they're all just fine, they enjoyed the trip. Being here is not about need or hope, or popularity. I have a different task: right now, to endure not knowing what it is about and what the transaction really is.

All I want to do today is to stand here honorably. Because I am not honorable. This morning I awoke calculating staying on the roadside forever, to use the money not for school but for drowsy comfort, plotting how I would spend my whole life doing this.

"Thank you. God bless you. Thank you. Is there any work I can do for you?"

Because she hasn't any work an East Asian lady shakes her head, smiling apologetically, sad to have fallen short.

I fear someone who knows me will see me.

Man in Monty Woolley beard is driving up—he is that man from my town! No, only someone who looks like him, different wife. They give me money. Fast-food miracle again.

Cars stop. In the third car, a pretty, well-dressed black woman fumbles in her purse. Don't look directly, Bruce, don't impose, she may be looking for a smoke; just see things edgewise. She turns to the back seat, it looks like to collect money from a woman there, and a man. But her window doesn't open. If the window's not rolled down, there's no money coming.

The traffic starts. As the car passes, long red fingernails slide two bills out the top crack of the window, along with a hyena of black woman laughter! The money falls on the asphalt. Why did they not hand it to me? Were they afraid of me, did they think me diseased? Why were they laughing? I chase the money in the road around where it blows.

Food comes only in the afternoon and it's still morning. Superstition 4B.

Immediately a man reaches out four cellophane-wrapped candies. Another fast-food miracle.

In standing here I fear I am indulging in superstition born of a quantity of self-concern that is slowly turning me into a crank—a man wrecked by the fixity of his preconceptions, an uninstitutionalizable soul cut off by the brain-damaging denial that there is anything wrong with such self-involvement—a denial strident that the wound of my spirit shall do the world great good—scoring Creation on a box of soap, one index finger raised to the sky, the other pointing at the crowd, both fingernails dirty. Inflamed with the crank's devotion to his own idealism, I take money on the grounds that I am engaged in Spiritual Transformation! Well, cranks are waterless canals, and if Spiritual Transformation is my alibi for being here, a car sits before you which is polished, gassed, tuned—but in a junkyard—a car that no one can drive—since Transformation is a very fancy but utterly useless and indeed vulgar ambition. If my ideal of going to school is justified by some high-toned notion of enlightenment, then it's just a convincing racket. In fact, to collect enough to save $40 a day feels like bunk half the time; it feels like Brendan's being a toy millionaire.

A young man gets out of a car in the middle lane. He holds out his hand, in it a package of cheese and crackers. He dashes back from me to his car, a fellow human kept from starving—and it's true, I have been!

I wish people knew what was on my menu though—a man hands me a Mars bar and a can of Coke, and I don't drink soft drinks. "Thank you, God bless you." I scarf the Mars bar right now because it'll melt if I don't.

I oughtn't to eat on the roadside, though. I'm not being paid to eat on the job. To dine and beg? Bad form. Besides, people will see I am fed and won't give. That car turning the corner tosses a Dr. Pepper, I catch it, too fast gone to thank him, wow.

From Appian behind I hear honking. I go over. A woman extends a McDonald's bag. She has no work either, she says. "Thank you so much. That's very generous. God bless you." She's so considerate, all these people are.

I don't ordinarily eat McDonald's. I myself would give something healthier, but people think I'm in an emergency. Fast-food is emergency rations. Half of America makes a diet of emergency rations. Still, I am grateful for the giving.

Cars come, stop on the red. The rise of the day moves toward lunch—a vacation indoors.

A black man in a pickup hands me a sandwich in a Ziploc bag. "It's fresh," he assures me, "it's from my lunch."

"But I don't want to take your lunch."

"It's all right, I've got two."

He and I are together.

I breathe in as I resume my stance. I look upon the wide vale below. Above, the mackerel sky slowly closes over like a rolltop desk. Unusual: the Bay Area doesn't have many skies.

At 2:04, I pack up and make my way to the hospital cafeteria, taking the rubbish to the hospital dumpster on the way.

The cement man left, I didn't even notice when. But he'll come back. The traffic cones guarantee it.

In the cafeteria, I eat the cold McDonald's and the black man's sandwich, which turns out to be pressed turkey and cheese, and read another biography of Wolsey. I want him to invade me, so that I can be good, so companies will want me.

I return to the office at 3:19—means I'll leave not at 5:04 but 5:19. I feel established here, like a bus driver on his route.

The Hispanic paver is back. He does a good job, self-enclosed, happy, responsible. No one knows his name, he's mestizo maybe. He deserves a medal.

I am happy too. The sun feels as good on the back of my neck as it did when I was a child, that certain flavor, baking it. I wish it to stay. It doesn't last past the wish. My smile is cherubic, I can't help it. Cars come up; let them see me; I don't mind. I'm so happy, cars, if you only knew. My spirits so rise with bliss I'll burst. Can they notice, do they think I'm nuts?

Of course my feet do ache after four hours without sitting.

And what about too much sunshine? Get one of those peaked old-boy baseball caps I hate? Nah.

What about gasoline fumes? Nope, I'm standing on a hilltop where fumes blow away.

Cars stop. A thirteen-year-old boy dodges through them to give me money. "Thank you. God bless you." He dodges back.

Lots of cars stopped in all three lanes. An older man in a van way down there beckoning. Aw, the patrolman told me I couldn't be down there—but what the heck—I'll nip back before I'm caught. I bow courteously. The man gives me a five-dollar bill. "I gave you money yesterday."

"Oh, thank you. I'm sorry. I didn't recognize you," I blurt out. He seems hurt. I go back to the sidewalk. He's right: he has a right to be remembered. I note him down behind my sign. That means I'll remember him there but it doesn't mean I'll remember him here. As his car passes I smile and bow, hoping to remember him, but I don't remember him from thirty seconds ago.

I don't know what to do. Because already people are starting to give me money regularly, but I don't recall their faces.

A car beckons, two men in it, the driver a man of forty who hands me a bill. "Thank you. God bless you. Any work I can do for you?"

"The only work is the steps it took you to get to this car," he says.

That man knows the truth, and it's a kind truth and a ruthless truth, which is that on the roadside I am off the hook.

I want also to take note of the people who do not give, for, like the five eucalyptus trees whose shade does not fall upon me, those are with me also. Two men call out, "Get a job!" Another time, two girls applaud me when the man three cars ahead of them gives. I am not unmanned by "Get a job!" and I am not unmanned by the applause. I'm learning about survival and its relation to popularity. Eastwood is cheered and jeered. The girls don't give, but they give; the men don't give, but they give. The people who go through gyrations about seeing me. And those who wave genially. Or nod. Or smile. And those who simply do not see me. And those who see me and are not impelled one way or another. And those who call me names. Those who do not give, and they are in the majority, all of them and all of that is still the giving, all of it worth remembering.

Oh, that beautiful black girl from yesterday gives me two bills again as her car turns the corner. And there's the elderly woman who pulled off in the Cadillac yesterday. I place my hand over my heart and bow as she drives by. And screeching around the corner, that crazy woman in the beat-up brown Olds. She's with friends again, and they're screaming with laughter, and she waves. I wave back! She doesn't seem to have any business save the mad entertainment of turning corners on two wheels. Whether drunk and thinking me drunk too, they see me as part of them. This off-ramp is Grand Hotel.

And those two in the black van, they wave too—always make a point of it. I wave back quietly. They have nothing to give, but they wave. They give. Like many people. What they give is a salutation to a stranger. That's a gift. They've seen me here some days now, so now I'm the man on the side of the road to whom they wave.

A woman in the lead car rolls down her window, looks up and says: "I can't. I'm looking for work myself."

"Okay, well, good luck to you."

"Same to you."

Another stop of cars. In the second lane a gray-haired black black man in a black black sedan beckons me to take money. "Stay strong," he says. A woman says, "Have you tried the County?" She thinks I'm homeless.

"I have. There's nothing there."

She realizes advice is not what's needed here and hands me five dollars. That was a good thing for her to do.

In a tiny car three cars down, a big bald man beckons. He opens not the window but the door. He has the corporation and imperiousness of a tycoon and he grandly instructs a little boy next to him to hand me three small coins. Intimidated, the little boy does so. "God bless you both," I say.

The off-ramp is filling up, people off from work. Someone waves. I trot down, I take the money, and that one over there sees and joins in, and it catches on, and the man over there hands me a bill, wrapped around a big bright orange—three in one stop—a record! Maybe I'm going to make the $40 after all.

A commercial van I saw yesterday, a Middle Eastern couple in it. In hand-painted script: Osman. He beckons. "Do you have a valid driver's license?" "Yes."

He gives me a number. I write it on the paper on the back of my sign.

I ask if he's Pakistani, no, and he's not Osman either. I can't figure out the business. I'll call. Add to the

COMPACT

• Call about all jobs.

Down a ways, a black van pulls onto the dirt. There is no activity from it, and because the windshield is dark I can't see who's in it. Do they need help? Don't impinge; if they want me, they'll beckon. Everyone does not pull off because of me.

A hand out of the driver's window waves me forward. When I reach it I maintain a respectful distance.

Children in the back. Their mother reaches out a big Peet's Coffee shopping bag with a red plaid thermos. She's a plump, pretty, sweet-faced woman in her thirties wrapped up in a parka.

"I saw you there," she says. "I feel for you. Here's some soup and hot potatoes."

I reach forward to relieve her of its weight. I want to say, "What an angel you are!" but there is something in her more than the occasion warrants. Still I see her kind nature, and my own heart feels amazed and made glad by her action. This woman has cooked this food herself! She is well-off and has given amply, for two bananas rise out of the bag. I thank her deeply, "How sweet you are! You're an angel." She starts to cry. "I'm all right," I say and set the bag down and reach my hands toward her so she may understand that she too is all right and she reaches to me and we clasp hands for a moment and see one another. "I'll be here Monday so you can get your thermos back."

"No, that's all right, keep it," she says.

I back away, thanking her, blessing her, and bowing. I watch to make sure her car isn't hit as she resumes the road.

What imagination people have! Not just she but everyone who gives! In all of life this is the strangest thing: people are completely irrational and, at one and the same moment, kind.

Of course I see that people, seeing me, ascribe to me a frame of their own devising. One woman from a middle-lane car calls out: "Thank you for your courage!" She's a strapping young woman and grown up, but I do not feel my being here is an act of courage. What I do feel is the willingness of people to connect.

I put the bag in my backpack to hide that in food-gifts I am a millionaire.

A wild-haired, black-haired young woman jumps out of a car in the middle lane and quarterbacks her way through all sorts of vehicles and hands me a five-dollar food stamp.

"I can't use a food stamp. You have to tear them out of a book at the store."

A look of doubt in her eye, "I think you can," she says and quarterbacks her way back to her car.

I shouldn't have said that. I wanted money instead of food stamps. Besides, now I think of it, I know a store that does take loose food stamps.

I feel bad about saying that to her. So I put down my sign and take time out to apologize to her in my mind: "I apologize to you for not saying 'thank you' properly. I appreciate your bravado in running the traffic to give me this; I appreciate your wit, your beauty, and your odd bounty! Please accept my apology for my poor manners. I do thank you for your gift and will use it."

An East Asian woman gives me money even as I apologize to the food stamp woman who ran the gauntlet of the cars for me; what a rotter I am. I demand a love perfect for me; Perfectionism ruins love. Be alert to it next time, Bruce, pray it won't jinx you today. Add to the

COMPACT

• Accept all gifts.

WestCAT vans (the door-to-door transportation here) won't give.

School buses won't give.

People who smoke don't give.

A blond woman stops. "I've been there," she says as she hands me money. She's good-looking—young and inexperienced somehow. "Keep happy. Take care of your health."

"I will. I do." Good counsel under the circumstances.

Then I notice her right hand holds a cigarette. Another fast-food miracle.

"Do you do roofing?" a man in a truck asks.

"No," I apologize.

Not interested, he drives off.

I should have said, "I can do anything." I lost the job by telling the dull truth.

Lots of activity up here, the wide round hills and all the cars going to their homes and the two shopping centers and the hospital, and all the cars below zooming to Sacramento and Berkeley and San Francisco, and the five lady eucalyptus trees and the dirt beneath my feet and the weeds and the passing of life.

I stand here tall in the sun, and I feel masculine. I'm a balding, gray-haired, middle-aged man in an old green parka, but my masculinity has no age. It's odd to feel it here, you wouldn't think I would, you'd think I'd be beaten down.

Meticulously the Hispanic paver man scores lines on the fresh cement where it meets the street. We've been neighbors all day, yet I haven't addressed a word to him; it's improper. Taking a break from avarice, I walk across to him.

"You really do beautiful work. I've been watching you."

On his hands and knees he looks up and smiles, pleased that someone knows this is so.

"What are those lines for?"

"For blind people so their canes can feel where to cross."

"Look at that: in spite of the ribbon, someone walked on your sidewalk."

"Oh, they always do that."

I ask him how long it takes cement to set up and he tells me but I don't copy it down; I want to get back to the money. I go to my side of the street, happy.

The beautiful guy in the fiery black pickup waves back as he turns the corner. Does me good to see him here. Our contract's a wave.

A young woman in a burgundy business suit walks down from the hospital, and out into the road to skirt the new sidewalk. This is an unusual sight, for if this sidewalk is used by five people a day it's used by a throng.

"I have no work for you," she says. "But here," she says, "for you." She walked all the way down here to give me this! Modest and businesslike, shy even. But that is her delicacy in the situation. I'm stirred by her coming. The good thing about not looking at the money is that I can look at the person.

A tall, four-wheel-drive pickup pulls off onto the dirt with three youngsters in the front seat, every one of them Huckleberry Finn, none of them over twelve. How can they manage this big truck? Of course they're not stopping for me, twelve-year-olds have other business in this world, have no spare bucks, are too young to give one money. Maybe they need help. I am summoned.

A plump rosy-faced boy in the driver's seat leans out. His face is covered with freckles which the boys inside have passed around among themselves as twelve-year-old boys will do. "Do you take change?"

Now that's a civil question and a smart one—for all they know I might be insulted to be offered charity. Wouldn't have thought kids to have the social imagination to ask, particularly kids with freckles who might more want to haze me.

He reaches me down a big fistful of change they've collected among themselves.

"Thank you. God bless you," I say and step back, aware of receiving from those much younger than myself.

Five hours.

My feet ache, but, so what, you pay a price for any job. This price is called Tired Feet.

Car in the first spot. I catch the man's eye. Middle-aged. He sees my eyes. I look away. He waits. The red light waits. It is as though he had a lot of money but won't give it. Or resents having to imagine my case, doesn't even want to give the imagining. To him it's my fault he has to go through all this.

"Will you take change?" he eventually says, still uncomfortable.

"Yes, indeed." And I take it and thank him and bless him and ask if he has work even though I know that he doesn't. He needs to be asked so's not to feel cheated.

At four I figure there will be no more money before five when I leave, but it pours in. Even so I think I'll make only fifty dollars. But that's all right. Anything is all right.

I have promised to leave at 5:19. I look at my watch frequently as it approaches five. Add to the

COMPACT

- Don't look at your watch. You'll leave at the right time without.

At 5:19 precisely I close down shop. Though my parka pockets are stuffed, I want someone to give me more, as happened that other time. Stop that, Bruce, and it stops.

The money is so bulky that, as I go on to La Pena where a friend is dancing and to another friend's house to pick up a letter of recommendation for acting school, I'm so afraid it will be stolen that I keep my parka on all night. Turns out it's $145, the most I've ever made, at any time, on any job, in one day.

I write this record before I go to bed; otherwise I'll forget. Being on the roadside occupied six hours, and now it has occupied three more because taking notes means I remember more, and that made this the longest entry yet. I am lost in the roadside when on it and writing about it now when I'm not. Will the amount of time enmesh me? Will the money? I want to go back tomorrow and make more. And even if it's not a lot, I don't doubt that I can make enough to get by. Besides I want to. I like it. I like what I am when I'm there. So is the roadside a seduction? Or is it a passage of destiny? I feel I'm being slowly liberated, but maybe I'm just becoming licentious? Are my going and my not wanting to go to the roadside simply the greed of laziness—for the energy of laziness can have great digestive vitality? Or is my survival here a calisthenics of my soul? Or maybe my character will become worse than before. Or maybe freedom and degradation is just the dance I dance. Certainly I who wanted to be popular when I was in grammar school and never was, now never will be, for having been on the roadside, who would admire me, who would not dismiss me as an unfit animal? And I myself am ashamed.

Will that shame ever leave?

What is the transaction going on here? Should I be going to the roadside at all? No, that's a stupid question by now. The question is for how long? I'm afraid I may have to stay forever, my life cut off from everyone but passersby. On the other hand, because of the passersby, I feel less cut off from humanity than I ever did. Anyhow, for the moment I have no other choice. Because what miracle will eventually make my leaving possible? Is it actually some job? Or if it is not a job but acting itself, how could acting do it? There isn't enough money in acting in the Bay Area to support one. Acting would be ideal if it could pay the rent and if it were a calling. But I don't know. What's going to become of me? I may never leave. I may just go to sleep there forever.

Yes, and if I don't go to sleep, if I stay alert, what am I to learn? That East Asian people will or won't give? Or discover the foundation of prejudice? No. These questions pursued would be dead ends, they'd just be answers. I need another, different room of truth than that of questions-and-answers. But what truth? That, that is the transaction, if I can live it out. But I haven't done it yet, so I can't speak of it yet. Maybe I never will be able to.

At least I don't entertain any hope; that's something.

I am also dog tired. It's late. I can't think. And if I could, thought would be wielding a cabbage to hammer a nail, the wrong tool for the job. I stop.

I have to record the food before I refrigerate it, so, item by item, I empty the shopping bag the lady who cried gave me.

Two bananas, two apples, a can of green beans, a can of green peas. A new plaid red thermos filled with herb tea, which is still hot, and which I drink before bed. A little container of hot soup. In a Ziploc bag four slices of delicious brown bread. In an orange terrycloth hand towel three baked potatoes still warm. She has put in a Ziploc bag of spices with a note: "Put this on the potatoes." This is a complete and nourishing meal.

On stationary with yellow roses:

Dear Sir:

I don't know who you are, or where you're from but I just saw you the other day standing there and it breaks my heart to see you there. You could be my father.

Three years ago—my father committed suicide because he just couldn't handle whatever it was. He has left us all in a lot of pain.

I just want you to know—Do whatever it takes to get back on your feet. I can't offer you a job but I hope a little food will help. I saw you again while I was headed to the grocery store—decided you were more important!

Love to you—you are in my thoughts.

                                                    Your Friend,
                                                    Linda Lee

For a napkin she had folded a length of paper towel. On it the paper towel company had printed:

> The best and most beautiful things in the world
> cannot be seen or touched
> but are felt in the heart.
> Love is sharing.
> Friendship is a special gift.
> No act of love however small
> is ever wasted.
> A gentle helping heart.

I sit back in my old swivel chair and curl my hand over my mouth and shake my head. The sweetness of humans is unfathomable. There is no end to it.

30 January, Saturday

I'm first generation and have a touch of that English accent my parents brought to America just after they were married. So, while I was born in New York City, I am half alien, born without the ingrained mental American idiom. What I am is mid-Atlantic. Which means I could play any character but a popular American character: I could be in a film with Clint Eastwood, but I could not play his part. Neither of us could play Willie Loman, but I could play King Lear. There are other differences between us too: the fortunes of life and time-in-grade.

In any case, the pieces I have chosen for the Theatre Bay Area audition and the acting school tryout are Henry Higgins and Alfred Doolittle from Shaw's *Pygmalion,* Antonio from Shakespeare's *Twelfth Night,* and Lord Illingworth from Oscar Wilde's *A Woman of No Importance.*

To rehearse Wilde's *Lord Illingworth,* I move the chairs aside in my living room, establish an imaginary set, with Gerald, the character I am speaking to, over there with his back to the window, and start in.

> My dear Gerald, examinations are of no value whatsoever. If a man is a gentleman, he knows quite enough, and if he is not a gentleman whatever he knows is bad for him. Don't be afraid. Remember, you've got on your side the most wonderful thing in the world—youth! There is nothing like youth. The middle-aged are mortgaged to Life. The old are in Life's lumber room. But youth is the Lord of Life. Youth has a kingdom waiting for it. Everyone is born a king, and most people die in exile, like most kings. To win back my youth, Gerald, there is nothing I wouldn't do—except take exercise, get up early or be a useful member of the community.
> But then there is the question of your mother, and whether she agrees you shall do this. I should imagine that most mothers don't quite under-stand their sons. Don't realize, I mean, that a son has ambitions, a desire to see life, to make himself a name. After all, Gerald, you couldn't be expected

to pass your life in such a hole as Wrockley, could you? A mother's love is very touching, of course, but it is often curiously selfish. I mean, there is a good deal of selfishness in it. Your mother is a thoroughly good woman. But good women have such a limited view of life, their horizon is so small, their interests are so petty, aren't they? I suppose your mother is very religious, and that sort of thing? Ah! she is not modern, and to be modern is the only thing worth being now-a-days. You want to be modern, don't you, Gerald? You want to know life as it really is. Not to be put off with any old-fashioned theories about life. Well, what you'll have to do at present is simply to fit yourself for the best society. A man who can dominate a London dinner-table, can dominate the world.

Then I go to the coaching session.

The coach at the session is kind and astute. She says I am perfect for Lord Illingworth. But she points out things I am doing that don't work, and I despair to look at them because I'm so low in morale I'd have to go even lower to see them. It is as though in acting Illingworth I am looking for a formula—not someone else's but my own, but still a formula. It's so hard to hear I don't even remember what she says, and she said it sweetly. All I know and don't want to face is that as Lord Illingworth I am *not* GREAT, or NOT GREAT YET AS AN ACTOR. I went to this coaching session to practice and to be told I am good. I should have known better.

So I come home and eat too much, and watch Garbo in *Grand Hotel*. Now there is an actor! She summons her depths right up through her spine—and it is so economical.

I don't know what to do about Illingworth. It is as though I am encased in something when I play him, as though all the moves were canned—my own can, but still canned. There is some stricture around me, a fear for an impropriety of soul. Something not courageous in my heart, or rather a seizing up of my heart, a scorching of my heart, no real freedom Something. Something. What is it? I feel disappointed with it all. And baffled as to the cure.

31 January, Sunday

Last night I did not meditate. What am I fleeing from? Is it the February rent, I could only send part payment?

But, I sit on the couch in the morning sun. I can see the old hickory rocker. The sunlight on it shows the honest soul of it. Through the door to the studio the old pine chair before the typewriter is visible and I hear it. As I kneel I see the actor's center in me, the land whence acting is generated. I feel the difficulty of holding onto the courage to remain there.

Lord Illingworth.

I don't want to face how bad I am in it.

1 February, Monday

I spend the day rehearsing Illingworth. I have got to bring these auditions off. I have only thirteen days. I have got to be brilliant.

3 February, Wednesday

I notice my habit to postpone going on the roadside. I plan to come on Monday but don't come until Wednesday. Of course, I couldn't come Monday because I had to go to acting school for an interview, nor Tuesday because of rehearsing and because of procrastinating. Procrastination takes more time than doing the thing would. And no matter how noble may be my plan to use the money, something in me prevents me going every day. Is it a laziness? A refusal to change? I don't know. The roadside is a pilgrimage without a step. I do not know the answers until the pilgrimage be done.

I settle myself at the roadside like a farmer picking up the plough where he left it the day before, like a farmer seizing the reins of the weather into his eyes, a farmer who recognizes the dirt, the mare, where he is and what he does, and is satisfied.

The hills are winter green that by late spring will turn beige. They are too high to be planted with developments so they smile in their still-performing task, free as antiquity.

Today I arrive with the thought, "I am looking for a handout." I have to be here to contribute, but the thing that comes up first, is to be contributed *to*. I say my prayers and begin.

Bless you Onion car, and bless you Ford, and bless you Ford, and you too Ford, and bless license plate WALLY, and bless you red truck and other red truck and still other red truck except not so red, bless you, maniac, yes, maniac I say. No one's coming, no one's coming ever again, oh here they come, but will they come in my lane, bless you whether you do or not, bless you black van, and you peculiar green, nameless green, a green so nameless you can't even name it nameless. Bless you, boxy car and other boxy car, you should get married, look at all those cars on the freeway, a million cars, not a million but a lot, bless you all. Bless you cars on the overpass, let none be omitted, bless you and spare you. Bless you, apple truck, are you an apple truck, not an apple truck. Bless you— oh, no one is coming, yes, there one comes, come on, come this way, well bless you nevertheless, bless you, will the light be red so they'll stop or will it—?

Passing cars semaphore money, in the first hour three only. I don't worry about it. Let it float away, spend more than you earn, eat out!

Yesterday I noticed an Indian restaurant in the mall with a buffet. I ought not to. On the other hand, an Indian restaurant at lunch is not expensive.

I leave at 2:15. The Indian restaurant is not open. I go to the Thai restaurant instead. Feeling good from the cold on my skin, feeling it the more indoors. Two patrons. Wonder if they recognize me and what they think of me spending money here. I take off my backpack, conscious of not being dressed like they are, an outdoors man here with white tablecloths. I order the least expensive thing on the menu. I'm not like these other lunch-hour diners, but I still know how to behave so they don't throw me out.

Wolsey. I'm overloaded with reading of Wolsey. I fall asleep over him at table. I wake and leave a proper tip.

Coming back from lunch at 3:15 I see a car stopped down the ramp. I meet the driver, a well-dressed black man walking up to the exit. He's out of gas.

I tell him I have a gas can, and all he has to do is walk me to my car for it.

He agrees, but there's something odd in the fact we don't say much as we walk. He suspects me. He says he'll wait on the corner of the hospital parking lot instead.

When I come back to the corner with the can I see him across the street with a can from the gas station. My feelings are hurt. He didn't keep his word.

"I was pressed for time, I just took the can they gave me," he says.

He could have said so beforehand. Maybe he thought I wanted a handout.

COMPACT
- Decline handouts when helping people with cars.

I set up my backpack and sign once more.

In the middle lane a stocky young man jumps out of his car and gives me money and says, "God bless you, man."

From the middle lane a black man turns into my lane to give.

In the same stop, a young man in a gray car in the middle lane opens his door. His window is open, he's blond and idle looking. "How much you earn doing that?" he says. He has a baby in there and he is smoking.

Such questions arm me to a reprisals alert. Any low amount might be too much for him. His is The Research Approach.

Gesturing to his pickup, I ask him nicely, "How much you earn doing that?"

"Not much," he says, shamefaced, realizing the impropriety of his question.

What some people want to think is that I am salting it away in a Swiss Bank Account, whatever that is. What they want to think is that I am an addict feeding my habit, I don't smoke or drink coffee any more, never drank, gambled, or took drugs. What they want to think is that I am a cheat and earning more money than they. What they want is to believe the worst, because the inviting thing about the worst is that it's concrete.

We have a long conversation. He drives away, friends.

A low car driven by an East Asian woman with two silver front teeth. She has a black child in back.

A pretty young woman with strawberry blond hair hands me two tiny boxes of raisins.

A woman stops, good-looking, sexy, forceful. She tells me to call the Budget Binder Company in Emeryville for a job. "Who shall I say told me?"

"My husband owns it. Tell him I told you to tell him to give you a job."

I will. I call them all.

The weather is cool on my face. I face north after all. I forgot to look at the mascot tree. There she is, still in place on the hilltop, like the postman, every day doing her job. The long sweep of the cars that peel off down there offers a question, a possibility, and it is a happy one. Even though I want money, the possibility is for something else, a charm.

I always stand right-angled to the road and face the oncoming cars. So, when cars stop, I don't see into the car next to me, but rather into the one behind it. Through its windshield I face the driver. So when a woman stops second in line, I see this woman's face now. She sees me the same moment I see her, and each of us as though knowing and indeed actually knowing exactly what the other was to do does the same thing the other does in the same way at the same time, which is to nod. We laugh. It looks like she is not going to give me anything, and that's all right. What is right is the human coordination. I stand and rejoice in it, as does she. But I don't look at her further. She hands me a folded bill.

An East Asian young man hands me a low-fat chocolate milk and says, "Bless you."

A couple in the middle lane want to give. She takes money out, but the light changes. He stalls for me to get to them, but the traffic starts so I can't cross, and he has to drive off. The $1 bill that got away.

A black man with reefer shrugs and says he has nothing. I laugh at him nicely. Before he goes he hauls out a loose one dollar bill from his left pants pocket. He's a dealer, my dear, and a jerk just like the rest of us.

A pretty young woman in a red car, but I can't record her properly because the next stand of cars is here and I jot this down since part of the job is jotting it down. My desk is jammed—six telephones are ringing, and my secretary just walked in and dropped her teacup.

Senators of clouds above convene, adjourn at will. I stand in secret with them, no one knowing about us being here together, just the two of us, the weather and I: outdoor people.

I want the $10 that couple couldn't get to me!

An older man gives me $5. He sits in the car rocking back and forth, without rocking the car. "I've got a deadbeat in my house," he hollers as he starts to roll.

Did I hear correctly?

"I've got a deadbeat in my house," he calls over his shoulder as he turns the corner, "My son-in-law!"

A small young man and woman, with delicate feminine features, skin as pale as porcelain, they are married but they look like children—are they Vietnamese?—the blackness of their hair so black it turns black inside out. She says, "Have a nice day, okay?"

I feel happy. I feel so happy I can hardly bless the people who don't give. Why? Maybe I was meant to be happy and to stand here and be blessed. I want to give blessing and good wishes to all, but I am the recipient of this bliss and cannot give back into its avalanching cornucopia. Except to smile.

I stand privileged. "Prive" means private and "lege" means law—a private law. I am in touch with a golden rule within myself: do unto myself as I would do to others. The first thing my mother put in my baby book was that I had a sunny disposition. Here it is again. The rule in me was to shine like the sun, and for me it is easy, I never liked the overcast. I feel everything around me is kind. The bedroom communities shine with care, the hills sing—yes, to me, to me the hills are generous. Oh, they are so to everyone—but they know I have an *ear* for it.

In the middle lane, a guy in a yellow and brown van addresses me: "I'll see what I can do for you. I myself am working for reduced wages."

I wonder what he has in mind or if he's talking well-meaning bunk. Standing here by the roadside feels like being molested, the same sense of having to go along with protective authority, of being scared to say no. Most people are not molesting me here, but I fear it could happen any moment and I have no defense. He doesn't give.

I want the $100 that couple couldn't get to me! Boo hoo!

In the middle lane in a four-wheel-drive, a teenage boy in a white T-shirt. At his age I did not drive, and in my sixtieth year I still can't earn my living. I wonder if other roadside people can't grow up either even if they want to.

Are these the pains of being here—the pain of being eight years old, of never having been able to be any stronger than the greatest weakness of the age of the damage? Is this what trauma means: what once happened is held outside of time and inside the body, the Then that rules the Now?

I stand taller than these cars. Why are my eyes kind right now? No one is frightened of me. I have an open face, a baker's face.

Which probably does not conceal my notion, for instance, of BMWs not giving—because people who own them go psychically broke, because the eyes of the grill are set close together, and you know what pikers people with close-set eyes are, and because BMWs are German cars and Germans are mean.

People become like their dogs and their cars: red cars are expansive and openhanded, Volvos suburban, BMWs pursy. Such is the menu of my prejudices. Prove me wrong, God, make me rich with BMW takings!

Immediately a yellow BMW with a black man. He and the man he's with are drug dealers: you can tell: they are unnecessarily savvy. They do not give. How wonderful: people are diminished by BMWs, and is there a Mercedes made that does not make its owner bourgeois? They scoot around the bend to be replaced immediately by a poor young man in a poor yellow car who does give.

I still want the money that couple couldn't get to me, my $1000 bill! Weep, weep!

The man in the yellow and brown van who said he would do something for me calls to me on Appian and beckons me to follow as he drives past the exit and stops.

He's a middle-aged man with tobacco-gray hair. Is he on the up-and-up? However, I am obliged to find out what he has in mind. It's 5:15, I can call it a day here, and job interviews are part of the business. I get in. Now I feel in prison though I've never been in prison. To redress this, I talk so he can see I have some maturity, am reliable, well-spoken.

We drive to the McDonald's parking lot, grab an outdoor table—we're not eating—and I wait for the job interview. Again he tells me he's earning less than he used to. I tell my story briefly and listen to his.

There are people who drink a lot of coffee and smoke a lot of cigarettes and swallow a lot of beer because when they were teenagers those were the first adult things they did, and also the last. Addictions hold you in the place you were when you first assumed them, and the decline of life through subsequent ages is marked: as each age declines, none are fulfilled. People don't become wrecks at fifty. You are a wreck at fifty, at forty, and at twenty. The twenty-year-old wreck just doesn't look it because he's twenty, but he's a wreck all the same. But all this means is that this man my own age may be lost. He's lost with his wife, he's lost in his trailer, he's not a bad person, but he's lost.

He says custodial work needs doing at the mobile home park where he lives and gives me the number of the manager. I wonder at this man. Did he just want to hear if my story is the same as his own? It isn't. His is a hard-luck story. I'll call Friday morning.

The unisex bathroom at the hospital is a decompression chamber. The world I have left is a good world. The world I am going toward is a good world. To be enclosed in the satisfaction of the day's work done I use the good world of the john.

I always put the money into my right-hand parka pocket as I get it. The pocket has pleats so it expands, and I can't tell by the bulge how much is in it.

$51. I was here three hours, I earned $3 in the first hour, so this means I earned $24 an hour the second two hours. A twenty-dollar bill, and two fives— a Scottish generosity—when they are generous they are exquisite. I'm astonished. I no longer want the $10,000 that couple could not get to me.

As I walk down the hill to my car I feel like a businessman with his job well done and I drive away tired and comforted.

When I get home, a message from the landlady. She says she does not accept partial payment. Hard, because I've always been on time. I may be evicted.

5 February, Friday

I telephone all the job offers given me on the roadside. None of the people who offer me jobs has one. Wheee! Don't have to work!

I spend the morning on the monologs. I imagine I can just run through them and then get on to the roadside, but the monolog work is itself work, and as such, a world in itself, not readily entered and not readily left. I am unable to go on the roadside.

7 February, Sunday

I'm excited all day: first *Catherine of Aragon* read-through tonight!

When this play was written everyone who went to it would have known who Cardinal Wolsey was; now no one does, so I expand a speech to Anne Boleyn: "I am the Lord Chancellor of England, I am Chief Justice of the Star Chamber, Archbishop of York; as Legate in Latere I speak for the Pope in this land, I am King Henry's mentor and also his oldest friend. He sometimes listens to me." I'm not trying to pump up the part, but to make this dumb play work. Camber, impressed, accepts it.

However, we can't read the play: they haven't cast Henry. We all have to go home.

8 February, Monday

I spend the morning on the monologs, which I put ahead of the Wolsey lines because the monolog auditions come before the *Catherine* opening, and because it's grinding gears to work on Wolsey lines after I work on the monolog lines, in fact grinding to move from one job to another. My body rejects it, I don't know why.

I am holding down five jobs: 1, being on the roadside; 2, transcribing the notes; 3, preparing to get into acting school; 4, rehearsing the Bay Auditions; 5, preparing Wolsey.

They conflict with one another, and the one easiest to do that day will take precedence over the one that ought to be done. I also work at temp work when I can get it. The one job that cannot be postponed, though, is to record the road-side, because otherwise it slips from memory and because gratitude demands it.

COMPACT

- Enter the day's notes into the computer that night or at least the next morning.

And record them to *honor* the people—to *honor* them, that's the point. It's right that each of these people be remembered. Yearning to do it is not enough.

Eventually I get to the roadside where I stand—every day the same—here on my business. As I prop my backpack on the tan dirt next to *Do Not Enter* with the second sign bungeed to it, I settle myself inside to beg. For the daily winter rain I bring a big blue umbrella, which I never use and which I slide behind the strap holding the *Do Not Enter* sign.

My own sign's cardboard is wrinkled like a camel. The note paper is clipped to the back. Sometimes I clip the pen back there, sometimes I keep it in my left parka pocket. The money goes in the right.

I police the area for trash. I set up my windshield wiper. I greet my mascot tree on the far hill. I say my invocation. Then I turn and begin. I am already smiling.

I have not worked on either the monologs or the Wolsey lines today.

Clint Eastwood comes and stands next to me again.

Actually I saw a snatch of another film of his once—bullets polka-dotting the air, he never hit, his weak upper lip curling as though distaste were sufficient for exterminating someone. I turned it off.

I watch the cars sweep up from the thruway below. Slowing as they approach the light, red or green or yellow, feeling out one of three lanes.

An old East Asian couple in a white van right away—a good sign. When I ask her for work the driver says, "I'm not from here."

A beautiful black woman in a ruby car. Ruby lips—a chocolate cherry woman.

A beautiful blond woman in a red car with four kids. People in red cars are more generous. I like positive superstitions, but I harbor both kinds. If I get rid of the one, do I have to yield the other? Yup.

I'm forgetting to say "Bless you" to myself. Bless you, bless you three ladies in a taupe sedan, bless you Mustang, bless you purple-hatted lady, bless you salesman with your collar open, bless you Triumph.

A man drives up in a big brown car. He makes moves possibly preparatory to giving. I monitor myself not to run expectancy, and don't, as he shifts out of the seat-belt, hitches back for the wallet (he could be reaching for a handkerchief), opens the billfold (he could be getting out a business card), opens the window, and hands a bill out.

A white truck, machinery laced to the top, stops, and the driver jaws with me as he waits for the light to change. "I do fencing. I just got squeezed out of a union job," he says.

I help him get it off his chest. Do people tell me their hard luck stories as an alibi for not giving? Do they want commiseration? I don't think so. I think they want to talk to someone who is in a fix too.

An old couple in a white car give me $5. When I ask if I can do any work for them, he says, "No, that's good, that's good."

I still have a prejudice that old people either have no money or are all Republicans.

A fat black man in a red car: "Hang in there," he says.

I feel drawn to the black men who go by. Why is that?

Curious: I don't know any black people well: I see black people as slave-machines—of sex, sport, and song: yet separate from that I've always liked them: this country is unthinkable without black people: I've always been prejudiced, even when I was a little boy, in their favor.

Curious: now here on the roadside I feel a draw to the males. Yes, I sense a survival power in black males, and the lack of it in me draws me.

What survival power do black males have that I don't have? What am I envying here?

A sense of being in their skins, is that it? A spontaneity? A rejoicing? An abandon? Some connection to themselves that does not ask permission and that is guilt-free, that is not even subject to their belief in God?

A law unto itself which is a good law?

Properly shameless.

What am I drawn to here?

Black women have it too, but I'm a male so what I'm drawn to is a male instrument of survival. I have survived but I have not prevailed, and I have not, as black men have, mined the humor of not having prevailed.

But how is this survival humor of black men a financial power? How do I assume that even black workmen who pass have a financial capacity that I do not, when I know black people often to be poor and reft of opportunity?

Or is it a survival power based on their presumed sexuality? No, it's not a sexual draw I feel: it's a draw that's presexual. I don't get it.

Oh there is a power in black people that astounds me, all right. Their ability to have lived, under the circumstances. And to have come out, gay, vigorous, hymning loudly, wailing rudely. To have come out exuberant. Cackling wildly. To have come out saucy. On the ground. To have come out strumming, twirling, yakking. High-feathered. Warm. To have come out. To have come out of it *alive!*

Or is that vim a screen over a demotion?—a demotion not even the blues reveal. "Whiteboy, you think black folks in Africa don't sing the blues? You think the blues is caused by white oh-ppression? You white-folks-fool, you think you so im-*po*tant. You not *that* im-*po*tant."

Or does this draw to black males have something to do with my manhood, something that I am not connected with?

What is it, what impotence is abroad? Addiction is everywhere—sex, food, spending, entertainment—all addictions are addictions to oblivion—and the oblivion I am sensing in me as big as a race.

What impotence is abroad? The inability to save Mother Earth?—disgusting phrase.

The inability to *care* for Mother Earth, then, the house we live in. The Earth, the air, the trees, the animals are our responsibility since Eden. The Earth is the Paradise we inherited and that responsibility makes Earth Eden. We must take care of every tree, every plant, every animal, the seas, and the soil itself, since, in the face of our depredations, they cannot take care of themselves. Care of the world is our whole task. There is no other task. Not to save these things for future generations, not for ourselves, but to care for them for themselves alone right now, simply because they have a right to live. How far from doing right by The Earth is wanting to be an actor! To be the vagabond and carefree actor . . . is the closest to impotence anyone can come. . . .

A four-wheel-drive screeching to a halt interrupts these thoughts. When I ask the big man within if there's any work I can do, he says, "No, no, no" in the most interesting way as though it were unheard of that I, a prince, should do such a thing as work.

A red car comes up. A young man, son of an older woman, gives me a food stamp. Then, looking up at me, they together segue into giving another. An unspeaking coordination between them gives both. There's a marriage like that between an old radiator and the window it sits under, the radiator giving no heat, the window not opening, a parliament of dunces who enjoy hanging out together.

Two in a row, too fast to record.

"I may want you to do a hit on somebody," says a man.

When I say to another man, "Is there anything I can do for you?" he says, "No, just buy something."

A good-looking woman in her late thirties, "Do you want work?"

"Yes. I do."

"Here, call me at this number."

"When shall I call?"

"Tonight."

Her car doesn't look too prosperous. She has loose brown hair. I'll call her though. It's in the Compact.

A middle-aged woman in a red car, when I ask if there is any work I can do for her, says, "No, just have a nice meal."

At the last instant before they take off, two boys in a big black truck hand over $3. Kids. I wouldn'ta thunk it.

I feel It Is Right that people should give to me. I stand here and resent those who do not meet my needs. Interesting: I resent them not as they leave but as they approach, I resent them for Not Meeting My Needs even before they have been asked to. It works just like Greed. When they arrive a second later, the resentment's gone. And I never resent those driving away who have not given. Only those who have not yet given. My human mechanism is so peculiar! Resentment in advance of rebuff is another version of my specialty: Doom Too Soon!

Although I stand behind his gray car, a Hispanic man awkwardly reaches money back to me. He took the trouble. Nice.

A white trailer truck gets stuck. There's no help I can give. They need big-time aid.

In a long, dark blue car from the '60s, an old black man stops. Because he leans up out of the window to speak, I think he is going to give, but instead he asks, "Where is Aspan Way?"

"*Appian* Way?" I suggest. "It's right here. This is it."

The light goes green, and he turns left this side of the island into the wrong lane. The cars kindly beep him awake and make allowances for him. Just in time, he veers to the other side of the island and away, an old man's responses carrying him through.

At 2:19 I pack up and go to lunch.

I welcome the vacation of the cafeteria. It's indoors for one. It's different. It's sitting down. It's taking off this parka and sweater. It's refueling with roadgrub. It's hiding out. It's a new Wolsey bio. It's falling asleep over it.

I awake as I usually do exactly on time.

As I walk back to the roadside I think: what roadside people need is to be picked up and carried off and given a permanent job. It's like coming out of prison being here. We need to be *given* a job. Except me. I want a job acting.

Two rough-hewn guys, one with a black beard, you wouldn't think would give but they do.

A black man with a white beard in a white car moving on the green—tricky for him and all the more generous.

Two young girls in a gray Mazda convertible shrug "broke"—then give. Others have shrugged broke. Some give, some don't.

Hispanic man with moustache with family. He gives, and they've got expenses.

Beautiful mulatto girl with beautiful eyes.

Food stamps come from a family returning—from what?

Two elderly people in a red car. "I hope something good comes for you," says the man, and the woman supports it. A marriage.

A black man and woman in a red car stop in the middle lane examine their wallets. A good deal of anticipation on my part as they direct their moves toward me, I, anxious about the light changing before I get to them. He calls, "Only got large bills. Catch you on the way back."

"Okay." But will they? They better. I keep watching for them the rest of the day.

The same man from the red car, who the other day went through such contortions of hesitation before he gave me his change, now looks frightfully uncomfortable, as though the only thing to do is to give more change, but he won't, because the only thing to do is not give more change. He's in such difficulty. Wonder if he'll be a regular like the guy in the fiery black pickup or the laughing lady in the old brown Olds. I'll call him Alvin Blum. If he could talk to me it would ease him, but he's got too much going on about me for it to occur to him to. His window is closed.

A pretty lady in a white car. "I see you every day," she says. "I gave money to you once."

"Thank you," I say but I don't remember her. Best not to say so. But she knows.

Man in a gray car asks how I do.

"I'm just fine," I say, and I am. "How are you?"

"Okay," he says. "You here often?"

"Often."

"I'll know where to find you," he says, promising work with the phrase, and drives away leaving the promise dry.

White man in a white car. "You all by yourself?" he asks. He means, am I alone in the world? I am.

I leave exactly on time, which keeps me honest.

I go home and eat pea soup I've made, and Ritz crackers—oh rightly named. I take a bath and in it I resume the Wolsey biography. I fall asleep in the bath.

When I get out, I call the woman with the loose brown hair.

"I'm the gentleman from the roadside you gave your number to today. You told me you had some work."

"Ya might not want to do it though."

"Well, say what it is, and maybe I will."

"See, I have this truck parked here, and I don't wanta use it, but I don't wanta get it ticketed. So what I need is a registration sticker from the license plate from another car."

"So . . . um . . . what did you have in mind?"

"Twenty dollars for a registration sticker."

"From another car? . . ."

"That's it."

"No," I say carefully. "I don't think I want to do that."

"Okay."

"I mean—why don't you do it yourself?"

"I don't want to either."

"Ohn-honh." I wait to see if there's anything else. "Is that it then?"

"Yeah, that's it."

Disappointment. To be asked that. And that there was no work after all.

Off to the first *Catherine* read-through. Will I be better than everybody, IhopeIhope. We sit around a massive conference table. The Henry is slim and is going to have to wear padding, but his voice is right and so is his energy. He also has red hair, which is good. But the two women, no: the actress playing Anne is too old, the one playing Catherine the wrong type. Baffling, it's not going to work: the play is about them. I also see that, although the company is rich, all the scripts have been photocopied, meaning the author loses his royalty.

Well, I need to be patient, though patience is not a virtue I much possess.

6 hours, $131. Also, a check for the Winkin job—good, I can pay my landlady!

9 February, Tuesday

Night. Rain.

My studio dark but for the computer's blue face.

A window next to this chair. Beyond that the cold black rain. I cannot see past the inky shine of the pane, its wrinkling glass. The glass is in a clear cold sweat. Everything outside the window rains. The animals of the rain disport themselves there. I don't belong in their clan.

The gray computer sits on a low, oak filing cabinet, and a low, wooden table borrowed from the landlord holds the printer. This secretary's desk from the '20s stained too dark holds the keyboard. Carved acanthus handles. Or are they scallop shells?

If I could see anything in the black of this room I would see:

The hoya behind me cascading.

Pictures: Captain Kirkwood, a New Bedford whaling captain—for moral guidance, a banana-wood Bali mask of a blue-faced jackass, a Bali monster mask, a photo of me that appeared once full-length in the *New York Daily News*.

And then the lares and penates of the writer's studio: four framed post-cards—a rhino statue for stick-to-itiveness, pelicans on a square in Costa Rica, birds of good omen, a raging red leopard statue for passion, the angels on the roof of the Costa Rica Opera House for angels.

A big picture of seventeen photographs of myself from babyhood to age forty-five.

A letter to me from Somerset Maugham my former wife had framed.

A picture of Oscar Wilde's son Vyvyan Holland and myself she also had framed.

Boldini's drawing of Wilde.

Two pictures of Mildred Dunnock.

A charcoal head of Pinocchio I drew as a boy.

An old slant-topped, pine desk stained dark. A golden oak, General Grant dining table with a shiny top. A golden oak child's desk with a hooded typewriter. Shelves of reference books and manuscripts. The hundred-year-old swivel chair I now sit on, tired.

I was too frightened of them to practice the auditions. Today, to work off a traffic ticket, I left at 5:30 A.M. to work gardening at John Muir's house in Martinez. I work in the mud and rain of winter dawn, clearing weeds. Is it a career?

Here under the single light of the computer I look at the roadside paper. My brains are too weary to recall all that happened. Who were these people?

A fruitful day, actually, begun by two large grapefruits handed out by a Filipino man and wife in a van, and ending with another prejudice dashed, that school buses do not give: from the high seat of one a black woman swung down a beige plastic supermarket bag at 5:00.

I turn to her bag on the window seat. A container of orange juice, a piece of chocolate cake, one turkey croissant, a bakeshop loaf of sliced bread. She has bought these for me especially.

I stood out in the current rain. The seven-year drought has broken and I can't begrudge it.

Two lovebirds hand me their bag of hot fresh bread.

Many food offerings come in these three hours, which I write of pleasantly enough here in the warmth of a different place within me, one unlike that one out there in the rain, which today was painful.

I put the bags of food all around me to record every item.

A young man pulled off below and parked. I walk down to him. He gives me this big paper bag saying, "There's money in there too."

"What's your name?" (I ask only men's names: a man wouldn't think I was being familiar, where a woman might.)

"Bryan."

"Thank you, Bryan, God bless you."

"There's something else in there too."

"Thank you so much. Is there any work I can do for you?"

You would think I would not be in charge here, begging, but it is not so. Indeed it is agreed that in our transactions *my* agenda is the focus, because of a psychic balance inherent in begging. When Generosity meets Need, Generosity tips its hat to it. This is the natural mechanics of charity, and people enter into it humbly or as equals, never disdainful. If they're disdainful, they simply don't give.

The young man drives away. He's a handsome young man of good physique, and I wonder how it is he comes to offer me so much here. I sensed an unspoken question in his giving, an uncertainty.

Standing on the hilltop today I could not smile. It rains, but that's not it. Long periods when no one gives—they seem long though I'm only there three hours—but that's not it. And, surely, when people do give, my spirits rise and I am glad being given to. When I send out blessings that feels good too, but it's hard for me to remember to keep doing it today, and all my time here is not benedictive. There is a pain in my body, a pain of soul.

A young black man in a hurry hands me a bag, "My sister just cooked it!" I peek. Chicken wings!

A black man stops and gives. He has that proficient black energy which spurts through, an impatience controlling and volatile. When I say, "God bless you," he says, "God bless you too, my brother," so emphatically it moves me. Interesting how I can learn from people whose personal style I don't like, for I say, "God bless you, my brother" to everyone for the rest of the day.

Afterwards I drive across the hills to a warehouse for a costume fitting. I do not know where I am in the rain but drive on and on over the empty highway in the dark. I sense there is something mean in this acting company, a belligerent indifference. There is also my own infantile nastiness at not having all carpets unrolled before me, a toxic ego exaggerating slights. How am I to keep hidden this poison for which everyone will hate me and which will cause them to exile me?

Once home, I practice Illingworth. Audition in 4 days. I fear I cannot do it well, I fear I don't know how to act, that my acting is just an elaborate recitation, and fear belays the work.

3 hours. $31.75.

I look at the rest of the food. Ah, that Chinese lady left me a little white bag of those delicious, flaky crusts and sweet dip. I refrigerate them for meals to come.

Then I open the young man's bag carefully like a Christmas present. Each thing is separately wrapped.

Wheat Thins, a crabmeat sandwich on a Kaiser roll wrapped in what looks like old foil; inside two separate little packages, two cookies; another sandwich, on whole wheat (I eat it as I type); and two books of scripture: Doctrine and Covenants and The Book of Mormon, also wrapped. Not bad. In fact it doesn't get better than that I be given what as he believes is God directly.

In an envelope is $20. That must be a lot in a young man's salary. I am loath to take it. On the other hand he may make more money than I suppose.

And a letter:

Please do not disrespect this letter or the books.

Bryan Boe

There is a god and I found him out through reading in the scriptures and praying for the truth with an open mind. With an attempt to really know what is the meaning of life, I, two years ago was not involved in religion or Christ or God. But through faith, I gradually learned the truth. I will tell you something it was not that easy to believe in this and find the truth, but through the faith I had and the need to know if there is life after death, that Christ is the son of God who really died for our sins so we can repent and be forgiven I say that if you really want help this is no joke. That you really read the scriptures and don't hold any negative thoughts against the gospel I [beg?] you that our heavenly Father will truly bring you and guide you out of your troubles. I have seen and witnessed the power of God. In this time the world is so blind to the plan of Salvation and God and Christ that the

Gospel is a joke. I say unto you that I know that the lord will help you through your troubles if you have faith and ask truly for his guidance. I say to you it won't be easy but it will be worth it. Amen.

The Christ of Jesus Christ of Latter-day Saints.

Our church is located on hilltop drive by 7-11 & Chevron gas station.

His spiritual pain is sweet as it is young. I am not a churchgoer. I know I'm not going to become a Mormon; I don't want to lead him on. Still, he must be responded to. He has left his number, and it's not right to disappoint him of a response.

I call.

"Hello, Bryan? This is the gentleman you spoke to today on the roadside."

He talks to me candidly as an interested stranger. He tells me of a failed love affair that led him to his own conversion. I wonder how the young lady could decline a fellow so handsome. A part of me also has contempt for his love affair and for his religion, for I have neither. And there is a part of me that also listens with respect. What does it matter that his love affair and his religion do not serve me—what does not serve me is not therefore to be condemned. He is hurting, young, beautiful, idealistic, and sincere. He needs to tell his tale to an older male perhaps. Or perhaps he just needs to bring the message. I treat him civilly and thank him, saying I will consider the contents of the books. When I put the phone down, I read in his scriptures a bit, but they are for me impossible. But what does that matter? His very act was scripture.

10 February, Wednesday

My life as a beggar is the life others do not have to lead. Here for the grace of God I do go.

Every day in front of the health food store in Berkeley stands a tall old thin black man begging. I have the notion that he should not be there every day but should move on, or that he is a drunkard or drug addict and would either waste the money or does not deserve it, or that he should get a job, or stop conning people. I have given him money before, and I also have the notion of not giving to the same person twice. Yet I know that people give to me twice. I've always given to street people, but I'm also stingy and have notions, and I've never given more than change or a dollar. So I've decided to seek him out and give him five dollars, never mind what use he may put it to or what I may think of his life. I don't know anything about either one, and it doesn't matter. The only thing that matters is that he is begging; that should tell me all I need to know.

What's interesting is the flavor of my shortcomings. If I could capture the tang of how boring I am, how weak, how selfish, I might be an interesting actor. If I could write about those things they might vanish beneath my hand.

I think of Dickens. He remains our greatest novelist—because the drive of his life and work was the restoring of the wounding of his whole life and whole country at one and the same time and he always fails. He is our greatest novelist because he attempts more than anybody and because his failure is gigantic.

Here I stand, on the roadside, likewise, in a struggle I cannot name.

Day after day, I stand and do not much look at the office walls, which are of heaven. For on the roadside a world surrounds me to which I am autistic, a world like the inside of a house all made of wood, the wood showing, but the house has sky for beams, for wallpaper round hills, cars going by for sofas, carpets of gravel under my shoes, every morsel of which I would denominate, save, and spare. But which I do not look at or regard.

And yet can you say that this gravel life is not my real life, since it may be the life that saves me?

Is this the story of a man whose life is being saved? If it is, he records the drivers-by as the saving grace. Giving or not, to them he accords it. He records them as grantors of his greed, knowing nothing better than greed, not knowing that something else saves him maybe. That wood house. That sky. That air. If he is being saved. If that's what this story is.

I arrive at 10:03, say my prayers and beg.

COMPACT

- Have your phone number ready to give so people can reach you.

So I have made a paper with tear-offs of my number and clipped it behind the Will Work sign to give to folks who ask.

The first stop—no money.

I shift the sign, curl my fingers around the bottom, wondering if I should hold it up with bent elbows or hold it down over my privates, to eliminate any sexual ingredient. Ahtahellwithit, bent elbows feels more comfortable.

What do we have for the weather today? The sky paved gray. But that will spare my balding pate. I am warm inside my blue sweater, my fir green parka. My body is strong. Where's that mascot tree? Ah, there you are my foggy companion. The cars come up from below. What's in store?

A strong old man in a moustache. "Buy yourself a sandwich or something."

A girl swings out a beige plastic bag of canned goods.

A boy yells something from a flatbed as it passes—a curse, I think. It sounds like "Wriggly tires."

At 11:05 I look from the workbench of the roadside again to my mascot tree—whom I do not wish to pester so I look away.

Usually there is good giving at the end of day—except Friday.

Interesting I should say Friday's not the best day: I have formed that superstition having stood here too few Fridays to warrant it, four including the first day, when I stayed half an hour at dusk. Superstition arises from a ready matrix in me like a phoenix from fire, a machine already existing in me and wishing to form such opinions, a machine that turns on by itself: The Superstition Machine.

Is the Superstition Machine a capacity of scrambling for certainty, like the Prejudice Machine—my survival desperately manufacturing water-logged logs to keep me just above water? Or is the Superstition Machine assembled by the very passivity of this roadside standing? That is to say, does this inability to move from this spot give rise to and produce Prejudice/Superstition? For surely these machines are created by another machine, like dew at dawn. Is this Superstition Machine a flower of the inability to work for myself, soul-torpor, the nightmare that one's life cannot move? It is natural for the soul to fear death, for the soul needs the kinetic life of the body to do its work in. But standing here is all the movement I am allowed. I stand still, I stand erect, I set myself up on the exact same rim of sidewalk on the same windshield wiper every day. But inwardly I am scared to move. I Do Not Know Where To Turn. And this immobility being the only movement I am capable of, this standing in one place the only gesture my soul can make, this standing my parade, inertia my twitch, immobility is still easier than facing acting—and failing. And at least standing here does not involve hope. I don't hope to be a good roadside-stander. I just do what I have to do to be one. For the roadside at least is doable.

What time is it, I've been here over an hour, where's my money! Oh shut up, Bruce; you're talking as if God is paying you a wage here. No, kiddo, here you earn any old way.

Think of God.

God.

Take a look. $3 right? No, $7. One of the men has given me a $5 bill!—what a honey—and if I count the canned goods (I tend not to count the canned goods), I have well over $10.

Let's bless these cars. I don't want to. What I want to do is calculate the take. It's more than a calculation. It's a mood, a hunger, a whole approach, calculating when business may be good, when bad, how to manage an attitude to generate the most bucks. Which is odd, because in my life I've been a person not much interested in money. And odd also because I know better: God doesn't need Greed to keep His till.

So, Greed is the meditation.

Here it is, Bruce, Greed in your stomach again, feel it sitting there today like a beet. "Come on, God, eat it for me, do your job. I'll prove I'm greedy, God, I'll skip coming here from 10 to 11 when there is no money!"

Nah, it wouldn't do for me to stay away because the money is less at a certain hour. For less money primes the pump. Standing 10 to 11 may make 11 on prosper.

That's what you think, Bruce. You think you can figure how God chances it, you want to second-guess God.

Anyhow I am here to bless. That's my work whether people give or not—if I can do it.

The wild lady in the beat-up brown Olds sails by keel-up with a pal on a tear, both waving at me, both laughing. I wave back. I would never have known her had I not been here.

I look up and see the hills colliding with the fog. Fog and hills don't see me, they have business of their own, well worked out after all these years. Like a basketball game I'm not playing in, the hills play on. But I look only for an instant since I too have my task, one whose greed does not wish to regard anything that threatens its continuing.

East Asian man in a gold car with a little moustache as though drawn on hair by hair with a brush and the vulnerable neck of the East Asian, which suggests they are weaker, incapable of business, meant only for sacrifice, and cruel.

Man who gave $5 that time and who the next time reminded me he had passes again. Or is it he?

I can't recall the faces. It's a defect of character.

But why should I feel guilty for a talent I do not possess?

I feel guilty for having no talent for baseball, bridge, chess, high finance. For sixty years these guilts have been going on. Because God did not make me such and such, I engineered a permanent chastisement by turning Guilt—a memo—into a life sentence.

And suppose I did explore, bridge, say, I might gain competence, but there will always be someone better. There is always a way to make oneself feel bad. Envy is a big way. Prejudice and Guilt and Greed and Superstition are other ways. Maybe I am here to find them out.

For the good I feel saying "Bless you" makes an ordinary ecstatic alternative to guilt. Even though I want Guilt, Opinion, Envy to correct and better me, they do not. I demean myself with them. Guilt has become a resident, thoughtless addiction. "Bless you" sets this habit behind a wall of ecstasy. "Bless you" is another side of the coin of self-curses I had never flipped but which by tossing shows itself to be a coin.

So here I stand, and what is my mind actually doing while it is waiting? I bless and cannot tell.

You know what happened?

Last night on TV I caught the tag end of a film. A tall, middle-aged man has

TB, and he has a kid, a son maybe, and they're broke and traveling through the rural South in a touring car—this is the Great Depression—and there's a teenage girl along for some reason. They land in Nashville; he's a singer-songwriter who is there to make his first record, and it becomes clear that he's on his last legs physically. But he sings an audition at the Grand Ole Opry, records a song. He sings marvelously. Is it him? He acts *marvelously.* He's a marvelous actor. I don't even recognize him. What's happened to this person?

Everything in his acting is musical. How could I have missed this? Or maybe it's come into being since I saw him years ago. His delivery, his attack, is musical. It's not a music you can hear, you can't hear it, his voice is breathy, quiet, slow-paced—that's not what I mean, no, what I mean rather is that as a scene is played, the energy underneath the voice and his moves consists of an *instrumental* grasp of scenic ensemble. His acting of a scene is *conducted,* not performed, and he himself is an instrument, important and modest, in the composition. To get it you have to listen to something you can't hear. You can hear him listen but you have to listen very closely to hear him do it. You have to drop your notions of what acting is and what listening is. His acting is not related either to histrionics or to showbusiness. It's not stage acting, it's film acting, and it's not Marlon Brando, and it's not Betty Grable who was also a good film actor. It's not how he plays the lines, it's how he plays the scene, or rather how he *participates* in the scene. He's an ensemble player, and what he is playing is jazz; the rubric of jazz, the most self-reflective and baroque of all the arts, is the foundation of his craft, except both the baroque and the self-reflection are missing from his because his is cool California jazz. With him you can see the things he can't do. But you can hardly see what he can do, because it is taken for granted. Indeed since what he can do seems like it isn't anything, it becomes lost in what he *can't* do. Delivery of lines is secondary to his hold on scenes. His hold is rhythmical, silent, as rhythm is silent, as the rise and fall of a wave is silent. His acting is instrumental. You have to understand what instrument he is.

What instrument is he?

A clarinet.

He must have directed this piece because in his death scene he cuts from himself to other actors' reaction shots, which is a mistake. But never mind that. For me, what a treat to get rid of this resentment about this person! Clint Eastwood in *Honky Tonk Man.*

Again, the handsome young man in the black truck with the fire painted on it—I wave, he waves. We are cohorts here.

The shine of the day is old silver rain.

Hispanic man in red car. I turn my sign and write, "H m r." Perhaps the drivers-by see me writing.

"Hey!"

I turn. Behind me on Appian Way a man in a Roundtable Pizza car.

"I have a leftover pizza. Do you want it?"

"Why, yes, thank you." I am grateful and surprised. I hold the foolish box in my hands while he drives away.

Lots of pretty girls full of girlish sexual charm giggling in a VW van. They give some money, and then some more. "Have a good time," one says.

"Looks like you are," I say.

An East Asian man from the middle lane calls, "Go to Kentucky Fried Chicken."

"What do they pay?"

"$4.35 an hour."

"Thank you," I call back.

Every day a fellow walks by—slender, young, blond, and mad. He has a farmer's homely face. You can tell he's off by his jittery energy. He lives in the neighborhood and passes toward the mall and then later back again—I don't know on what business, and it does not occur to me that being mad he even has any business. He is often the only pedestrian all day. I want not to relate to him for I feel put off by mad folks, fearful lest they drain me.

But he is a part of this landscape as am I, so today I say hello, how are you, and ask him his name.

"Bob," he says.

"That's my name too."

"No, Steve."

He covers his traces, escapes while standing in place. In him is the underlying anger with which the mad keep the world irrelevant to their purpose, which is to keep the world irrelevant, for madness is selfishness continually completing itself. Madness is a career. It takes doing.

But I set his madness aside and address him as though I did not notice it. This however is also wrong. To treat a nun as though she were not in a wimple would be just as wrong, and Steve-Bob is wimpled in madness. Madness arranges for other people to never get you right. He discounts me and bounces on his way. By talking to him I achieve virtue, so I think.

"Sir. Oh sir!" I turn to Appian Way behind me and walk over. A young woman hands me lunch from Long John Silver's. Also a soda—the second today and I don't drink soda. I wish fast-food joints sold nourishing drinks. Soft drinks are made from used tires.

Young man in low, orange car waits there until the last minute. He is heavy-set, macho, withdrawn, controlled, the sort of man who gives nothing emotionally but has a lot of emotion.

"Is there any work I can do for you?"

"No. Try to help yourself though."

People assume I am not trying to help myself. I wish to correct them, for I am an exceptious person yet I accept their words without correction.

A lady pulls off on the dirt below. I do not assume her turning off has to do with me. She may want to study a map, she may have car trouble. But she beckons me. I approach gingerly. She gives me a Taco Bell lunch for which she has gone to some trouble: she has had to see me, go for it, buy it with her own money, return to the freeway, drive off it, cross over it, drive on it again, and come back down to my exit—all for a stranger.

However, none of this is calculated by her in the moment of giving. That is the miracle of this place. The miracle is that for the gift no payment is exacted. In the moment every gift comes without history. Guilt, religious duty, fractious parents—none of that remains in the instant of giving. And that is how all charity is a gift of God. We smile. A gift makes us the same. The quality of a charity is equality.

I am happy and happiness gives me latitude, gives me psychic money to spend, so I think I'll engage in a bit of research to find out how many cars pass me every day.

At 11:29 I count the number of stops in 15 minutes—God bless you—in 15 minutes cars stop 10 times, which means 40 stops an hour, which means in 6 hours there are 240 stops. I average 10 cars a minutes which means 3,600 cars a day going by me, although not all in my lane. It means nothing, but figuring it is elating.

A plump, sweet, lower-class lady gives and says, "I might be next."

As I stand here I know I have a sweet face. My smile is God smiling through me as I bless. It's seraphic. I can't help it. Sometimes pain fills me, and, although I don't want to impose, people can see it. But today I smile, helpless not to.

A woman in a white car pulls over from the middle lane and hands me a bag from the supermarket bakery, full of crullers, one half-eaten. Mmm, I think I'll sample one. (I eat them all by lunch.)

Steve-Bob comes back from the mall and snubs me, but I say hi, and I offer him a lunch, for I have too many of them, among which are cheese and crackers and devilled ham. "Here," I say and, "Here." I give him the Taco Bell; I keep the Progresso soup for myself. He's fussy about what he takes, but I think he lives with his family and has enough food. He doesn't thank me.

"Don't you say, 'Thank you'?"

"Thank you," and needing to stay rude he bends over for a butt and without good-bye, he splits. He will clamber up the retaining wall, a shortcut home, but I have turned my attention to the roadside and I do not see him do it.

A man in a big old gold car screams out something: "Blank blank . . . you wouldn't have to beg." If you danced on linzer tortes you wouldn't have to beg? He delivers his words as though I have lived a bad life, which I suppose I have, but not the one he thinks I've lived.

At 1:04 I head for the hospital cafeteria. Once there I settle myself so as not to spread out in a place where my presence is questionable. However, the lunch counter has closed, so the cafeteria is empty at this hour. I open up a Wolsey bio but can't keep my eyes open.

I get back from lunch at 2:34, late; I wanted to leave at 5, but 5:34 it must be.

The rain touches down on my parka. I am safe, I do not melt, I have been long hours in weather before. And if I were wet, still I'd stay.

A sweet lady waits there a bit, then rolls down her window: "You really look like a nice man. I pass by you every day."

"I am nice," I joke.

She gives me some money.

"I just thought you looked like a nice man," she insists.

"So are you," I say.

But repartee's not fair coin here. Stillness in gratitude is sufficient. "Thank you" is sufficient.

I decline a Burger King bag from a couple who, again, must have driven all the way off the ramp and onto the highway and back up again to give it to me.

"I don't eat that," I say.

"You don't eat hamburgers?"

"I'm a vegetarian," I lie, "but thank you."

I should also have said thank you for your trouble and generosity, and bless you. But I was nice to them and I felt better for saying no to what I really didn't want, just as Brendan said no to a Christmas dinner. Perhaps beggars can be choosers.

On the other hand if I am fussy I'll thwart the giving. And perhaps I *ought* to accept everything. I don't have to eat everything but I should accept everything. It's *generosity* itself I ought to accept.

An East Asian woman calls out that help is needed at Pinole Valley High School. I make a note of it and will call.

Hispanic young man in an orange car. "Keep out of the rain."

"What you give me helps keep my head covered," I say.

Nice lady with slightly buck teeth in a pleasant face with white sunglasses gives me $10 with apologies that it isn't more. Many people apologize for what they give.

When people speak to me about work, I am delicate with them. A good-looking man in his thirties asks if I will be there on Saturday. He says he has work clearing up his yard. I ask for his number, which he does not want to give to me. We talk a bit, and when I ask how I am to reach him he gives me his work number. Name's Will. I'll call him. He seems genuine.

Coins from a black woman in the far lane, then all the cars join in, a merriment of giving, which includes a supermarket gift certificate. The first time four in one stop!

A lady with her daughter. They look hard but eventually they give. "Buy yourself some food now," she says.

"This will pay for a roof over my head," I say, but she looks sourly away. I imagine she imagines I am a drunk or an addict and will use it for such truck.

Passages arise in me, unaccountably, like landscapes outside a train window. It Will Not Be Enough rises in my chest as a disposition. Where does it come from? My parents? No. It's a natural contraption like Prejudice, Superstition, Greed. It Will Not Be Enough switches itself on as I stand watching the cars move into formation below and drive up toward me. At the moment they give, what I actually experience is that it is always enough. Yet It Will Not Be Enough arises as the next car comes.

People drive by. I don't know their work, nor they mine. Mine is to wait, to bless, to collect money for school. But just for fun I think I'll ask theirs.

A man in a red pickup chats while he waits.

"A machine operator," he tells me.

"What does that mean?" I ask him.

It means he operates heavy construction machinery. He's a union man and has a job. He does not give but talks about the many who've been laid off. Because he has worked for the same company for a long time, he has not been fired. I wish him well.

The rain drifts in and out.

A smoked windshield, an old woman behind it. Oh, not an old woman. A sweet pretty young lady.

A black woman reaches a loaf of Tastee Bread out the window. I decline saying I am allergic to it, which I am.

"I was the one who gave you the turkey dinner."

"Oh, yes, it was very good. I ate it."

"I don't have no turkey dinner today," she apologizes. She had gotten the loaf, an extra one, from an organization which feeds the elderly. If I took the

Tastee Bread, I'd either throw it away, which would be bad—or eat it, which would be worse.

Anatolian man in moustache smiles and nods.

A young man as soon as he stops asks, "Would you take this?" holding out a folded bill.

"Yes," I say.

When I ask if he has any work I can do, he says, "I would if I could, but I'm employed by someone else." He tells the mysterious, plain truth.

At the end of the day my blessings get sad. It's raining, is that it? Is it because the money is not coming in? I would rather have a lot of people give a little than a few people give a lot. My feet ache. I lift them up one after the other, as you do when you're cold. I'll massage them at home.

Sweet, tiny-faced, old Jewish man.

Plump black lady in red car. "All I have is this change." Black people are so attractive.

A red car on Appian Way behind stops. I have radar and turn before he beeps. I go over and am given money from an older man with a moustache, sitting in the passenger seat with an older black man. Maybe they're lovers.

Hey, what's wrong with that red car stopped down the ramp?

I pack up and go down and help the car to back off the road. I accompany the man up to Appian in the rain. But he doesn't want me to help any further. My feelings are hurt.

5:34. As I pack up to go I see a young woman walking off the freeway and onto the ramp. I hitch on my backpack and walk down to meet her and ask if I can help.

She's pretty, levelheaded, easy, amiable, with straight, dark, shoulder-length hair like Ella Raines. Her car is stuck with the kids in it; she doesn't need help from me really, all she needs is to call her friend. I tell her where the pay phones are. I put up the umbrella to walk her to them.

We walk inside the yellow line between the abutment and the three-lane. It rejoices me to be in the presence of such a pretty woman. I'd run off with her in a minute—and her children too. Along with my umbrella, I'd offer her my hand. As we reach Appian a man hands me folded bills from his car, an act which leaches virility from my gallant thoughts, which are: isn't your husband a workaholic wretch, isn't he dismal in bed, I'd love you forever if you'd let me. At the corner she excuses herself and we part.

Later, driving back up to Appian, I see the young lady returning to her car and I ask her if she wants a ride to it and she declines. She is young and pretty and wise not to travel with strangers.

I drive home in the rush hour traffic and the darkening day. I make for the slow lane, no need to get home fast, keep the speed limit. I feel a wide space around me, a confidence in being taken care of.

At home I get in a hot bath, slide down, read the *New Yorker!* Then I sup on Progresso soup—begging makes each meal a surprise. Then I look at the money: $163, including $60 in supermarket vouchers. I'll call the Pinole school in the morning.

I call the man Will who gave me his card. He says he needs help cleaning up a tree in his yard, says he'll call me when the rain stops.

The less you are paid the harder you have to work for it, and therefore the more obliviating your relaxation must be. TV takes the cake, so I turn on that blue moon which shines in the night of my parlor and watch as one would watch the midnight sky agog.

11 February, Thursday

The first sign of no talent in a director is his blocking the play before letting the actors explore the material together. It follows that none of us are going to get anything from this director. Too bad. I had been excited all day because it is the first day on our feet.

At 12:45 A.M. I wake, lie back in the stale dark. In my stomach a dread that life offers no promise, that every day will be like the one after it, no success, no future, no change. I jump into the kitchen and seize a box of crackers so as not to feel this. How long will I be on the roadside? If I get into acting school, I'll stay on the roadside for years. And if I don't get in, will I also stay on the roadside for years?

12 February, Friday

I forgot paper so could not record anything.

It was painful to be there. By that I mean my body hurt, not from standing, not from holding the sign six hours, not from age, but from a black inside sun, as though my soul were in discord with what my body is doing. I hurt in my being.

I want to be here for right work. I have got to forge a proper ambition; being here for bucks is not enough; in fact it's bad for me, but it is my inclination.

So I wish for each of the passing cars what I would wish for myself. I change the silent blessing from "Bless you," to "Bless you in your work."

"Bless you in your work," I say. "Bless you in your work," over and over. To each one of them, to this one, to that, to you and to you though you don't know it, though you don't see me do it.

But it was painful.

To be blessed in my work seemed so far from my situation.

I also sense not as much money coming from the roadside as heretofore. Is it that each day there is to be less? There's all the food of course. Yet I can't pay my rent with canned goods.

Catherine rehearsal.

The second sign of no talent in a director is rudeness to those around him. Saul Camber does not know how to talk to actors as people, or to people as actors. He is unkind. And who is that man sitting next to him, whispering?

13 February, Saturday

Maddy Fluhr is an actor friend I have known for eight years. She knows everything about me, but she does not know about the roadside. She's offered to give me some Illingworth coaching—the Theatre Bay Area audition is tomorrow. As we talked on the phone this morning I wanted to tell her—but not on the phone. But now as I drive to her house I wonder: there's something precious about a thing not told. Still, I'm so afraid to tell that it's probably best to tell.

As we have a spot of tea in her kitchen, I balk—I don't know how to broach the subject. I am a man who can right now forward his life in no way but by begging, and I am ashamed. "Maddy, you know I've been out of work awhile . . ."

Once over the hump I forge ahead. In the end I even show her the food I was given yesterday and forgot to take out of my backpack.

Maddy is a very good actor. One virtue of that is that she is capable of a dispassionate attention to dramatic situations not her own. I see this good actor in her now. She takes this roadside matter without being knocked over by it, weighs it, retains her humor. She is not horrified. She does not pity me. She does not commiserate. And she does not offer to lend me money, which she has already done and I declined. She treats the situation with old-fashioned, evenhanded respect.

Once I've told, I feel that being on the roadside is not a bad thing. That I imagined others should think it a bad thing was the bad thing.

Afterwards I go to a spiritual meeting that I have attended for many years. I had told the meeting about my job search, on the off-chance someone might know of a job. But I have not said I am on the roadside, for fear a stigma might attach to me.

Race Du Port is a firmly set man of forty with a pleasant, round, red face, and I'm surprised to see him approach, for I always thought he was afraid of me. "I saw you standing there," he says happily.

"Oh!"

"I work at the hospital. I've seen you there before but I've never been able to stop." He's smiling. He isn't disdainful or embarrassed or pitying. It's as though he is glad to make this contact with me finally.

"Yeah, I ran out of money so I had to." As I admit it, I don't feel bad—I feel relieved. We're humorous and practical about it. I feel closer to him. How can this be? The exchange is fun. He and Maddy and Ellen treat it as a brave adventure. No one treats it as a demotion.

So the cat is out of the bag.

When I got home I realize I have left the backpack behind at Maddy's. When I finally get it, I find in the Taco Bell bag a five-dollar bill, and when I call to ask Maddy if she put it there she says no. But you never can tell. Maddy is a very good actor.

14 February, Sunday

When the TBA audition is done, I walk into the marble lobby of the theater and down the sweeping stairs to the street, the tenderloin of San Francisco, and into the garish light of afternoon. The air is numb. I know the truth. While I have not disgraced myself, I have not been great, and there is no other reason to do this work but to do it greatly. I look neither to the right nor to the left, lest I see a further truth I do not want to see. What does this mediocrity mean in terms of my life? It doesn't bode well. But does it mean no? Don't answer.

Acting school auditions in 20 days. When I get home I'm going to find an audition coach. My former boss has sent me $100 for Christmas. I'm angry with him for firing me, so as to stop being angry that's what I'll use to pay for it.

And so as not to think, not to know a truth that might tell me to quit, I rent a Clint Eastwood movie. Because my estimation of him has changed, I now want to examine the collected works and give him full due. At the $1 video I rent his pictures one by one in no special order. To see what there is there. To see what I can learn. To see what I can steal.

But before that I go on the roadside.

I stand in the variable air. The wind blows its moisture on my face, but like a Nordic farmer my skin joins with it to make my face full as an apricot. If I were at sea my face would weather like jerky. I stand in sight of the sea and what the sun subtracts the soft day restores.

In a car stopped down the line a family of Filipino folks, the father driving, the mother in the passenger seat rummaging, children in back. She fans bills, hands some to her husband, they consult, the window opens, and the man beckons.

I walk down, smile, keep my distance. I bend and look in. Both the man and woman are smiling sweetly at me. The man hands me a bill. "Bless, you. Thank you. Is there any work I can do for you?"

"I'm unemployed too," says the man.

I see another bill in the wife's hand. "Is that for me?" I ask the woman sweetly.

Embarrassed she hands me the other bill. I thank them again, bless them, and leave.

They drive off and I turn to walk back to Appian—and then I realize what I have done. I have not been quick enough to listen to what the man said! That man was unemployed, and he had a family! I have been caught up in the agenda of my own greed—I might have given him money. I am disgusted with myself. How to make amends?

A boy from a passing car calls—sounds like "Meet me at the supermarket in the shopping center."

While something in it sounded rude, something suggested a job, and as a penance for taking that family's money, I pack up and go.

I reach the supermarket but do not find him.

Instead of going back on the roadside I protract my penance for 45 minutes—I talk to the owner of the furniture refinishing shop, I trek around the back of the supermarket for a shortcut, which brings me into the weeds behind the dismantled gas station, which I traverse as a kid's adventure on dirt, the Comanche trail, no mother-cooked meal in sight.

When I return, I resume my sign and the blessing of the passing cars, but when money-wanting energy appears inside me, I banish it. "Bless you, Greed, bless you." I keep saying it.

All at once I realize my energy has dropped to below my navel, the house of chi. I am deep in my life. I am living in another country. This is rare: usually I live in in the throat, which is the emotion level, or in the mind, the Coney Island of the soul. Now I rest in this room below my navel. Which Sees. From which Seeing is wide and old. It is old. It is rare. It is precious. I keep blessing. It is steady, assured, does not smile.

After a time a smile comes into my face.

The chi has risen, my awareness is no longer below my navel but back where it was.

Too bad, for the belly-chi is not a room I can shift to at will.

But now I know I can resume begging. My word has been kept. The penance is done. The boy's crack was a whip putting money-getting out of commission. He cooperated with a vow he never heard. I would say God did it, the Universe did it. No, those aren't my terms. The gray sky did it. How all things do conspire against me to conspire for me. Shshsh. The lint, the lint in my pocket did it.

3 hours: $46.31.

15 February, Monday

Right away a black man with a round face drives up and starts talking. He's just been laid off from the Lincoln dealership where he detailed cars. There is nothing to be gained and nothing to be lost in talking to him. He needs to get something off his chest.

Then a tough-faced guy in a black truck, a real meat-ax but what a honey. His cover has nothing to do with his contents.

I read this morning about the Sufi woman mystic who said, "If I love God out of fear of hell may I go to hell. If I love God out of desire for heaven, may I never enter it."

Yes. To love God for God alone.

And so the day is spent out under the sun and the moving clouds.

For the great blessing of this work is that it is out-of-doors. To be outdoors thrills me. (How awful if these freeways were subterranean.) And to think of God for God alone. And what is God? I am selfish, greedy, infantile, so God comes as someone who gives me the alternative to these: God fills my self with His self; God feeds me with the coin of bliss, who can count it; God nurtures my soul. And what I know in knowing all this is that God loves me. I know it because I experience it. And out-of-doors is the right-size cathedral for it.

But how do I love God? Not as much as God loves me, for sure, for when I think of God I feel happiness, shining ease, and clarity.

God Himself could not possibly feel this happy.

This morning in Traherne's *Centuries* I read how one must love each grain of sand, for the brilliance of God is in everything, and I know this is so. Yet I do not live it out.

Yet I have been given the chance here, on this hill by the road, to live my life exactly the way I most want it. To live my life ideally, never mind the circumstances. As my life is, not in any elected ideal of my life, but as it is. To do that, all I have to do is think of God.

Yes, I am a beggar, but I still stand here with God in me, breathing like a man, from my balls, and sending blessings to all I see and to everything about.

If I stand here, God will give me my calling. If I bless here, God will give me a living. If I am steady here, God will give me the dessert of funds. "You shine with God's smile," I tell myself. "Keep it up, it may make some dough."

It is my tendency to come from the position that if I do one thing then God will do another. But God is not to be purchased. All there is is God's direct love of me, my direct knowledge of God, the direct communication between God and myself. Nothing of necessity comes of this feeling of God: it buys nothing, it guarantees nothing. I know this by experience, but my mind constantly runs otherwise, and I am sad.

But my sadness is sweetened by God.

So as I stand here I try not to bargain with God, since such negotiations are disgusting, and besides I'm no good at them.

Fame is the last temptation of noble mind, perhaps, but what about the temptation to Paradise, John Milton, what about Doing Right as the coin to heaven? To me the afterlife is inspeculous, but the temptation to it rises in me, operates like a weather, this weather, which is rainy within me. My mind, ever unsteady returns to the drift and tide of mentation, which is to say other states than God. This is the nature of the mind, it is not the mind's fault. For I believe in Paradise on earth, and I know I am in it. God is that Paradise in me.

And I still want more, I still want God to make me money!

Rehearsal:
Saul Camber sneers, "You people should have learned that in Acting 101."
That's no way to talk to folks. He should have learned that in Directing 101. But does he mean me?

$76.41

16 February, Tuesday
I stand in the compact of the day.

An East Asian young man in a white car is the first to give.

Also on Appian, a young lady walks past and gives me money. "I see you every day," she says.

A bicyclist dressed in full armor. He's nineteen, he means business, and a terrible business it is, the chain mail of skin-tighting down the road on a treadmill. He stops at the curb, delves into a slim hip-pocket, extracts two dollars. Exercise is good for him. "Buy yourself a meal," he says. His commitment to biking has ripened him to a minimalist.

But instead, of recording those who did give, let these notes today again be a record of those who do *not* give.

How people do not give:

I have a nice conversation with a blond lady in a red convertible. She has no job either.

Twice people hold up money which they do not give because the traffic sweeps them by.

I help a man push his stalled truck; he does not even know I ask for alms. Good.

A big, fat black man in a tiny, new, expensive red car shrugs the "no-money" shrug. For there is a sign language of not-giving: this sappy smile, the head cocked slightly, and a shrug. Could this gesture be read in Tibet, in Patagonia? I would like to think so.

A man in a truck chats. He does refrigerator work. People need to Get It Off Their Chests, yes they do.

Other ways people don't give: to offer jobs one cannot take, to offer jobs that don't prove out, to offer jobs and not follow through.

But they mean well—and that is a gift.

A mature person is one who has given up dependence upon others and become dependent upon God. Is that true? Or am I just spouting sententious pieties? Yes. I am.

Other ways people don't give:

The main way is to conduct conversations with me. I hold the position that only those who give have a right to my conversation because only they have paid for it.

And is there the pretense in drivers-by that they don't know I need cash?

Three young East Asian boys wave. The one in the back seat wears an ID badge. Probably fast-food workers.

Why do folks wave? They wave to me as to the engineer on a passing freight train, that they be not, that no one be, passing strangers. Do people wave all around the world? If I wave to a Fiji Islander does she know what the work of a wave is? Would she wave back as I do to the East Asian boys in the car?

An East Indian woman says she will stop by tomorrow to arrange work. Promised work feels good. But I feel she won't pay me enough.

I feel miserable. It's 11:20. Not many have given.

A man with a cigarette in a bright yellow pickup truck stops and says, "God bless you. I got a car, but I'm the same."

Lots of people out of work stop to tell me so. Telling me defuses their unemployment.

A man with all four middle bottom teeth out says, "Good luck," another way of not-giving. "Good luck" is a balancing wish. Folks throw luck in your cup to balance you. I also have the notion that people, without giving, don't even have the right to say, "Good luck."

An older man and wife in the middle lane move around for money. He beckons me. When I arrive the man holds a bill and the wife holds $2 more. The man gives me his bill but orders his wife not to give me what she wants. My eyes move toward her money as though it were mine. I don't ask for it. She can't disobey her husband. This is the first time I have experienced not-giving as a wound.

A man in a pickup stops and rolls down the window. "How much are you makin'?"

I don't answer him. He spoke as though I were a scam.

"You a vet?"

He has seized authority.

"Yes."

"Make a sign, 'Homeless Vet.' Those guys really clean up."

Where does he get off, how dare he assume I'm here to clean up? And what does he know of homeless vets or what they make? His purpose is to crush others with knowledge they can't check up on, a know-it-all, a type I've not come upon here till now. Of course he doesn't give. And of course I *am* here to clean up.

Another vocational counselor, although more polite, says, "Why don't you go to McDonald's and ask for a job?" People think a mature man can live off the salaries kids earn living with their families while making just enough for their first secondhand car.

I stand here appalled at my situation.

I am a rotten fool. Every kindness God could provide me with here I have been given. A tolerance for outdoor weather and to breathe *air,* those are blessings. My happiness in the out-of-doors, though, does not fadge with my dreams of grandeur on the silver screen or the condescension with which I will receive the Nobel Prize For Radiant Suffering. So I dismiss the air, the weather, the vision of the hills.

Look at them, *look* at them!

I do not look at them. I have business with these cars, with their money. Even a glimpse at my mascot tree is time stolen from ambition. The wind records itself upon my face. I look right through it at the roadside only.

No one gives. I look straight ahead. I bless.

This morning I called up all the job offers: the bookbindery man whose wife said he would give me a job—no soap; the Pinole School District again—no soap.

I don't really want those jobs. But I have to make the calls, be willing to test unknown waters 'cause I said I would. Besides I'm curious.

The clouds moult rain. It is abundant on the face. And the absence of money falls no heavier than rain. Paucity is not solid. It does not drown. All about me is the air, the mist, the gray—not sun, but clouds, and these clouds prove out the gift of not-giving. From them, the bearable weight of the not-giving falls.

In the hospital cafeteria, I eat my takings and open a new Wolsey biography. I am afraid that they will throw me out for sleeping, which I know I will do when I start to read it. So I prop the book before me and sit so I won't fall, and bow my head so they can't see my eyes.

When I get back, I feel ill with depression. The way I am standing, my lungs are sagging on my diaphragm.

I pull myself upright, the lungs lifted off the stomach. I draw my head up. I lengthen my neck. I open my chest. Immediately I am no longer depressed. You stand here for hours, Bruce, in one place so it's understandable you should collapse into yourself. Remember, you are not here to pay for charity with depression, and the remedy is to hand: stand tall.

Bless you, bless you horse van (is there a horse in there), bless you old lady with the pink hair, bless you Hostess Cupcake truck, bless you flivver, bless you glass truck (will they stone you?), bless you cars down below, one two three four ten eleven fourteen, sixteen gazillion, bless you cop car, bless you and you and you and you . . . I am in ecstasy bless you—I am going crazy bless you—I am losing my mind bless you—my head is going to fly off bless you bless you I can't breathe! Why is this so hard? Stand tall and bless you, bless you I can hardly get the words out—I want to faint but I'm not a fainter bless you. You've got to bless them. But I can't. I'm all jammed up! Why? It's impossible. If God wants me to bless it's got to be more possible. I stop.

Why can't I do it?

What was I doing wrong in blessing?

Oh! I wanted to be a good boy, to *pay* for, to *earn* the money with blessing! I see! How pious! I'm not a holy person, who am I to be confettiing the world with blessings!

Blessing is pretentious for me then, or above my station somehow? Yes. I never feel good feeling Good. It lacks salt. For what blessing am I, that I may bless?

You are a dumb-cluck, Bruce, you like to work, so you chained yourself to the blessing chain gang, but you're not supposed to work here. Here God is giving you your survival as a free gift.

What can I *do*, then? What can I do if I can't bless? Stand here and do *nothing?*

Well, if that's what I'm supposed to do, I'll do it.

The cars drive, the sun shines down through the wind, the hills hill. They have work. I feel bereft and beaten. I am less than a blesser of cars. I meant well. Brendan Moon blessed every car! If I stand here and don't give back, I am the lowest of the low. The money!—I wanted to *deserve* it! But no—my ideals don't work. It's odd though, how God seems to ask me to do less than I am willing to do. But goodwill is still will. It's not Good Will but God's will that's at stake. Accept it, Bruce. The answer is no. Life doesn't want me to give more than I'm asked. The message is: this money is free. How odd. I desired to do my part, and ended up being merely industrious.

But what shall I do if I don't bless—I've got to do something. Just bless the people that give, maybe, yes that I can do. "Thank you. God bless you. Is there any work I can do for you?" But that seems so paltry. And yet to bless every car is to count the sands of the sea. I know! Instead—instead, I'll start the day with a general blessing, a one-blessing-fits-all. Let's see—

"God bless all who pass in sight of me today—on the freeway or behind me or on the off-ramp. May no person and no car their whole lives be involved in a fatal or disabling accident."

Yes! No harm can come from it and it means everyone's blessed, and if it works, two benefits: countless lives and vehicles will be spared; and I will also be spared, since, as I will never know whether the blessing succeeded, I will never be tempted to take credit for it.

I feel relieved.

What I may have to do is just stand here with God—if I can remember God. Maybe this is my task, a more modest one than blessing. God does not want me to be good—I've always known that—but to do right.

I open myself to the cars.

There they are.

You cars, all you folks in them, you may if you wish know that my blessing you has ceased. I've had a demotion. I wish I could give you more, but it's not allowed. You in the red car, you in the silver pickup, you in the car turning—God bless you, anyhow, but I have to tell you, I can't pay you back.

And so I stand here for the rest of the day in the sweet pain of this carefree wind, blessing no more. If this is in part a record of how others do not give, it is now also a record of how I do not give. For if it is all right for others not to give to me, it must likewise be all right that I not give to others.

I feel God loving me as I do it. Always here in the rain, in the sun, there is this beauty, when I remember. Love is God's fiction in me, the story God tells in me, the word that has no syllable, no sound. Love is God's fiction in me, God's imagination smiling that smile on my face. How can this be when I am so dissatisfied, have such poor character? Yet there it is, palpable as wood, God's loving me again.

For I do know that God loves me, now, here, nothing else about but the rain, these hills, a thousand cars, strangers, money, taking notes, difficulties. Simple as saying his name, God comes and my heart is full, my being shines. Just like that. And no one taught it to you, Bruce, you never learned it. God did it, does it.

Usually when someone loves me I don't like it. But God loving me I do not mind. I like it and am grateful. And yet this God is not some power that I can wield. I know that as I know I stand here. Even to influence others to this joy. Oh, no.

But do I love God in return?

I hear I am supposed to, that I am supposed to yearn for God. If I could love God back, what would that be like?

Maybe just standing here and saying "God" is loving God, maybe this bliss is both our loves. Maybe there's only one love.

If I could do that everywhere, maybe that is the lesson of the roadside. Maybe saying "God," I am doing all I need to do. Maybe God's name itself is the two-way street. How is it possible to feel such joy! How is it possible!

Love is God's blessing without the words.

17 February, Wednesday

I arrive late, 1:30. It starts to pour, and I put on my hat and put up my umbrella. No one gives. "The fichew nor the soiled horse—" Shut up—King Learing yourself in the storm, how contemptible. The rain comes on harder, and from behind drenched windshields they do not touch me. Incomprehensible. I become angry and put the umbrella down, take off my hat: I defy them not to give. "In the cold. In the rain . . ." Shut up. Here under the hills with nothing, I beggar by the road. But I stand tall.

Brendan Moon said alms increase in rain. But the drivers' windows stay closed. The element I am in differs from the element they are in.

And there is no cause that my being here in the rain should inspire giving. Compassion is not a cause. Compassion accompanies the act and surcharges it but does not cause it. "I would not treat a dog like this," I say to myself, "to leave him unassuaged in the cold and the rain. I would not pass him by." I might, though. Just not open the window. Just keep my cuffs dry.

But by what right do I ask *anything* from them? I'll tell you why: any moron knows that my sign means I need money now, and that no one needs "work" at four in the afternoon. So they are either fools or pitiless.

Or agents of God's indifference.

No. It is not that they do not give. The issue is that I cannot understand how God could have put me here. To what purpose?

I feel there is not enough energy to keep me alive. But that's not true. For one day there will be enough energy to make me die, and if there is enough energy for that, there's enough to make me live.

I laugh in the face of the people who do not give. I laugh at this mocked scene as they drive past the water dripping off my nose. I laugh. But not at them, but with the mockery of the world.

Everyone has his reasons for not giving. It might be that they do not give on a matter of principle, or to beggars, or they may have given to me once. I drink the mockery into my mouth, I drink it up with the water of the rain. Do they know what this smile is?

It is not the rain. Not the cold nor the winter. No. Nor that they do not give. The women go on with their lipsticks, men seek smokes in breast pockets, lighters igniting warmly within.

It is exile.

The man called Will, whom I called for work on his backyard trees, stops.

"We'll do it when the rain stops," he says.

"Good. I'll be ready. I'll call you again."

A woman and her daughter reach out two plastic bags of food. Oh, Lord, I wish they gave me money. I peek inside. Bread I don't want, apples, oranges, apple juice, snack crackers, and a little can of Vienna sausage. Vienna sausage?

A man says, "Do you like souflaki?" He hands me a foil-wrapped package.

A black man in the middle lane beckons me over to hand me his lunch: "I haven't eaten it," he says, and there at four in the afternoon I eat his ham and American on white.

Someone tosses high in the air a package of English muffins.

Two ugly boys making troubled movements in their car, throw some Chiclets out of the window. I leave them in the dirt.

A man squeezes out the ball of a dollar bill, it falls to the wet asphalt.

A woman stops down the line and lets her daughter of ten hand me a quarter. "It's her lunch money," she boasts disgracefully.

I return to my place over the windshield wiper. I stand tall and with the rain water falling down my face, I weep. Who can see it except everyone? What my anguish may look like is a smile. Am I supposed to keep a face on to receive money? No. I will not do it.

A gold car three down the line. I bend down and look in and see a young East Asian man with a trim moustache. In his eyes a query gleams. When I say, "Thank you. God bless you," he says, "God bless you too," as to exceed the keenness of sweetness. I place my hand on my heart, bow, step back as from an emperor. A crystal cross glitters from his mirror.

I return to the sidewalk. When I get back there, I see him in his car. I see in his eyes what we know. We know the same thing and it is terrible and funny. I laugh, and he laughs, we laugh at this, this predicament, this exquisite exile, this exile which breaks and is broken. I cry as I laugh. He can't see me cry. But he can. I stand tall and I cry.

He drives away.

I see the hills in the distance all day. That one tree, my mascot friend, which I mark as the day goes by, how the fog almost covers it at times or the rain, how the sky above blows clouds behind it from the east to the sea. I watch the skies moving fast and the rain coming on. You hills, you tree, you are my companions, the ones who stay.

And the rain does not bother me. Let it fall on my face, I am accustomed to it. One middle-aged man beckons me to the middle lane to give and says, "Put up your hood," but I shake my head no. I will not. The rain doesn't bother King Lear. I let the rain pour from me. I rejoice in this sorrow.

I am separate. That is all.

Does each day produce growth? Or is agony but a sign of misapplication once again, my being out of place, my forcing myself into a world I don't belong?

The answer's in the swimming it.

And likewise now as I write, I am detached from the roadside and from the people going by with all their motives to choose not to have anything to do with me. I write inside in the dark of the studio. Outside, the rain, which has stopped, has polished the night. The night is out there. I am not a part of it. The moments of being and not being given to are over.

I feel less connected to God in all this. What is it, this pain, this conflict, and these tears but that I have come expecting the rain would make me rich?

I know I cannot manipulate myself to appeal to folks. But I thought that the weather would do it for me. My whole position was that the rain goad them into a charity that would reach out a hand to my hand, a coin whose abiding excuse is that our hands should almost touch while I take it.

I forgot. King Lear is not subject to the storm—instead he mounts it like a warhorse, allies himself with it, asks no pity for it and asks no pity from it.

He is exiled. In the very heart of things. King Lear is one thing, *King Lear* is another. King Lear is a man melting. *King Lear* is a stone.

I see the amount is $66.05. Odd that I treated this as virtually not happening. What was happening was the difficult formation of another rule.

COMPACT

- Leave the weather out of it.

18 February, Thursday

I have about $500. My rent is $450, and I have telephone and gas and electric bills, petrol and food. Acting school auditions in two weeks. Before getting on the roadside I procrastinate. Procrastination, a sleepwalker leading Inertia's Parade, blares its mute coronet to the right and to the left, but never straight ahead. The Parade is designed to frighten Fear away with Distraction, and it succeeds.

Once I get there the rain prunes the paper so I cannot take notes. But at least I am there. The roadside is sometimes the only fight I can make.

At rehearsal Saul Camber sits in the orchestra with his stage manager in front of him and this other man always on his left, Billie Pierceye, Saul's plump, peroxide, forty-five-year-old lover, a man trying to look young by trying to look blond. Saul's relations are not to his stage manager, though, but to Billie who takes notes like a spy in the open.

I do not have my lines down yet. I try to remember the blocking without writing it down. But I am undermined and thrown by a death ray coming from the two of them toward me. Perhaps Saul now realizes the play is lousy, and, since he cannot change it, needs a target to blame.

20 February, Saturday

I arrive roadside at 12:25; I'll take lunch at 2:25, be back here at 3:25, leave at 5:25.

My rule is to stay no longer than six hours, and to stand no longer than four hours running. That's the best setup for strength and morale. I also understand that I do need to arrive at ten sharp, leave at 5 sharp. I need, that is, to be orderly in my business; it's good for my character. But, don't be merciless, Bruce; if you get there at 10:05—traffic and delay do that—just lunch at 2:05, get back at 3:05, leave at 5:05.

COMPACT

- Stay no longer than six hours and stand no longer than four hours running.

I make my invocation and begin.

It has rained and promises rain. But these blowzy clouds are the clothing of my soul, and I do not ask the weather to be otherwise. I have promised to be here and weather-what-may, I am. I am friendly to it, this one with its inconstancy of rain, sun, hail, and fog. The hills to the east merge with the clouds in a play I can see but those in cars cannot. Not being out of doors like me, they do not concern themselves with Constable's weather, with Turner's weather. The Impressionists never painted weather, but we English landscapers see weather's action, weather's cooperation with the earth. Like the trees, like the hills, like fishermen, we live in it.

Once again today I feel a draw toward every black male driving by. As though they would carry me off and take care of me. Did I need to be taken care of at some time and wasn't?

What lies at the bottom of this?
What is the transaction?

Again, giving goes down during showers, and being bareheaded wields no influence—and so I still question that it is compassion that drives people to give. People give for fun, they give to be generous, they give so as not to feel guilt, they give out of religious persuasion, or out of emotional imagination, they may give because they see me as someone to whom they can give unreluctantly, for I stand here smiling, maybe daftly, my little smile God puts on my face. They give because a voice opens in them and says, "Give." Or they do give from compassion. Early on, a man, dark-haired, opens his truck window and offers his folded umbrella!

"Oh, thank you. I have one over there," I say.

Something lyrical comes into my voice when I speak to these people. Why is that?

One lady looks up out of her window and asks, "Have you a place to stay? Do you stay at the shelter?"

"No, actually I have a small apartment."

"I was out of work a good while a year ago." She had been teaching college, had managed companies, had advanced degrees. "It looked good on paper—but there are thousands of people out there. It was humbling. But beneficial."

"Yes, it is."

The plainspokenness of people, their accepting me and the situation as difficult, yes, but okay, is ease-making, heartening, surprising. People do not judge one as often as I think they might. To many I am one of them. In that I feel safe.

The rain stands in morsels on my parka and darkens its shoulders, but, again, the sweater inside, it does not penetrate. The rain and I are reliable with one another. When I look to the far hill to see what my mascot tree is doing, the fog there has changed it to a ghost. The hills know the deep changes of rain. But who else would see what the hills and rain are doing together but me? Before cars it was different. Emily Dickinson looked out and saw the operation of the weather on the field, the sky, the bird, and to her generation weather from the window was more than a practical issue—it was an entertainment. The window was her TV. I stand outdoors in a show of weather that, like vaudeville, no one is interested in anymore.

I haven't brought lunch from home because I rely on someone giving me some, and so it happens. A man from the middle lane says, "Will you take food? You need it more than I."

A family drives up behind on Appian and the mother gives me a package from Taco Bell, with a soda which I politely decline, saying, "I don't drink soda.

But thank you for your generosity and God bless you." It's fun. People are fun when they give—at least I have fun with them.

A girl gets out of her car and hands me a bag.

"Oh thank you so much. God bless you." Tastee Bread and a package of salami.

I go back to their car and hand the bread back, saying, "Thank you. I'm allergic to it. But thank you." I put my hand on my heart, I am grateful.

A man holds out a big supermarket bag filled up, a rocket of Italian bread sticking out of the top, which I hand back to him. "I don't eat bread, I'm sorry, I'm allergic, but how generous you are, thank you!" On the back seat he turns to hand me another bag. I am so surprised I don't even say "Bless you."

He says "Bless you" instead, as he drives away.

"Bless you," I call after him.

On my way to lunch I go back to the car to unload the huge take of groceries, the third in three days. (Else I'll have no room in the pack to put what I'll get after lunch!)

In the cafeteria I eat the man's lunch. I lose weight out here too; it takes calories to stand, it also seems to have taken the edge off of my eating after hours. I read of Wolsey and snore.

When I return, the rain keeps up.

The owner of a restaurant in Berkeley tells me to call him Monday at 10. I fantasize running his restaurant but—ha!—is it likely that he is going to take a strange gentleman off the side of the road and put him in charge of his business? Actually, I *could* run it but, after years in the restaurant business, I am not meant to go back to it. I would disintegrate in the business and I would disintegrate the business, and I shall not call him.

An East Asian woman pulls off. She writes on a piece of paper and she hands it me with a $5 bill. I open it and read instructions about a place to work in Hercules, which I shall investigate.

A woman beckons and holds up a bill.

"Thank you. God bless you. Thank you," I say.

As I back off I realize that as soon as I see someone move to me, God disappears from my mind.

I speak the word "God" when I say "God bless you," and I say it from my heart, but *remembering* God is not in it. "God" disappears, replaced by the ritual of approaching the car, which is: waiting until beckoned and, if not beckoned, waiting until the driver passes and reaches money to me on the fly—for some people do not wish to give until they are about to leave, perhaps because they fear hijacking or an involvement. I see their left hand with the bill, I see the car veer toward me so I can reach it, I step off the curb to meet it, keeping one eye on the giver's eye and one eye on taking the moving baton of the money without hurting either of us, at the same time giving thanks and blessing, and, if there's time, asking if they have any work they need doing. I feel sweet gratitude, I bow, put my hand over my heart, and back away—all of which comes spontaneous and proper. I resume the sidewalk, taking care to face the cars so's not to miss anyone else, but when I get back, I realize I have to remember the word "God" because in all of this I have forgotten the word "God." Happiness has supplanted God.

If I can only remember. To surrender to God at every moment.

Of course, surrender to God means death.

I mean, do I really want to live my life as though I already had died and gone to heaven? If I think of God all the time I may become a saint—and who wants that? If I'm a saint, I'll never have sex, git nikkid, find a mate. I don't want to be a spiritual big shot; I just want to live an ordinary life. Why is that so? It occurs to me that all we were put on Earth to do was to enjoy life, but since we lose the knack, God gives us bliss instead. Why does He give it? Because it's God's nature to, and to keep us reminded who owns the shop.

Losing the knack of enjoying life. . . .

It occurs to me there is a distinction between natural virtue and the virtue of God. Many humans, I imagine, and I am one of them, believe their innate and natural God-given virtue will carry them through life. Common courtesy, common decency, common sense—these and such endowments we think will serve us, and they do. We think we are born with enough of them so as not to have to worry overmuch about God. We don't need God's virtue, he gave us our own, and that should suffice. Atheists and agnostics are supported in their noblest deeds in this faith. And God did indeed give us a natural portion of virtue. People are naturally pure, naturally kind, naturally faithful. We have a desire as humans for affinity and we are born with the tools for it. We get them directly from the knee of God. But something happens.

To some of us.

Some of us can't exercise those virtues. We lose the knack.

I am one such person.

And so God does it for me, if I think of God. God enters into me and I am constant once again.

For, without God, I can't say I enjoy life on its own. Oh, I do things I enjoy. I listen to music, watch certain films. I read spiritual books, I know acting and literature. But music is a borrowed ecstasy and reading is a spectator sport, all of it to savor another's radiance—Rumi's, Richter's, Brando's. But Richter,

Brando, Rumi are a special occasion. What I mean by enjoying life is enjoying not only what is special but enjoying ordinary life itself.

And so I stand here in the ordinary weather. You would say rainfall is bad, but I would say it is rapturous. For here alone do I have the chance to enjoy life for here alone do I have the chance to think of God only. I am not constant, I think of other things. As the day wears on my feet hurt, my knees hurt, I lose patience, I am distracted, I can no longer rely on my natural virtue, perhaps I never had that much of it to start with. But here I can rely on God. And the feeling I get from thinking "God" is not one of virtue, but of delight. I feel God as simple inexplicable undeserved happiness.

Still it would be wonderful to have a calling that paid, to have work that I neither dreaded approaching nor looked forward to leaving. On the roadside, although I am in bliss a good deal of the time, I do look forward to its one day being over. It would be wonderful if I had a job which was a part of my life, inextricable with it. Like Eastwood's.

I see more of his films. I write, comparing myself to him, what I have, what I don't. What I don't. Something in him in my bones that I need. Something to live up to that I don't live up to. And I don't know what it is. So why do you come here, Eastwood? I don't hate you any more. But why are you here? For your presence is a wound on my life. Though I look at your pictures without pain, your presence is a wound on my life that I need. I can't say go away, any more. But I don't know what to do with your being here, or what it means.

I contemplate staying past 5:25—but it won't do. Part of me justifies being here only if it is a punishment. Besides, I have to keep my word to my body about the hours so it can orchestrate my being here day after day. I am just as tired after four hours today as I am after six another.

I take myself home, a little heavier for the damp, but my heart is not heavy. I cross the road and tramp up the wet hill with my umbrella under my arm and things in my backpack, and I feel satisfied and clement.

When I get home and count the money on the bed there is a twenty-dollar bill folded around another twenty and around a ten—someone has given me $50! I say "God" but nothing surprises me since from every dollar I know that people are amazing. Not including the food, $132.87. I stash it in the yellow envelopes for rent, food, fun, charity, school. I empty the backpack of its food: 2 quarts of lowfat milk, 1 9-pack of Hi-C orange drink, 3 cans of Campbell's Chunky soup, 1 can of Dubuque ham, 1 pound of Colby cheese, 2 cans of Lady Lee solid white tuna, 1 dozen oranges, 1 dozen Granny Smith apples, 1 can opener. What benefice!

21 February, Sunday

I wonder if I should tell my sister Kathy I am on the roadside. We talk a couple of times a year, send presents. I haven't seen her but twice in twenty years, but I am close to her, and if I did tell her she would offer me money. However, since there's a creep in me that wants to be paid for being a fuckup, it's not good to tell. It's not that I'm too proud—although I am proud—it's that angling for sustenance from her is draining. Actually, I have never asked my family for financial help. Why do I feel like a creep then in the temptation to ask? Because Kathy's A Helper, so I know it's not good for her, and because the help I need is not financial.

A black man stops his black woman from giving.

A jolly, plump, pretty lady in pink who has been reaching in a cookie bag says, "Don't have any food left, wish I did."

Lady slides a $5 bill through the vent window as though scared I will intrude.

"Here's a cookie!" calls a young woman as she whizzes by and I take a Pepperidge Farm Oatmeal. "Thanks. What fun! God bless you."

A woman in a shabby, untidy VW wagon with a pink body and who knows what color top, rummages in her purse and finally hands me out two cracker packages: Peanut butter and cheese. I snack on them. Ghastly. I spit it out. I laugh.

It's Sunday. I shouldn't even be here.

COMPACT

• Take a day off. Sunday.

Didn't I say this before?

Catherine rehearsal.

Why am I doing this? Why am I acting? Why am I subjecting myself to this misery? Getting a part is just an ego-draft, I'll never remember my lines, and never be good in them if I do, where has the inspiration I had at the tryout gone, I am not meant to be on the stage, and everyone will see that, and the actors know it already, and all of them hate me. The director especially. The director and his sidekick who keeps sitting there and sitting there whispering.

22 February, Monday

Ramakrishna himself says that everyone must come to God as he is: a thief must come to God as a thief. So must I today come to God as a beggar by the road, full of dishonesty, weak of character.

Ellen left a message about a job at a camping supply store. She wants me employed, but I am employed—on the roadside until *right* employment comes along. Or do I hear Macawber speaking?

Maybe in this record lies a story—but a story of what? By the time I get home—who was the black woman in the red car, the first man in the white? Evidently the story is not of *them*, or even of my adventures here. But what is the story? Is it to be the story of things I find in my nature, discoveries by the roadside like the windshield wiper? Or the story of my soul, which is not like any narrative at all?

Why, for instance, should I today still be drawn to the black males who drive by. The draw is that somehow they will carry me off and take care of me.

But they're not going to do either. Nor am I angling for them to, nor do I want them to.

Is it possible there is a part of my life I do not know? And that I *dread* to know? And that, somehow, black males in their vivacity own that life? Is it possible that my draw toward black men is a Duessa or impersonation of something real in me, a draw and a force so far at the ends of the earth as to be unknown to each other, poles only guessed at, two ices, but different, one north, one south, one a frozen continent, one a frozen sea? For this draw, absurd by the roadside, asserts, that another force is in play.

But what?

When I was little my family would go to a restaurant called Gordon's Cupboard owned by a middle-aged black couple who picked me up and hugged me with their plump bodies, a living alternative to my family's English reserve. They had the warmest hearts I have ever known. Gordon taught me to walk.

Once, in a past-life regression I was a fifteen-year-old black boy in Africa carried off by a spear. . . .

Ah, these speculations lead nowhere, Bruce. There is no way to ask a delusional urge to yield a real answer. You don't even know the question.

What's true is: I am at survival. Black males are at survival.

But they are safeguarded behind their blackness somehow.

I wish I were safeguarded.

But how—how are they safeguarded?

Because . . .

Because the blackness of black males gives them the shield of an inalienable excuse. Because they are black, they have a right to be poor, undereducated, rash. Because they are black they have a right to have no job, or not a good one, to be vagabonds, braggarts, thieves, and rogues. Opportunity deprivation scores their skin, but that same skin gives them an out. Being black becomes an I-Was-Elsewhere-On-The-Night-Of airtight alibi for not being able to prevail. And that alibi puts them higher on the pecking order than me. I have no such alibi.

I am the lowest of the low: I am a white anglo-saxon protestant male and— what is worse—I went to Yale.

So, you black males, your blackness lets you off the economic hook. Your blackness excuses you from trying to prosper. And the desire for an alibi is my draw to you. White, I have no excuse. And I desire one. It'd mean I could stay here forever. For a piece of me would rather be excused by an alibi, carried off by an alibi, taken care of by an alibi, than prevail in my life forever at all.

This is the foundation of prejudice.

Yes, even if I am prejudiced in favor of black folk, it is prejudice just the same. Prejudice is envy of the superior.

At night the world fills with garish rain. The waters of my life gather about my house. But outside the window the Sacramento River walks down to the sea and will not reach this eminence. It glisters in the night. That's not my danger. My danger is being too afraid to do what I must to enable my soul to give its gifts. But that's not my present danger, my danger today. What's my present danger? My danger is not knowing the gifts.

23 February, Tuesday

I awake in the dead of morning in the dark. Fear drives me from my bed. Acting school auditions. I don't want to know how little I've got to start with. The cat wants petting. I get up.

I light the sage, invoke the guardian animals, pray, play the drum, lie down in the dark living room, and cover myself with the afghan.

My intention is to find new spirit guides.

I enter the blasted tree and go to the upper realm. When Oscar Wilde arrives my body shakes in waves. What I need is old male mentor energy. I need male guidance and have always needed it, so I think. It is never to be found. So I think. There are no great men. So I think. The thing a male needs from another male he needs like a screaming baby needs it.

The spirit guides are here. But they do nothing. They display the gift. But they do not bestow it. "You can have it, if you can take it," is the message.

No sign of Keats.

The power animals say nothing.

I return to bed, where I worry that Wilde is roaming about like an unhappy ghost. I expect God could send Oscar Wilde down to thousands of people at a time—what fun for us all—except Oscar Wilde doesn't utter epigrams any more. He once was heaven on earth, but heaven would have changed even him.

It is pouring. I go to the roadside nonetheless. I said I would.

Walking up the hill from Poquito Court I pass a ten-year-old girl putting her foot in the gutter to part the rain water flowing downhill. Her mother and she wait for the bus, and she beguiles the time with the fascination of the excruciating routine of the water around her boot, a brook around a galosher, the curious personality of water, ordinary, mysterious, monotonous, and entrancing, entrancement taken as a vacation from the parental load, a disappearance into the infinite, right under her mother's nose.

When I have gone twenty-five feet past them I hear: "Sir?"

I turn.

"Would you like some money?"—it is the little girl walking up to me under her umbrella.

"Oh, no, that's all right." After all, she is a little girl. She hands me two coins, dimes maybe. I smile at her. Her mother backs her up.

I refuse Tastee Bread but take this little girl's coins?

Once on the roadside, I stand forth in the shifting weather. By now I am accustomed to the rain on my bare head, by now I am content in the rain, it will not hurt, I won't catch cold. Basically it rains every day, but today it does not rain continually. Rather the clouds above bundle along, shifting their various burdens of light and water.

Behind me way across Appian I hear a horn, someone shouting my name, I can't see who.

I pack up my things and cross over.

It's a friend from my meditation group—in fact I'm his mentor. He looks as though maybe he ought to be embarrassed to see me here. "Hi, man, what's up? I seen you there and I wondered whatcha doin'."

It must be funny for him to find me, as someone in some authority, having to stand here. But as I tell him the story his embarrassment passes, and by the time he drives away neither of us are any the worse for it. The more people know, the easier it is, it seems.

Later, a bearded man addresses me, "Bruce."

Who would know my name?

"Hi, I'm Raymond from meditation group."

"Oh . . . hi! I didn't recognize you out here."

He is concerned to find me employment and he gives me his card. I do not want a nine-to-five job right now. What I want is money for school and for fixing the car. I take it and thank him. I'll call him tonight.

A lady gives me her money. "I'm out of a job myself."

"Oh no, here, that's all right," I offer her the money back, "You need it," I say.

"We're sharing," she says with a smile, and it's true.

A teenage boy wants to give, but his mother shakes her head. He feels impotent.

A certain Harry Newman gives me his card to do house painting. He says to call him after Monday.

When I get home I reach all the people who've offered me jobs, but they're all gestures of goodwill they can't follow through on. $25 an hour today. Three hours: $75.81. The important thing is not to expect this every day.

But I do expect it.

Rehearsal:

"More authority!" Camber yells at me. Doesn't he know that if a figure of authority yells at one, one loses authority. It's too early in rehearsal to ask for finished work. I don't say anything.

24 February, Wednesday

Scared of the rehearsal atmosphere, I take the lines with me on the roadside today and peek at them behind the cardboard, but I can't learn them there. In fact, I am met by a sequence of thrown food. A bag of potato chips that could have been handed to me. A man reaches out an orange but tosses it instead, and it falls. It feels odd—disrespectful.

"How are you today?" a big voice booms right behind me. I jump out of my skin and out into the road.

"Wow, you scared me!"

"How are your feet?" He comes and stands right close, a well-set, good-looking, dark-haired man of thirty-four with a big voice.

"My feet?"

"Can you walk?" he booms.

"Yes I can walk."

"Do you want to distribute some posters?"

He hasn't apologized for scaring me. "How much does it pay?" I ask because I am angry at him for scaring me.

"$5 an hour."

"I can't live on that."

"It's just temporary."

I turn back to the road. Wait, I have done wrong; I should not have turned him down. Where is he? He's nowhere to be seen. Posters would have been interesting. What am I thinking of?! I am supposed to accept every job.

Well, he scared me silly, so I was miffed. Why the heck did he not apologize? Jesus Christ, didn't you see me jump into the traffic, you nearly killed me with that voice of yours—you've lived your whole life with that voice, moderate your tone, man. He wasn't discourteous though. He was succinct and masterful. I ought to have negotiated with him. My whole position was immediately No. I have a No foundation. I'd like to replace that with a Yes as the starting place. Or a Maybe. Or something. This No hampers my wits. Please let it be dissolved. Please God. Or something.

I feel disturbed by the wrong I have done by turning down the loud-voiced man's work. I am so upset that I am frantic, I can barely stay put, I can't concentrate on the cars or—I've got to get out of here! But I've promised never to leave this place early. I'll stay. I'll stick it out. But I can't stand it! I can't breathe. My whole body hurts. I want to do the right thing in the work, everything depends on that. I've got to leave! I'll seek out Brendan Moon. The only excuse to leave is to see Brendan Moon.

Brendan listens with a still, assessive gravity. He's younger, but I accept his seniority. Since the poster man drama is over and the job's no longer there, once I tell him the story and my frenzy subsides, I turn to questions that have been bothering me about the roadside in general.

What to do with extra food?

He says I might overeat on this job, but don't feel guilty about throwing it away.

About refusing bread and soda? Because of my courtesy, he says that, for me, declining food is all right.

My sign? "Will Work For Food Or $" troubled me. Since "Need Work For $ For Shelter & Food" was truer—that's what I wrote on the back of the other sign—but I was just being a stickler so I turned it over again. Brendan says any sign is all right if I feel right about it.

Brendan's answers are just. And now, done with my worries, we sit on the curb and talk about him.

Brendan looks overpacked, he's gained weight. I wonder about it but don't ask.

He's been on the roadside a long time, and I wonder if he's due for a promotion. I ask how the toy plane business is going. He hasn't called the kiddy furniture woman.

He changes the toy subject to his being a roadside healer, "These people need me," he says.

I wonder. Yet as we sit there, a man of sixty waiting for the light in a silver Mercedes tells him all about his marriage. "My wife won't have me back," he calls out to Brendan as he drives on. "She doesn't have another man. She doesn't give a reason."

I laugh. There is Brendan smoking a cigarette with his buccaneer's beard and bandanna giving therapy to passersby in cars.

"I know these people. I care about them," he says.

Yes, you do, Brendan, I say to myself, but is that your calling? I look at him narrowly.

"I want to show you something," he says.

We get up and walk to his camp in the nearby woods where he has never taken anyone. It is a Swiss Family Robinson compound—tent, tarps, a closet of orange crates, a shaving station. He shows me these for the approval that, though on the roadside, his shanty is shipshape. I stand back within myself and view him; I withhold approval. We sit on a fallen tree and talk.

"Looks like you've gained weight, Brendan. You've been drinking?"

"No, I don't drink. A couple of six-packs a day."

He goes to a bar at night where he has a platonic romance with an alcoholic beauty whose boyfriend beats her.

"I'm saving her."

"Saving her from him or saving her from the alcohol?"

"She doesn't drink that much."

"Yes she does, Brendan. They all do."

The violent boyfriend strong-arms his way into her place and Brendan stares him down: "You touch this woman again and you'll be hanging up your ass on a coat-hanger in the cemetery," all the more dangerous as the opera enters sequels. I listen to him under the arching trees of the forest where we sit like pioneers of yore, the grizzly of the traffic behind, the condor of the plane above. Brendan the star of drunk dramas, Brendan the therapist by the roadside, the man who passed on the tools of the trade, the maker of wonder-toys for children, the savior of damsels in distress—something's off. He's sawing the wrong board with his goodhearted and virile life. The bottom line is he's fought with his wife about not being with her, she's got his child and she wants him by. They're on the outs, so now she's got a feller. He loves his son and he loves her but he has less drive to restore himself to them anymore. Besides, the money he gets these days is less: people are used to him, they've used him up as a charity, they think he should have a job by now. And I imagine he's now standing there just for the easy money. I call him on this, but I don't want to shoot him with it hard, so I don't take it all the way.

I call myself on it too. What, like him, am I avoiding by standing here?

You have to want right work more than you don't want wrong work to survive being on the roadside. Otherwise all you'll do is turn down work for the easy money no matter how little it is. Wanting right work is the only strength you've got apart from God. Like Brendan I too want easy money.

After I leave Brendan, I go back to the roadside, and as soon as I get there someone throws a package of Oreo Cookies out of their window. All I hear is the splat on the pavement as it breaks and scatters in the gutter like contempt.

When I get home, I find I have earned $4.50 an hour—less than the poster man promised.

Rehearsal:
Bad blood. There's snacks and I eat too many—my version of a six-pack.

25 February, Thursday

It pours. I stay indoors, watching this Eastwood and that. I pick over the buttonbox of his pictures.

26 February, Friday

I forget my mascot tree, where are you, there you are, my baby. Are you happy in your work?

I look at these people passing by. Are they also happy in their work? It would be presumptuous to suppose that simply because they live in the suburbs that they hate their jobs. That woman is a housewife. It would be presumptuous for me to suppose, just because she is not a concert pianist, that driving the kids around is hateful to her, that buying the groceries is a degrading calling. Every job in the world has its tedious passages, its dullness, its concrete repetition. It doesn't matter what people do, what matters is that it is right that they do it. So, Bruce, don't wish for their work to be different. Wish for them what I wish for myself: "May everyone who passes by find the work that suits them and do it well. Me too."

A black woman says, "God bless you. You take care of yourself." Such care. Such kindness.

A loopy man saunters across the freeway, right through the traffic. It's hot and sunny but he's in a black snow hood, black glasses. White long johns peep out from under his pants: overdressing is the agoraphobia of the homeless.

"Boy, no one picks you up here," he says.

"Take off the dark glasses," I say. "People have gotta see your face."

"The sun blinds me. I wanna go north."

"North is the other way." I think, just for fun, I'll give him the money in my pocket. "Hey, can I offer you a bit of money?"

"The worst thing is horse vans."

Well, he didn't say no, so I delve into my parka, pull out what's there without looking at it. He hasn't paid any attention till now, and he doesn't pay attention to the money either, which I am relieved to see is only $1.30. "Here ya go," I say and lift up his hand to put it in.

He looks at it. "Oh yeah," he says as though at a fond memory. He doesn't acknowledge that it came from me, doesn't say thank you. It's as though the money just popped up there.

He then lets me set him on his path north. And off he bops.

Today I get lots of job offers.

Wally Goode, a big-spoken man, gives me a piece of paper with his number on it and tells me to call him.

Kate Piersanti pulls off the road in her van. She wants me to clean her roof gutters. I'll call her.

A man in a black car wants me to haul concrete. "You look like a strong man." His wife in the passenger seat has an Oh-Harry-not-this-again look on her face. He does not give his number, because the traffic moves, so all three of us are spared.

F. E. Briganti says he'll hire me to build a wall.

I break my code and ask beforehand what he pays.

"Seven or eight dollars an hour, depending what you're worth." Not exactly a green field with cows in it, but I must accept all work.

A gray man in his seventies looking up from his black car says he wants me to prune his trees. Says he'll come back. Says he has an appointment at 1. I'm not quick-witted enough to ask when he's returning from it. When I come back from lunch the man does not come.

During the afternoon my pen runs out and I can't take notes. I have $40 at the end of day. I like making less, but doing the job well. Lots of food.

No rehearsal tonight, thank God!

I call all the numbers. Kate Piersanti and Wally Goode both have jobs for me. I feel I'm in business.

I resume rehearsing the acting school auditions. They go well.

27 February, Saturday

Wally Goode lives in the bobcat town of El Sobrante—horse barns and lower-class homes save it. His house lies under tall cool eucalyptus trees whose bark descends in stripes. Wally lives in a redwood shingled '50s ranch house in the broad sun, with a wife and her two teenage daughters by a different husband. They, separate solar systems from Wally by their own election, are in charge. Wally has a truck and does hauling off the books.

He has a deal of dead lumber in a lean-to in the backyard. The job is to organize the lean-to and take the lumber up front to the truck. "I'll let you do this work so I can see if you work well. Then I'll decide what to pay you," he says.

The suspense of that is interesting. Like it says, I have not asked his wage beforehand.

The sun is hot, but Virgo-ing that shed I know exactly how to do. I'm a good worker; in an hour I am done.

Wally's a big, handsome, masculine, middle-aged male with a bad back and a former drinking problem, his voice still in combat boots. A male but no longer a man, he has all the appurtenances, but he uses them to bully, and he's too old to. His wife finds him ridiculous, she keeps a wise distance from him—a divorce on the burners. I can tell this as he brings out two big bags of groceries she has packed for me. "Do you like fish?" He hands out from his freezer three frozen trout he's caught.

"Oh that's plenty," I say as he thrusts two more upon me like a drunkard pushing drinks.

He asks how much gas is in the car. He pulls out $4.

"No, that's all right. You've given me enough already." I am moved: all this for one hour's work. He tries to ham-hand me into being his truck driver to Canada. To get out of it I tell him I go to school. He wants me to come back the following Saturday, to weed raised beds. That much I will do.

28 February, Sunday

Catherine rehearsal.

One of the cast has left, and I've given Saul Camber Maddy's head shot, and when I get to the theater tonight, there she is.

Let's hope bringing him Maddy will put me in his good graces.

Afterwards I drive to San Francisco to the coach I've hired for the audition at the acting school.

For one moment, I come alive. But the rest of it is dead. The coach doesn't do me any good. I have spent $100 on a cold plate of spaghetti.

As I walk down Geary, with its gum-smeared souls, I am not thinking of art, I'm thinking of money. All my life I've thought of the art of acting—"the most beautiful, the most difficult, and the most rare of all the arts," as Voltaire said of it—all my life I've thought of the art of acting, but now? Now all I think of is the money it will earn me. And in all this, in fact, I fear art, its great transformative power. I just want to make sure I can pay my bills. I am paralyzed by fear of future poverty.

Once home, I watch another Eastwood picture.

1 March, Monday

Kate Piersanti is in her late thirties. She has the controlling jollity of the stout woman. She has been a singer in nightclubs and now sings for the Mormon church. Two teenage sons. A husband who works at home, his office in a back bedroom of their home on a hill near Appian Way. I tread gingerly around Mormon, which I sense to be a kind of cult. Briefly I tell her my history.

Kate does not question this history. She does not judge it. She does not counsel me about it. She keeps a respectful distance, and I suspect that it is her theatre background, rather than her religious background, which makes her nonjudgmental.

She wants me to clean the rain gutters on her roof and wash the flashing beneath them where the over-drip has stained. She gives me rubber gloves and all the equipment, and says she is going to leave on an errand and will be back at four.

"I'll pay you between twelve and fifteen an hour. Is that all right?"

I am surprised: the money is out front, it is also high as a wage. She is noble-spirited and she has recognized that I am too. She leaves me to it. She can tell I will do it right. She says if she's not back in time her husband will pay me.

I've never cleaned roof gutters before, so it's interesting to set up a ladder, haul up a moustache broom and hose, walk around on the roof, and figure out how. Here I am, high up in the sunshine of a balmy spring day. A pleasant situation, really, doing something new for good money and earning my way. I'm happy, I'm out-of-doors, the world is green. I wonder if I could place an ad and start a roof-cleaning business. A high-minded thought, but saddening. I want to earn my living at my calling. Still, it feels good to earn my living at all.

I work without a break, as is my custom. But as the morning wears on I figure if I get only twelve an hour I would be cheated.

Why do I think this? She said anywhere between $12 and $15. Also I do not think of God much here, but only $15. I have a good job in a pleasant neighborhood. My employer is friendly and liberal and trusting. The wild plum tree in the yard is blooming. I am even up in the air. When I think of God I can hear the birds sing. And yet: all I hear is $15. Mercenary! And crazy. I would be happy if I didn't think. Thought is a form of insanity for me. Is there sane thought? When my mind is thinking is it always mean?

I figure the gutters need mesh to keep the needles out, and when Kate stops back during her errands, she authorizes me to drive to the hardware store to get it, and I do. But when I try mesh, it doesn't work. I don't charge for the mesh and I deduct the time it took to get it, for it was my inexperience that caused the mistake. Besides I want to make a good impression: she has said she might have me clean the grouting on her hall tiles. She goes out again.

When I am done I ring the front door. Kate's not back, so it's her husband who comes to the door when it's time to tell him I'm leaving. He pays me at the rate of $10 an hour. I know I have to leave without a word and I cross the street to my car.

But I just can't, I go back.

"Your wife said she would pay me at the rate of between twelve and fifteen dollars an hour, and I was wondering at which rate you paid me?"

"How long did you work?"

I feel cheesy. "Four hours."

He goes back into the house and gets $10 more.

That's still not fifteen, but I have to swallow it.

Driving away, tired, I feel good at having earned my own living though.

Acting school audition 5 days away. I am nervous, nervous, I don't want to face it.

Catherine opens in 3 weeks.

At rehearsal a death ray coming at me from Pierceye, the more it comes the worse I get.

2 March, Tuesday

Wake at three A.M. Don't know why.

Kate calls me to tell me she's found my red checkbook; I didn't know I'd left it. She asks if the money I got was all right, and I tell her about my exchange with her husband. She said she was very happy with the work I did.

When I go to get the checkbook, she hands me a big bag of groceries. She wants me to clean the hall grouting. I tell her I have never done it, but that does not bother her. The one quality I never expected to feel from people on the roadside, but the single greatest quality I have felt from people: respect.

My gas tank leaks, so I can only put 10 gallons in at a time. To get enough money to buy a tire, I drive over to work at Wally Goode's as I have arranged.

Four raised beds full of weeds must be cleared carefully because of herbs. The day is low and sweltering, hard dirty work this time—four hours without a break. At 1 P.M. I'm done with three of four beds and I want to have lunch, so I go around front where he's been working.

"I have to leave in an hour," he says; this means I must go too. He reaches in his pocket for his wallet and fishes out $10. "I'm short today."

I say nothing—that's the rule. How can he look me in the eye? He can't.

He says I should call him to finish the job, which of course I won't.

I clam up and go to my car.

I drive away angry. I feel ugly and cheated. $2.50 an hour for all that hard work—it isn't even minimum wage. Tires. Gas tank. I'm surprised at him because he had given the fish and groceries the day before. Or his wife did. Right. She knew he would shortchange me, so she made up those groceries for me. It shamed him into giving the fish. His wife, yeah. Besides that was that pay for that day's work.

When I drive to buy the tires I can't make up the sum. Vince the tire man says he'll reserve good ones from a load of used coming in.

At night, I go to rehearsal. I am not getting any better. I dare not ask for help from Camber.

When I get home and look in my checkbook, I find a ten-dollar bill tucked away. Kate.

3 March, Wednesday

Rent is late again, and I've got to scrape the money together for the tank and tires.

Rehearse for acting school audition. Takes hours.

"Bless all the cars that pass by here. May none of you or those in you suffer a harmful accident as long as you live. May everyone who goes by here or down on the freeway do the work you desire in this world, and as you want to do it."

The day is fair. My mascot tree—after so much rain, I forgot to say hello to you. You've been lost in the mist for days. As though you went away, as though, had I walked to the top of that high hill you stand on, I wouldn't have found you.

The money is slow on a cloudy day.

Superstition 4c.

Superstition 4a is: The money is slow on a rainy day.

I say "God, God, God."

Saying "God" makes me smile, and smiles may invite the giver.

I have no proof of that.

And I never will have proof of it.

Others may bless and not smile. I bless and smile—I cannot help it.

None of this is calculable. I am so happy I do not care to calculate a thing.

My mind does go on—figuring God as a business enterprise, though. The lesson, as I have said more than once before, is not to figure it out. Figuring-It-Out rises like a mist befuddling me. *Cogito ergo non sum.* I think therefore I am not.

God, God, God.

I'm tired. Heavy as a fruit tree that does not bear, I stand here passed by.

When I leave, it comes to $8.98.

4 March, Thursday

An East Asian woman, who has white hair but is not old, hands me an envelope. "How long have you been out of work?"

"Almost a year."

"What sort of work do you do?"

"I can garden. Or edit a book," I jest.

When she drives on, I wonder what the discretion of the envelope must contain. I open it. $10 of absolute consideration.

I feel pain today though.

The cars peel off the freeway below like birds, drive up, peel off again into the lanes they need.

I have to remind myself that all I have to do here is stand, wait, and think of God.

I do this and things are good.

This work is about being heartened, when, through long experience of it, I have dread and expectation of failure. The way I am doing the parts for the audition on Saturday has no touch of genius.

To stand here is a relief from that.

I take off my green jacket and stand tall in the cool March sun. I think of God, and I feel that shine in me.

Rich or poor, successful or failure, all a human has is a thought of God. I am no worse than anyone, and no better. I move toward the auditions as a failure, but here on the roadside failure does not count, here everyone is as beyond failure as I am. We—I who stand, those who pass in cars—we are in another realm than success or failure. Our hands held out are a respite from all that.

He dresses down. He never sits behind a desk. Or if he does, he doesn't have a desk job. He'd jibe under it. He's on the move, on the horse, on the road. If he weren't an actor he'd be a trucker.

Only as an actor does he smoke. He doesn't smoke. He hates it. He never did smoke. There he sits affable as a forest. Waiting. Waiting for you to make the move so he can do his part to fulfill the expectations of the form. One leg crossed over the other. What does that tell you? And sitting. For once. Sitting is a civilizing position. Don't trust it for a moment.

I hated him for having turned into something so far distant from what I am. In what garden would we meet? But even now that I don't hate him, I envy him—not his accomplishment, but something in him that got him there. What? A fortitude? . . . a simplicity? . . . a luck? . . . I seek to connect my self with his self. But at a certain point one cannot learn from anyone. One can only learn. And six degrees of separation are still separation.

I remember to look at that mascot tree again, sweet tree on the top of the hill, sky behind it, not symmetrical. I too am not symmetrical. Am I a fringe person then? No. I'm not peripheral to anything. I no longer stand outside look-ing in. I am not in relation to the inside or the outside.

I envied the popular when I was a boy, but popularity is created by its satel-lites and I never would be one, I snubbed that, I would rather be alone. I wasn't just popular, worse: I was unpopular, which means the other kids minded that I wasn't popular. Now no one passing minds that I am not popular. People see me as I am. People give—never for the matter of popularity.

But even Quentin Crisp is popular now. He deserved to be, God love him, he deserved some hearts ease. I once took him to the Pacific Ocean. I thought it would heal him to touch it. We walked quietly on the sand of Muir Beach, then stopped. From the sea he turned back, refused to actually touch the water. "The Ocean is my enemy," he said. There was nothing I could say to that. He'd crossed one once and that was enough. (Once when I took him to dinner and suggested salad, he said, "No thank you, it might do me some good.") On the standing sand I said to him, "You have achieved the ultimate masculine virtue, tenderness." I don't think he understood it, although my sense was that he took it away with him to consider. He used to be unpopular for his effeminacy; now he is popu-lar because of his bravery about his effeminacy. I called him San Quentin after a prison and a saint, both of which he was. But I? If people came up to me as though I were popular, I would wonder, "What are you doing here?" Popularity is not an ocean I need to cross any more. I no longer exist in relation to it as a force. I define it and depart. To have related to it as a child was a miscalcula-tion not of absolute value—because for some, popularity is a transformational arena—but of personal value. Because popularity was the first and most bla-tant of social survival forms, I thought it was the only form survival took. But my true arena was neither in popularity nor out of it, but completely other. And standing here now I know this.

Great events cross the skies. Vessels of state go down with millions aboard. Plagues raid the globe. Moloch avarice becomes a moral style. Deep, oh yes, concerns in the political arena. Sport becomes entertainment, entertainment religion. And news, news, news. And all that concerns me is none of that. Terrible bigotry, terrible injustice. I don't think of that. I never did. I am not part of that either. I am not part of the theatre, nor any profession. I have no family. I am daughterless as a straw.

Out here on this island that says *Do Not Enter* I reside. This is where I belong, wishing bottles into being with messages in them. And I find them too. This is where my history is rewritten. It bobs by. But rescue from this by the passing liner? I do not pray for it. I don't need rescue. This is not a desert island. I pray, but I pray for nothing.

In the second lane a burly man in a bandbox blue semi leans down and gives me a tightly folded bill. It's unusual for truckers to give, and I don't catch his whistle until just before the traffic starts. What is his life? Inwardly. That he would think to have anything in common with me. But he does so think. I can see it in him as he turns the corner, making a connection to me even though he drives a semi.

"Why don't you get a real job?" a young thug hollers out of a truck stopped far down. There are other catcalls during the day. One East Asian man says, "Haven't you got a job yet?" He gave me money once.

A good-looking young man hands out a beautiful green apple as he drives by in his truck.

"Thank you. God bless you. Thank you. Do you have any work I can do?" But he's gone.

I see a big carton held out of a passing car and have to take a carton of 17 Corn Nuts boxes. I don't want to eat them. What'll I do with them?

Give them away to drivers with open windows. What fun. Male drivers so's not to alarm the ladies. I get rid of five before it occurs to me I can bring them to rehearsal tonight—maybe it'll buy me some brownie points, God knows I need 'em.

No sooner do I start giving Corn Nuts away than money starts coming in. People beckon me from all the way down the line. Two cars in a row—women—give me money. What a merry dance.

I just stand here with my heart full and wait.

I realize what is happening at rehearsal. I have known it often before. I didn't want to face it: I am being scapegoated.

The principal players are fighting with one another, the actress playing Catherine is an alcoholic, the play stinks, and these problems cannot be addressed because it's too late, even if Saul had the talent to—which he does not—so he and Billy Pierceye turn their cannon on me. As does the actor playing Wolsey's secretary: he wants me to relate to him when I enter with him, but Wolsey relates to no one but monarchs and popes and because he doesn't, just as this actor sabotages me, Wolsey overlooks the man who will sabotage him, the very character this actor plays.

Something in me that makes me a sitting duck. The death ray of blame seeks the victim waiting for it to happen to. I am once again that duck.

Well, I won't speak up; it's beneath my dignity. Besides these people must stop when they realize how badly they are behaving, and that black cape of chaos and old night—death to the scapegoat—will disappear.

"I know what it's like," a man says as he gives me money. "I hope I don't get there." He doesn't mean it meanly.

An overweight young man with a spotted complexion in a beat-up old car reaches to his passenger seat and hands me a paper bag out the window. It contains rolled up coins. "I was on my way to the bank with them, but what the hell." His energy is mighty sweet. May he meet the lady to love him forever.

For here I stand with the sun. The smile God sets upon my brow is one of a pain made happy. If I would say, "I am happy," I would lie, for this pain's indistinguishable from delight. My smile's the cry of a bird whose note is mixed. But there is more joy in my breast than the pain it does redeem.

A middle-aged man in a dark van comes to a halt. I wonder at his face, which I can see less well than the face of his old father in the seat next to him, which is set, closed off, and dour. Old men come to conclusions about life which figure in their faces. Such grimness is never hard-won. They drive on.

An old couple stop. Her husband explains why I am not to be given money. While he talks, the woman regards me over his shoulder with studied suspicion, a suspicion which she is unashamed of. But I look her right in the eye. I stare into her wariness which is as tough as it is old, and what I am arrives into her directly, behind his back. Her expression does not change, but she learns that leathery suspicion is not the proper response to me.

A good-looking young man on a motorcycle turns his wheel to the side, slides into his left front pocket, and hands me $2.

The black man with the gray moustache who drives by every day in the silver Jaguar and gives me dollars, does so today.

A van pulls off way down so I don't know whether it is for me. The driver gets out with a bag and beckons, so I walk toward him as he walks toward me. When we meet, he stands directly before me and reaches out for my hand to shake. He gives me the bag saying, "I don't have any work, but this'll be good for tomorrow anyhow."

I thank him and bless him sure enough. It doesn't feel like a loaf of bread at least.

He says, "Lord bless you."

Then I realize. It is the middle-aged man with the dour father. Up close his face does not resemble his father's. His face is broad, good-looking, spectacled. What is that dour father doing there, how can the son tolerate such a mean-faced papa? Well, the answer to that is that that same tolerance brought me these groceries today.

A car of people give me a five dollar bill, and everyone is kind, wishes me well, as I do them.

A young man stops and asks how's business.

"How's yours?"

He tells me he's also looking for work. "International Relations—you have to have a Ph.D. to get a job in the State Department nowadays." Says he'll be going back to school.

For people stop right beside me, and I am as close to them as a reader to a book, their windows open below me, which helplessness sets them at a disadvantage of which every one of them is aware. I greet them to defuse that. "How are you?" I say to a stout black man.

"Fine. Yourself?"

"Very good, thank you," and I look away so's not to milk it for $. He waits a moment and asks me if I want some change.

"Oh, yes, that would be fine."

He gives me all that he has about him—$2.25 as it turns out. I think I hear a dime drop under the car and I look for it as I thank him. Greed for a dime.

Oh, here's Alvin Blum, the guy who was so scared to give, but gave. Oh, look, he's doing the same thing: going through his contortion. He's my pet. He's here too just like me. I nod; if I spoke to him, he'd not know what it meant.

When I get home I sit on the bed and count. There are two tens, six fives, and twenty ones, plus the rolls of pennies. I find when I unfold it that the man in the bandbox blue semi gave me a five-dollar bill. The man with the spotted complexion gave sixteen rolls of pennies of 50 cents each—$8 worth. $81.03. $27 an hour. I thank God and them. I divvy it up into the yellow envelopes. Most of it goes into "Rent"; most of what doesn't goes into "Schooling."

I go to the computer so as to record the package the man with the grim father gave me. It contains a really good ham sandwich, which I eat while I type, plus a whole lot of other things, along with a napkin and an invitation to The First Baptist Church in Pinole. They thought of everything; well done! Maybe I'll save all these invitations to church and go to them one by one.

A day of unusual delights.

Off to rehearsal
Not delights.

5 March, Friday

His card reads Francisco Effendo Briganti, Landscaping. I call him, and yes, he does have work, although toward him I feel the reluctance of a fish at a worm-less hook. He's unscrupulously monosyllabic.

His directions also mean a long drive—$5 worth of gas—and I am to meet him not at his business but at an 8 A.M. rendezvous, which proves to be a dirt lot in the foothills, serving five shops stampeding with lack of business and a Reno-huge defunct neon sign. He's not there.

I hang out for fifteen minutes. I call his number from the general store, no answer. Good, I don't have to work.

When I go out, his pickup is in the parking lot, him in it.

"Hello."

He doesn't greet me.

"Shall I get in?"

He doesn't shake my hand. He sits inside drinking soup out of a thermos, saying nothing: Threat By Taciturnity: a gun with a silencer. His is the boss energy of a good-looking, five foot six, dark-haired Italian about to go to fat. If I hit him over the head with a mallet and drove him into the ground I'd say he was forty-three. But I have no experience landscaping, none for dealing with domineering Italians who are late, don't cop to it, don't say good morning.

But he gives the impression of a certain mastery. He's dressed in a smart rugby shirt and pressed jeans. I've seen these spiffy construction company owners before: fashion-plate casuals grant them an elevation: if you can run a construction company and still have clothes catalogue-clean you must be an expert.

But we don't drive off. And he doesn't say anything. Instead he drinks his soup from a cup, its wide-mouthed thermos open on the seat between us. I put the sleeve of my coat in it immediately. Like a mouse in an owl beak I am brain-numbed—but I have to fight for my life, or at least for my manhood, or at least for some handhold. To do which I now make myself careful of the soup, in aid of which I immediately bump it over on the seat.

He doesn't say anything.

He starts the truck with one hand and drives away.

He doesn't say where we are going, what we are to do, and for how long. I'm not to know a thing until my fate is before me. I feel kidnapped, maybe he will leave me stranded, or murdered. It's not my place to inquire though, if I inquire I might be fired. His strategy is to make me feel impotent, which may be at one with something else: his pay practices. I better ask. But I daren't—yet. I'd better ask soon, though, else I'll swell up like an adder. We drive up into the forested hills. I stare at the road, afraid of the person next to me.

Briganti has dark brown hair expensively cut and a dashing moustache, but around him is an aura of disorder, breakdown, and belligerence. Pride in his person does not shroud a man in disarray. His silence is not ignorant: he is deliberately inconsiderate as a subordinating tactic, the only strategy he has to organize the territory as his.

One of my failings is to be grandly familiar on first meeting so as to claim territory too. Therefore, I ask, "Soup for breakfast?"

"Every day."

And I find I was wrong: he has not one but two strategies: the first taciturnity, the other logorrheic confidentiality. He now does not stop talking. I hear the whole story. He's a former alcoholic.

"Before that I was miserable. Now I wake up in the morning and I can hear the birds sing." In his long story, it's the first thing he has said that is not a tragic boast.

Interesting: his recovery is solid and valuable. His addiction to liquor—a substance which gives men the illusion of being fluid and therefore of being cunningly adaptable, divinely flowing, sparkling, deep, of another element than flesh—has been relinquished, and the strength of abstinence for him is that dry is not barren but a separate improvisation entirely. He is crude and dangerous but he is not nothing. As we drive through the woods, his eyes exude naughtiness and fun. He looks to see how great I think he is.

I cannot bear to look at him. But I look at him.

Crude Italians have a lure for me. Their crudeness scares me, but that is the lure. I was scared when I was a kid of crude Italians. I still am. I sink into stagnant mute servility before them. As a form of protection. A finicky center in me turtles in and makes me more finicky and less potent still to clear the fuckers out with a pitchfork. When small, instead of contending with them, I cast myself as the hero-victim in an opera of self-pity and vindication, a strategy that came so quickly I thought it was natural and to which I thought I had no alternative. A determining strategy formulated like a curse at twelve at summer camp where those Canarsie Guineas got me.

What's a determining strategy? A determining strategy is one that says, "This is how you will handle your life in this vital matter from now on," but you don't say it consciously. Trauma says it. Trauma offers self-pity the salve of a sure thing forever. "From now on" are the key words. You fix on the strategy because you're in a situation calling itself hopeless and because you decide the hopelessness will always obtain, so it's safer to say "always" or "from now on." That's how you get back at life for the hand it dealt you. You pay future protection the coin of immortality. You call "always" a salve, but actually it's a Scar. A Scar never forgives and never changes. You can always show your Scar—"See what they did"—and thus punish them forever. You also give the Scar plenipotentiary powers: a determining strategy is a flower suitable for any occasion. You start to practice it at twelve at summer camp—and it takes practice because that's how you contend with a situation you think you can't get out of—and eventually your strategy becomes habit. You cower and sing romantic self-pitying songs. You run away. You know what? At twelve I shoulda taken a canoe paddle and brained the sons of bitches. Then they would have gotten it. Because bullies are not going to get it any other way. I know, I've been a bully in my time, and eating crow's how I learned not to do it. Bullies are on this earth to learn their lessons by being brained with canoe paddles. Perhaps. I mean, perhaps they learn it. I too have had to learn a lesson and I have to keep learning it—that belligerence against bullies preserves the soul.

After fifty years this strategy of collapse is still in me as I ride next to one more crude Italian. And this one has the edge: he's both in the driver's seat and the boss.

So, that he may erect his answer as a shield between us, I ask him a question. "How do you like the landscape business?" I don't give a fiddler's fuck what he likes.

As he whines on, I maintain the hireling's compliance and say nothing. I long for dead silence. I fear him and I hate him. But we have to work together. Can I give him the benefit of the doubt—is it possible to actually have a friendship with him? No. How to keep him at arms length then? How to achieve a balance—like the pole of a tightrope walker, its ends far separate from one another? Maybe if I talk, talk will hold him at bay.

So, as the front seat of his pickup now holds a third entity—a silence filled with crummy fear—to cover it, and that he not think I'm queer, I tell him about my first novel and that my wife was the model for it. He takes over and starts talking about women, his ex-wife, his ex-girlfriend: "Fucking gold-diggin' pussy" is his mot juste. I prude up. I hate it.

A killjoy? I just don't want to hear this man's sex life. I don't want to hear anyone's sex life that I haven't asked to hear. I don't have a similar sex life and I certainly wouldn't impart it, why would I? Besides, my sex life is sacrosanct. Besides, my confidences would be met with his throwing me out of his cab because I'm *nice* to women, I *like* them, and I'd be rejected by a tough superior wop one more time. I'm also a physical coward around these types.

The truck drives on, and I gaze neither to the right nor to the left but only on the road before us.

Silence is my loud response to him, silence my punishment, all kinds of silence, especially that most silent of all in which the noise of other silences cannot be heard.

After a time, I coolly change the subject, I ask about the job. He tells me we're going to Moraga to build a retaining wall.

Moraga, once orchards, is a smear of upper-middle-class suburb with pool, the walnut orchards gone.

I unload spades, hose, picks, wheelbarrow and haul them round back. I dig a trench for the boulders. I use a miner's pick to perforate the soil, but he says,

"Use a shovel." I know the pick's quicker but I must abide. He has the experience and is the boss. He hasn't brought the right shovels, though.

What can I learn? If I tip the shovel toward me, the dirt won't dribble into the pool. I note that Briganti, although he has said he wants to keep dirt out of the pool and despite his twenty-three years in the business, doesn't know this. As I dig farther he warns me I'm in danger of cutting the pool lighting wires, so I am not so conscious of what I am doing either. Fear makes me inept. I blame him for my fear.

"It goes pretty quickly," he says, a practical, wise observation. Sometimes he has something to him. The sun is out but not uncomfortable; the work is hard on my body but at least out-of-doors; I work in terror but I'm careful and strong.

When we are done, as we go back to the truck, I observe his stocky gait in front of me. He walks exactly like a landscape contractor, a needful reminder since he has in fact neglected to bring the proper contract for the owner to sign.

We leave the site and drive to a landscape store to pick up boulders.

In its yard lie heaps of stone—for walls, paths, decoration. We gather moss rock—boulders with lichen adhering—but although he knows what sort of rocks he wants, he doesn't let on what sort, then tells me I'm getting the wrong ones. When I ask, he speaks arcanely.

I heave boulders, hand-carry boulders, lay boulders on pallets, label boulders with tape. The sun pats the fine dust up into the nose. It's a bare, hot yard, but it's all right. The work's physical, which is good. Maybe I'll learn the secrets of wall building, rock choosing, negotiating in the landscape world. Is this the life's work I'm meant for?

We go inside to arrange for the shop to deliver the boulders. He asks for his black briefcase from the cab of the pickup, and when I return with it I hear they can't deliver until Tuesday. Why didn't he find that out by phone beforehand—he could have brought his dump truck. He says he'll be back later today.

His dump truck has a flat. With the agenda of fixing the flat we drive back to his contractor's yard.

Briganti's yard embraces a dead fork lift, six wheelbarrows with flats, two extinguished pickups, a rent boat hull, a broken dinghy, a trailer with an ancient flat, a rusted flatbed, a warehouse of turkeyed gear, and the defunct 6-ton dump truck.

I still need to find out about the money. I'm pissed he hasn't made it clear. So, I ask.

"I pay on Friday." His voice is empty.

"It is Friday."

"Next Friday."

There's a form to fill out. I fill it out. When I'm done he says he won't use me any more today. I'm flummoxed, it's not a full day's work, and it takes time and gas money to drive here. "We'll work tomorrow," he dictates, "or maybe the day after when I get the dump truck fixed. It's Friday, so this means I can't take a new job until after Tuesday, and maybe longer. I hate him but I fear I won't be paid if I don't complete the job.

I drive home. What have I learned?

I have bad feelings about this man, his operation, and his manners but I stay. Because I am to learn a new trade? Because my code says accept all work? Because I'm supposed to work out my fear with crude Italians?

Or does God put me here to raise my hand against it and say, "No"?

6 March, Saturday

Acting school audition today at 1:30. I'm early. I am courteous to the guard by the elevator, courteous, courteous.

In the green room where we wait, I resolve not to dissipate myself in chat. It is a long room, and the auditionees, mostly young females, either practice their parts quietly to themselves or gossip. And one of them, a spider-thin Hispanic girl, speaks excitedly to a friend how she is going to play King Lear. She's thrilled. She's full of passion for it. She knows it's right: a young woman playing the part of an old man. And because of her intensity, her commitment, and her nervous excitement, I think she's right too. Different from me. But then I am not in my early twenties; I am contained. And I am also less sure than she. And certainly less passionate. Because passion won't carry me through. It will not do the job, as it will for her. I'm glad to see her, and silently wish her well, among so many other females whose audition pieces are banal, safe, usual. For me this one woman has the earmark of what an actor should be. On fire.

When my turn comes, I find myself in a studio with a man and a woman behind a desk, on which are papers and photographs, mine among them. They ask me to sit down and tell them why I want to act.

I fall into the trap of telling them about my relations with Mildred Dunnock and Elia Kazan. I realize as I talk that I seem to be dropping names, appearing familiar with people far more famous and accomplished than any of us. I sense I have made a mistake with a story separate from acting, as though I am going into acting to prove something. I talk about Marlon Brando and James Dean, and my passion for them and what they brought me, but not about a passion for acting and what that brings me. Once started I cannot stop this story.

Then I do my audition.

When I finish, the woman is kind. She says if I am not chosen, this audition means that I am accepted for a summer school. I realize I have not been chosen.

I leave the building. I pass the elevator guard. I am courteous, courteous. But I want to freeze dry myself, not feel, not face what I am facing.

I walk through the tenderloin. All theatre districts seem to be in the tenderloin.

7 March, Sunday

As I come into the theater, Saul asks to speak to me, so we go outside.

He tells me about a version of *Moby Dick,* in which the actor playing Ishmael wandered wherever he liked, driving the other actors crazy. "I should have fired him but I didn't." My stomach fills with dread.

I go on listening to him, but I do not hear him. I don't wander, but I tell him I realize my work is messy just at present but that's just my way at this stage. I say all this, but what I do not say, what I am afraid to say, is that he has a created a condition of dread in which I find it impossible to work. I don't have the guts to tell him. What I have got to find the guts to do is to override all this and do good work.

At any rate it is clear by the end of the conversation that he is not going to fire me. I go inside and talk to Maddy, and she will watch the rehearsal.

My scenes come up and I nail them, and when I am done I know I have proved I can do it. Maddy agrees. Thank God that is settled.

8 March, Monday

I work another day for Briganti.

I'm afraid of him and I hate him. On the way home he talks about our next job and the next, assuming I have no say but to do them with him.

I want to finish the wall job, collect my money, and see him again never. But I don't have the guts to walk out. I haul all the bags of mortar and boulders.

Catherine. I'm not quite as good as I was on Sunday, but that's because I take three steps forward and one back, I can't help it. I hope they have enough experience to know that's how some people work.

All I have to do is hold on.

Just.

Hold.

On.

9 March, Tuesday

Today Kate Piersanti sets me cleaning the grouting of her tiles. It's a day-long job and I have to buy knee pads to endure it. But Kate pays for the pads. She goes out on her errands leaving me to work on my own recognizance. I put my head down and do it.

Catherine rehearsal.

The attention of Saul Camber and Billy Pierceye is so ugly I lose my entrance, lose my lines, so ugly it occurs to me to quit. But I'll stand here and take it until it breaks. I'll endure it, I'll outlast it, tomorrow I'll be better, I'll be great by dress, I'll be great opening night and in the run.

I can hardly function.

10 March, Wednesday

Nile green, faded, bashed, decrepit, Briganti's dump truck shakes us over the forested hills while dully I listen to him as he recounts his love life. He lives in a world of Naugahyde intrigues, gold-tipped amours. The more crude he waxes the more prudish I get. In Lafayette we sit in the high cab of this dump truck looking down on various Mercedes. At that moment, the woman in front doesn't turn left soon enough for him. "Fucking dumb bitch. I bet she doesn't even suck dick." He tells me about his girlfriend: "Pussy, her cunt smelled like cheese, fucking gold-digging bitch." Is this the sort of man who pays his bills nobly?

As we drive around, he talks about the next job we will do together, and the next. I say nothing.

When we are done we drive back to his yard. I get out of his truck. I stand in his yard, looking up at him. "I'm going to call it a day here," I say to him. "I won't be coming back."

He's quiet.

"Here's a stamped envelope." I hand him a stamped self-addressed envelope. "You said you pay on Friday."

He's still. Maybe he's hurt. Tough.

"So you'll send it out on Friday?"

"Yeah. Put it in my briefcase." He wants a reason, but he doesn't want to hear the reason, so he won't ask the reason. If he did, I'd lie, I wouldn't say, "I don't like you."

"The form's inside. There's a bill saying what hours and days. I worked fourteen hours."

"Okay."

"Did you decide what you were going to pay me?"

"What did I say?"

"You said seven or eight dollars an hour depending on what I was worth."

"Seven."

I don't inquire why: I don't care. "So you'll mail it Friday?"

"Yeah."

I drive away knowing as sure as nails are hard that pay from that quarter is dubious. But I have done the business, thank God. I have quit.

I drive directly to the hospital and change into my roadside clothes. I walk down to the Appian exit bitter. No, not bitter. Hard. I stand there. Pain is in me. I am in pain.

Do you understand I don't care that I am? I'm reporting on the weather. I'm reporting on a stone wall I built.

And as to the weather, what might that be today?

If you shot an arrow into the air it would turn into flowers before it hit the sun.

But I don't think about it.

I am not thinking of God much either. I came here because the roadside is comfort, solace, home.

A boy right away throws a cigarette butt at me.

A stern-eyed boy in an orange sweatshirt gives me coins.

A lovely blond girl in the middle lane beckons with her index finger, holds out to me a dollar, I nip out for it, nip back before you know it. Kind of her.

Next to her, a young man in a wallpaper truck eyes her. Under the secrecy of his black moustache, he glances slyly and then away, intending to make his mating energy known. He knows exactly how much to throw without being offensive and just enough so she'll notice him, exactly how to turn away if she starts to look, so as to be seen to turn as though nothing could be further from his mind, and then how to look again and spread the next layer of the cake. It is a courting move, vulnerable, confident, a tipping of the hat of his maleness. No one had to teach him how to do it, it came with the territory of being male. But she never looks. Without looking, she knows he's doing this. Picking up on such heavy male mating energy and not returning the look comes with the territory of being female.

What appear to be two older lesbians stop their VW van on Appian and hail me. They ask if I do odd jobs, like moving.

Yes, I'm good at it.

Would I be free on March 24?

Yes.

They give me an old BART ticket with their number pencilled on the back and ask me to call closer to that date.

I stand there in my changed jeans and an orange shirt today. It's been warm. And my straw hat—regular condottiere's hat, the hat of an exiled South American dictator. I look at my mascot tree. Why did I bring this hat? I brought it for the sun. But it's too fancy.

Someone throws a dime out the window at me. Not good.

Someone else calls a nasty word, I don't know what. Where do I belong?

My faith in humanity is restored though.

And in myself. People who know me now wave and are kind. The man in the black flame truck salutes. I have positive relations with these people. When a man in a white Cadillac gives me $1, I want to weep.

A gray car pulls off down below. A woman gets out to rummage through the hatch. It's too far for me to know if she has to do with me. Then she walks toward me with things in her arms, beckoning to me as she walks. As she comes up, I see a barroom sort of woman—young with an old face, a long cigarette sticking directly out the front of it, a goodly ash depending. She gives me two oranges, two health bars, and a blueberry muffin. In her sharing she is solid as a can of beans.

I leave at 4:30 for a bath. Only one and a half hours, 2:45——4:30, and I still don't have the rent. I am so tired, it feels like I've been moving boulders. Oh right, I have been moving boulders. I take out the mail from the mailbox by the road and go into my apartment. There's a letter from my sister Kathy. I go to the answering machine.

On it is a message from Saul Camber firing me.

My stomach sinks with shame.

I call Maddy. I can't tell her because she's at work, busy, she'll call me back.

To distract myself I go into the living room and open Kathy's letter. Handwritten, not from Rochester, New York, but from Houston, Texas.

She is dying of cancer.

I put down the letter.

Being fired is demoted, dismissed.

Immediately Maddy calls.

Kathy is in Houston for radical therapy. Her lymphoma has returned and is in full flood. I read Kathy's letter to Maddy. It is amazing in its lack of drama and self-pity, in its pure informativeness. Kathy is valiant and positive. She is positive on my behalf even, she, in such circumstances. She is balanced and her balance is health-giving, but I am not balanced either generally or in this matter.

I start to cry. "I can't believe she is going to die." I double up, kneel on the floor, and bawl and learn what anguish has to tell me. Kathy is the only person in my family who has not abandoned me. I will miss her as the only person who has consistently loved me. But all this is self-centered. I do not think of Kathy. I do not think of Gerry LaMarsh, her husband, and their children, or her community, or the effect on my parents. Only of myself and her loss to me, and I see I am incapable of responding any other way. I will miss her as someone who gave love to me, presents to me, but especially as someone to fall back on (not that I ever did fall back on her). I do not weep because I will miss her because of *her* life but because of *my* life, because *my* life will miss her. My self-centeredness is like a disease; I am no good. I say none of this. I am bent to the floor by weeping, my head on the carpet. Maddy hears it out.

When I hang up, I put a call through to Gerry, Kathy's husband. I am frightened. I want to weep, to shed drama over the scene and steal it. But what right do I have to weep? I must keep a grip when he answers. Besides, who knows that she is to die? Why do I adopt the worst option first and then wring it for every tear it will yield? When he answers, his equanimity does not differ from hers. I cannot imagine what horrors he is privy to on her behalf and in himself. And I am not made privy to them.

He describes the treatment in Texas of reprogramming cancer cells. Kathy is to wear a bag under her arm with a catheter that drips a liquid into her. Just last night he caught a TV talk show in which an oncologist said that while there are no new therapies for cancer—and of course the old ones, surgery, chemotherapy, and radiation work in only limited cases—that the reprogramming of cancer cells is a bright spot. This gives Gerry hope, and gives me hope too since I have always supported Kathy's preference for alternative care.

But I am frightened. My sister is like to die. As I hear Gerry out, I find my mind wandering. I feel overwhelmed by what I have to take in.

But I can muster enough to say that I'm glad my sister married him, and that he is a good husband. I say what they are going through is an adventure. I can feel his stalwartness and his manliness. In their shoes I would collapse, I think, or try to run it all on emotion. But my sister has informed herself well. When the doctors said to take chemo, she asked which version, and when they told her, she knew it was for temporary cure and told them it was. They admitted as much, and said they could give her a year or a year and a half with it. She wouldn't take it. Because she wouldn't give up.

Gerry asks how I am doing. He knows and Kathy knows that I have been out of work for a year. Because they have more important things to think about I haven't told either of them about the roadside. But because a certain confidentiality opens between us, I tell him about it now, asking him not to tell Kathy because I want to tell her myself when the time is right. And besides I don't want her to worry.

He says some money just came in, a check from some stocks or something, and he wants me to have it. I say no, he's to keep it. But he says they're fine financially, he's going to send it. I tell him I don't need it, I don't want it, and I don't. They have medical expenses, don't they; I don't know what their insurance covers, and neither until after the fact, I guess, do they.

Her illness has done something for my sister. From the start she has educated herself about her cancer, has molded her recovery, chosen her own therapies. This has made her more selfish, and I am glad of it, because I feel her character gaining strength in that. That she has become more like I would wish her to be is less true than that she has simply become more herself, and that makes it easier for me because authenticity is always surprising, and it is easier to deal with the surprising than the boring. Talking to me about her illness over the years, she has become just and firm and forward-looking.

I admire her, I am amazed at her soundness, but still frightened. It would be terrible if I lost my sister.

I kneel down, put my head to the ground, and pray for her.

My life is so useless, and her life is so useful. She has two young children, twelve and ten, and a husband and family, and many friends who love her. My life has none of this. My life is baffled—so unsuccessful. But would I give my life for hers—for what good is my life? Still, I do not make that rash passionate offering. "I will die for you!" does not cry out from my lips. I have become so inefficacious I cannot even say, "If you live, I will live for something other than myself," for if I tried to live for the trees, say, I fear I would be expelled from the woods soon enough.

I sit back on my heels.

I can't believe it: she is to die.

I can't believe it. There must be a way to save her.

I must find it.

11 March, Thursday

I cannot sleep. To keep myself together I do something, I do the dishes.

As I wash I feel tempted to think badly of my sister, supposing she has left me last to be told of the return of her lymphoma—which began in December. I think badly of my whole life for being worthy of nothing but disregard. Then I think badly of myself for so thinking. I want to weep for my sister and then I want to weep for myself for being so self-centered.

I want everything for myself. I don't want anyone else to have anything. I want not to earn it but to be given it. Without greed, my center is not strong enough. I look out from a center in fear for its own survival and unwilling to take sufficient steps to learn to survive.

As early as I may this morning I call Houston.

She picks up the phone. She and her roommate are about to leave for a session at the clinic. She says she'll find out today whether the doctor wants her to stay a week more.

I tell her I couldn't get along without her.

She says she wants to live at least to raise her daughters.

I say I want her to live on her own account. I want her to live no matter who may need her. I cry a little. My voice sounds not my own, whatever my own is. She has such a cough—dry, grating—it makes my heart stand still.

We talk only four minutes. And I have the sense that at the moment she doesn't have the breath to talk longer. I make a date to call her back in Rochester.

Kathy is a gentle person, but also is stalwart and optimistic and in action. Good. She is in action.

But, oh it is dire, it is dire.

This drama is not about me, however. I am not the focus of this drama. My sister is the focus. I am not even next in line, her husband, her children, our parents are next in line, anybody who is ahead of me on that line is next in line. How to participate in it without drawing attention to myself?

Stand by. Say little.

Decline to say the "right things" because they will redound well on yourself.

Send love and prayer.

But how I always do revert to myself.

This may be why I have been fired from the play. No. The reason I was fired was because scapegoat energy requires a death.

Someone calls me with a film offer, no pay, never been in a film before. I accept it script unseen.

I call Saul Camber. I am owed an explanation, and he knows it. I insist he give it me eye to eye. I do not taunt him by telling him of my film offer. Getting back is going to take a form that does not involve him at all. I fantasize him begging my forgiveness. "Crawl outta here, buster; the only amends I want from you is for you to become a good director."

But of course it is wrong to impose an impossible penance.

I go to Kate's and finish the tiles. She wants me to come back and dig up the garden on the south side so it can be planted with vegetables.

Harry Newman, the man with the painting job, calls. He says he will pay me $12 an hour and he has no trouble in saying it. Of course, one doesn't want to work even for $12 an hour.

Tonight I record the work with Briganti—hours, tasks, promises, and circumstances in the event I have to take him to court. According to my Compact, I am supposed to accept what I am paid, which in this case may be nothing.

On the other hand, maybe I'm not meant to be so supine.

12 March, Friday

Harry Newman is a man in his early seventies who has had a stroke, which disarranges an arm and makes his walking odd. He is a quiet, contained man. He and his wife own a house in Pinole, which needs painting by Monday for the agent to rent. Harry is slowed by this disability, and a deadline is before them. So here I am.

They do not pry into my situation, but I tell them anyhow. Hi wife is out buying lunch, which they offer me while Harry and I paint along in the bedroom. As I chat him up about his life in World War II, I notice how fastidiously he paints. This not a function of his stroke, but of an ease and completeness of attention to the task itself. A bit later while Harry is not in the room, I remark to her how well he paints and she says, "Harry is a master at whatever he does." My ears prick up. This is not a statement a competent mature professional woman long-married generally makes of a spouse.

When we are alone painting again, I tell Harry what she has said and that I believe her. Since I may seize a lesson from a master, I ask him what mastery in painting is. And he shows me, but it's nothing that can be shown. He works without patience and without impatience. "Of course it's nothing," he says afterwards, and returns to rolling the wall.

I keep my eyes on him. He doesn't need to talk or listen to the radio. I do what he's told me, but my brain goes jingling on and I splash. Harry is occupied, not preoccupied. He is composed. He can't get up a ladder promisingly, he hobbles when he walks, and when he stands he stands on one side; but in the activity of painting a wall, he is a Zen master. The stroke simply gave him another koan.

When the day's work is done, they pay me more than they had contracted for and give me the leftovers. When I get home a check from January office temp work is there, so I send the rent. Good.

13 March, Saturday

Saul Camber's six-foot-seven bald head bends through the jambs of my rooms like a tyrannosaurus. He's interested only in my photograph of Oscar Wilde's son Vyvyan Holland and me, my framed letter from Maugham. When I settle him down I do not offer him tea. I do not mention his abuse. All I am interested in is what possible excuse he could have.

He says he fired me because in a previous show he directed there was an actor he should have fired but didn't.

Is that all?

He'd already brought in another actor the Sunday he spoke to me outside.

With this there is no way of continuing the discussion.

I walk him to his car. I tell him about a play I have written to see if he will direct it. There are no depths to which I will not sink. "Oh, no, I'm only going to direct opera from now on." What a jerk I am!

In the afternoon, I meet the film director, a young fellow living on friends' couches, all his money going for film stock. What am I acting for? Who says I should act? I got fired. Isn't the message rather simple? When we start, I'm camera-conscious.

14 March, Sunday

I see *Unforgiven.*

The performance is taken with something seldom seen in an actor, a territory virtually free, so still and ample that the actor hardly has to use a thing. And older, he's more open, you can rest in him, there's lines in his face to enter him by, he allows it. What I see is riveting. To be allowed to see inside anybody is riveting. Some things he can't do, but some things he can do superlatively, and he is *interesting.* The camera devours him. It goes right inside him and he lets it. He does not use it opportunistically, nor does he use himself that way. He allows a careful attention to let what is supposed to happen in the character, happen. The inside story. There is no difference between him and the camera. In other words he is without vanity. Practically. (He's probably vain about his hair.) And there's something else besides.

His popularity comes from having a working class look and a temperament working class people might fancy themselves to have, but now something else has ripened in him—what?—I'm not sure.

He can act like a junebug.

Vary inneresting. Of course, the temptation for Eastwood in all of this, the danger to his soul, is to use his instrument to remain emotionally stingy.

I wonder what I gain from gazing into the ravines of his face. Inside his depths of age and life, I see one thing, which is that he is willing for us to travel inside the depths of his age and life. Is it because he is just himself? As an actor he is not there yet, but the distance he has travelled is great.

As an actor I am also willing to be open and for others to enter in, but for me acting always means being invaded by a character not like me at all.

But I don't want to think about my acting. I don't want to think about it because I'm not good in this film I'm making. Every acting test I fancied myself passing I am failing. I am up against a wall. And there is no door. Looking at Eastwood is no door. Whatever gift and fair chance he may have been given are his.

And anyhow, maybe for me acting is a cop-out. Maybe the evolution is not to be some character that has invaded from the outside. I long for the authentic. Maybe I am faced with a different riddle: to be not someone else, but to be myself?

"If not, get out of it! The exit gate has been opened, you've been fired, buddy, slam it behind you, and go."

Is that right?

No answer comes. Only the standing still. If I cop out, I'll be doing again what I did all those years ago with Kazan. Only right now I can't move forward. All I can do is stand still and hold my sign.

15 March, Monday

As the weekend has gone on, I mobilize to do everything I can to ensure my sister recovers. It is not medical technology that I can offer, it is a different intervention: to bring healing from the spirit of nature itself, from the spirit of healing itself.

My plan is for Gerry to set up a bank account for medical bills, which friends and family know the number of and into which they send money anonymously.

People living far away could give. People with not much money could give. Members of her extended family could give. Young and old could give. Everyone could be a part of her recovery. And anonymity would mean that no one could take credit for a large amount or be embarrassed by a small and thus would gather to her the widest number of people focusing their prayers on her in angels of money winging their way toward her. And that's the key. Prayer in the form of a kitty.

But will the family go for it? Prayer. While I have no sense anyone practices prayer, they're too intelligent to discount the power of it. And will Kathy accept? As the love-giver of this family, she might find it hard to.

Gerry picks up the phone and I tell him I'm hatching a plan and that I'll mail it. He puts her on.

"Hi, Kathy, how're ya doin'?"

"Well, pretty good. The doctors in Houston have put me on this medication, and if all goes well, the problem will clear up in a matter of weeks."

"You think so!"

"That's what they tell me and I sure as heck want to believe it. How are you doin'?" she asks. "I'm doing fine," I lie. I would love to tell her how badly I'm doing, but I am too proud to be so damned dull. And she's got enough to handle.

"How's the money situation?"

"I'm getting by so don't you worry about it. How does this medicine work?"

"Well, it's something new. It drips into me from a bag that I carry around under my clothes, which isn't so easy, but I'm not complaining—except a little bit. And the idea, if it works, is that somehow this medicine reprograms the cancer cells to function in my behalf instead of against me, if you see what I mean. I don't quite know how it works. I don't quite know how any of this stuff works. Nobody does, I think. But I've got to go along with it, and I am. The trouble is that it's real expensive and I have to go to Texas to get a refill because it can't be sent interstate."

"Does health insurance pay for it?"

"Well, we don't know yet, because it's so new, but we're hoping."

I tell her about the prayer-kitty plan.

"It sounds great," she says.

"I thought you might not go for it."

"Brother, I'll take whatever I can get."

"Well, you talk it over with Gerry. He may not want to relinquish his role as provider, and I understand that, but the important thing is that we all get together and do it."

"But never mind me, how's Amanda?" she asks, characteristically turning from the more important subject of herself. It annoys me.

Oh but I wish I could hold my sister. I wish I could lie next to her and hold her in my arms as we did when we were kiddies and she would come toddling into my bed. I have the notion that just to hold her I could heal her.

"If I were there," I say, "I'd take your footsies in my hand and I'd give you a foot massage."

"And I'd take it," she laughs.

When we hang up, I feel my sister is on her way to recovery. "I'm optimistic," she said, and so am I. For I believe miracles are normal. I believe alternative care will work with my sister because my belief in it gives my sister a special favor with God with whom I've got connections. A part of me makes this call to hear Kathy say she is doing fine, and another part of me gears up to man all stations, because I could not live with myself if I did not.

Afterwards I get a gas tank at a wrecking yard. Then on to Big O for tires. Thank you, Harry.

16 March, Tuesday

Writing the prayer proposal takes all day. I'll let it sit a day, like bread.

No envelope from Briganti. Mailed on Friday, should have come last Saturday.

17 March, Wednesday

I haven't spoken to my brother and sister-in-law in years. I feel it would be wiser not to present the prayer plan on the phone, where they could refuse me out of hand, whereas if I write it they can sleep on it. On the other hand I am eager, so I phone. My brother is wealthy and probably means to be generous with Kathy and Gerry anyhow. Still that matters less than the communal prayer, since the only thing that matters is that Kathy recover. And the idea is so good, how can they resist it?

No one is at home.

I send the prayer plan to them and to Gerry and Kathy.

It's a week since I've been on the roadside. I drive back to it eagerly as to the house of an old friend. The day is a blue drum. The hills parade, some on the other side of the county with the hills on Mount Diablo. When I get there a man stands in my place with a sign saying, "Stranded."

I never bargained on competition.

I park and, nasty with trepidation, walk back to Appian and my place on the roadside. However, I see a red car broken down on the off-ramp, so I walk down to see if the driver needs help. The help is already on its way. Perhaps Stranded will understand what he has to do here besides collect money. Then, that the authority of these tasks may drive him away, I walk up to the spot and without a word put my umbrella behind the *Do Not Enter* pole, take my sign out, and set it up.

As I do this he makes as if he does not see me, a tactic that makes me fear the confrontation.

He is a square blond man, five-nine, mid-twenties, with a block face, and narrow inset eyes, an old look to him. I face him and I say nicely. "Hi."

"Hi," he says hardening.

"You know, this is my place."

He does not respond but keeps looking at the oncoming cars for money.

"I've been working this spot for three months."

He doesn't speak. Then, "First come, first served," he says.

"I did come first."

He doesn't answer. I wait.

"I don't think there's room for two of us," I say.

"I got a wife and baby stranded. I gotta get to Oklahoma City," he says as though these credentials would give him precedence. "I'll be gone after tomorrow." He keeps his eye on the cars coming, holding his territory. He has a level monotonous voice. He holds it with that, too.

Yesterday my friend Audrey Taylor told me about a conflict workshop. To exert resistance, neither buckle nor fight back, just stay in place. Don't give an inch to sentiment.

"This is my place of business. It's my office." I walk around behind him and talk to his back. "If you had an office and went out into the field, would you like for someone to move in and take away your business?"

He makes himself a block.

"Besides, these people are my clients. I know them, and they know me."

I walk around in front of him again, screening him from the traffic. "What's the matter with you, don't you have any decency?"

For the first time, he looks at me. "Do you want to scuffle over it?"

I don't want a fracas with people watching, we'd be arrested, business is business, and I don't want to queer this spot. I back down.

He's slow-witted. Maybe the injustice of the situation will register with him if I wait.

A car stops and gives him two bills. I'm getting nothing.

I walk back up behind him again and say in his ear right firmly, "I want you to leave."

He doesn't answer. He's not going to go. The point is not to lose self-control, not to sputter. But inwardly I am sputtering. The only fight I can make is to set myself up to solicit. Maybe if I stand in front of him I can ice him out. Trouble is he's standing on the dirt, where the patrolman told me not to stand, so standing there might ice me out.

So I set myself up on the sidewalk behind him. Now no one will give us money because to give to one and not both would be immoral, and two's too many. But that proves wrong. A car hands him money first and not me.

A big smiling black woman with me in her eye reaches out an industrial size can of strawberry jam with a dollar wrapped around it. As it passes him, he takes the dollar, and I am left with the jam.

People give $1 to him and $1 to me, but all the money handed out just to one person he gets because he stands ahead of me. He's stealing my survival! I'm fuming. I'll stand here like a thundercloud until he leaves. My energy will be so black he'll be death-rayed off the premises. Maybe he has the same notion.

I see his square back in the sun, his short stiff legs, his gloves on against the cold. He has the body of a small miller. He has no neck. He's a clod.

Wait—what's that?

He's whistling.

He's whistling quietly, I can't quite hear it, what's he whistling?

Oh. He's whistling hymns. He's whistling "Amazing Grace."

Oh. He too has a spiritual life. He's calling upon it now to fortify him. Things aren't so easy for him either: two opponents not talking to one another, standing within ten feet of one another, in need of God.

I realize that the only thing to do to the man in front of me, with his monotonous voice, narrow eyes, short and stolid stance, is to send him a blessing. He's not like anyone I would ever know, he's country, I would be frightened of him in his own setting. I have nothing in common with him, least of all English. But here we are and not because I am a saint but because it is the only thing I can do besides curse him—and I have cursed him, and my body feels bad from it. God bless you, I say to myself toward him. God bless you. God bless you. For all his miller's back, he is a man as I am. He is a human being and he is in difficulty as I am, and it is the same difficulty. God bless you. Let him stay.

Blessing him may make him feel so guilty he will go. No, just let him be here, Bruce. Entertain no notions of his going. Let him stay.

He's stopped whistling.

"What's your name?"

He does not answer. He doesn't turn around.

"Dave."

"I'm Bruce."

That's all. He's not sure of me.

I don't know what to say next.

"Why do people hand out such an odd piece of food as a huge can of jam?" I say finally.

"Same woman gave me a can of that jam yesterday," he says.

"She probably had access to it from her job."

He has a grocery bag someone gave him earlier set against the pole.

I start teaching him the ropes, telling him the code so he can do it better. I'm talking to his back and I can tell he isn't listening.

"I'm only here until I can get enough money to leave this here state of California," he says. "I got to get back to Oklahoma and find work." I don't ask what work. Every hitchhiker I ever pick up says he came to California to find work; why didn't they ask first if any work was here. "40,000 Bay Area families homeless" is perhaps not in the Oklahoma papers.

I give him the Compact information piecemeal. But he's not listening. It's as though he is here for the money only and ethics might compromise that purpose.

"Dave, is this work good for your spirit?"

"Good for my spirit? No."

"It's good for mine."

"The Lord is my spirit," is the hammer he lands on my thumb.

He's part of some sect maybe. Otherwise we are friends, very different, mind you, but not enemies. Love holds us in arms larger than we are, animosity goes. He's a stolid man, his wits are recessed, warily counting coins behind his eyes, but since I do not wish to undo him, that's all right. What we have is an accord for being here. We have no agreement about money or whose place this is, but we both agree to be here, nothing said. When people give me money for both of us, I give his to him. I feel in possession of myself again.

As he stands with his back to me I see his knees are locked.

"Hey, Dave, standing like that's going to make you tired." I go around in front of him and show him how to stand with his knees flexed a little.

"I have arthritis in this knee," he says. His whole body is stiff. He tries to stand the new way but doesn't persevere.

So the hours wear on with Dave and me.

The sun blusters about. The dry yellow dirt of the roadside and black pebbles of the roadside. Flinders of glass and refuse. Money still comes to him more, a piece of me waits him out, a piece smiles and lets him stay.

"You!"

I turn around. A short, rough man of thirty-five stands on the sidewalk.

"Me?"

"Yes, you! I got a job for you." He walks away without me.

Who is this guy? I've gotta get my things. I catch up with him. "What job is this?"

"Your sign says 'Will Work,' right?" He neither looks at me nor stops walking.

I catch up. "What did you have in mind?"

"Weeding," he says as a challenge, plowing on ahead as though defying me to follow, as though wishing I wouldn't follow, as though walking away from me would mean I hadn't.

I trot up along next to him. Hoes make blisters. "Do you have any work gloves?"

"You won't need work gloves," he says straight ahead, stalking on faster than me.

Maybe he has a tiller. Or maybe he means tiny low weeds. Again I hustle up next to him. "Why did you choose me and not the other man?"

"My father seen you there."

I don't get it, but its threat I do get. I catch up again. "Where are we going?"

"A place I own," striding like a five star general.

I catch up. I want to nail something down here or get him to shift modes. "You own it?"

"My father owns it."

We hurry on two blocks more, in silence, I trotting next to him. We stop by an empty lot, an acre of rubble and weeds. "Weed it."

"Now?"

"Whad you say?" he threatens.

"You mean now?"

"Yes I mean now."

"But it's huge. It's lava. I have nothing to kneel on. Do you have knee pads?"

"You don't need knee pads."

"Of course you do."

"You refusing work?"

"But that's a job for a rototiller."

"You refusing the work?" he says, hoping I am.

I don't have the tools, it's a huge dull backbreaking job that would net me less than the roadside; it would damage my body; I don't want to do it. "What are you paying?" I say, disobeying my code, but to hell with it.

"Five dollars an hour."

"That's not even a living wage."

"Are you refusing the job?"

"I can't pay my rent on that."

"Can you pay your rent with what you make on the highway?" Threatening me makes him stupid but it also makes him more cunning than I am.

"What you are offering a sixty-year-old man is hours of hard labor at slave wages. What kind of person are you?"

"Are you refusing the work?"

I don't want to do the work but mainly I want to get out of this man's presence. I also want to get back on the roadside, but there's a danger here to see to.

"What's going on here?"

"Your sign says, 'Will Work.' If you refuse work my father'll call the Pinole police."

The man is mean and the father is meaner since he inspires nastiness in others, but the son's meanness is worse: it isn't even his own.

"You refusing the job?"

"The job's impossible."

"You refusing to work?"

"I accept jobs all the time."

"You'll find the police visiting your island."

"Is this the way you treat a destitute person?"

"You refusing to work?"

"No."

"Yeah, you're refusing to work," he prepares to walk off.

"I'm *not* refusing to work! I'm refusing to work for *you*."

He turns to go. It's useless to argue, his mind was made up before he spoke to me. I feel terrorized and unstrung.

"I'll talk to your father if he wants to hire me."

"You'll see," he calls after me.

"Fine." I walk away, back across the freeway overpass. The police might come and take me away, they might be as bad as the man. I can see myself in the jail-house, being grilled. I have no money for a lawyer I don't even know the law. I have never been arrested in my life. Maybe I should have taken the work just to show him he was wrong and that people on the roadside aren't cheaters. But, no, that sort of meanness finds situations in order to flourish. My working there would have satisfied his father nothing. What's more, the father probably wouldn't have paid me. People who fear cheating cheat.

But the compact says I'm supposed to have taken the job.

When I get back to the roadside I tell Dave what happened.

"I'd tell him to kiss my white ass," Dave says.

That's certainly a healthier attitude than mine.

"I don't work for sex," I say to Dave, "I don't do work that's illegal and I don't work for rattlesnakes."

Dave continues to laugh at the man. Dave himself isn't interested in jobs; he just wants the bucks, which actually I consider rather admirable.

And so we resume standing, he in front, I behind. In time I calm down. Something about his stolid blond stance settles me.

Keeping his face to the road Dave tells me his stories—how he lives in a tent in Oakland at the end of a road. "The police know I'm there. They saw my fire yesterday and told me to put it out, and I told them I had to cook food for the baby, and they went away." He wields that baby like a weapon.

"What does your wife do when you're here?"

"She hangs out in a bar with the baby. The Seven Seas. She drinks soda. They let her run up a ten dollar tab then she has to pay it. She can receive phone calls there. One day she took a dollar and rode the subway all day to keep the baby quiet." Although it's all true, it's a sob story.

"What denomination do you belong to?" I ask.

"Baptist."

Maybe if I alert his church they'll foot their bill home and I'll have this place to myself again.

A big pickup truck pulling a horse van comes to a stop in the middle lane, driven by a blond woman big as a bale of hay with massive arms, a bunch of kids in the rear, another big blond next to her.

"See them two in the horse wagon? I'd go to work for either of them."

I'm amazed, but that's his taste—big cow women. Somebody has to love them, though.

"I'd put another kid in that back seat." He laughs, a naughty man, a roll-in-the-hay Baptist, pious but not penis pious. "'Roll over, doggie,' I'd say."

"Meaning?"

"Finish with one, say to her, 'Roll over,' and get onto the other."

Dave takes a break for lunch at one. He crosses the street and sits on the concrete barrier to eat the Taco Bell and the roast beef sandwich I gave him. He
takes a bathroom break after that. When he comes back I let him stand again in
his place of priority. And so it goes. The cars go by. The day goes by. We wait
for money. He mostly gets it first. We don't say much.

"Pity to be married with so many women in the world," he says.

"How old were you when you got married?"

"Nineteen."

"Whydja get married?"

"Thought it was a good idea at the time."

"Whose good idea?"

"Hers. She said, 'We should get married,' so I did." Behind his slits you'd think
he saw nothing, but he sees. He's not such a clod after all. He's twenty-three
now, but that's an eternity when you're doing the wrong thing being married.
Maybe it isn't the wrong thing. He just has the distance of a husband from a
wife that the righteousness of her dependence puts between them.

So we stand. I am second in line but I'm also out for all I can get, so while I
share what is to be shared, I take what comes my way.

Three cars down a man in a gold car beckons. Dave's ahead of me, so I go
and stand behind him. A young, nice-looking East Asian man with a fine moustache hands Dave a dollar, maybe there'll be something for me. When Dave
leaves I step forward. The man hands me a bill. "This is all I have today," he says.
He smiles. "I gave to you before," he says, to remind me not of his generosity
but that we have met here before.

"I remember you, yeah. You and I had that laugh together." It's that same
man I connected with when I was crying in the rain, the kind of laugh you have
once in a lifetime with someone, and you are joined forever because of it. He
seems different today, someone I already know. My head is bent down to the
window so I can see into his eyes. "What's your name?" I ask.

"Angelo."

"I'm Bruce."

We shake.

"God bless you, Angelo. Is there anything I can do for you?"

"Pray for me," he says.

"Okay, I will!" As I withdraw I notice a cross glimmering on his rearview
mirror turning on a golden chain. The traffic obliges him away.

As I walk up back to my place, I wonder. Why should I pray for Angelo? Is
he in such passionate difficulty? Yes. I could see it in his eyes. So I pray for him
by the side of the road then and there. It's easy to pray for Angelo. There's a
Christian good soul indeed.

In fact, I'll pray for him every day. I'll pray for Angelo, and, through him, for all the people who passed me here—those who gave, those who didn't. "God bless Angelo," I'll say, and let that stand for all.

The day wears on, and, although I have come to peace with Dave's being there, I still want him to leave the world to darkness and to me. I blanket him with blessings, but I hope he does not have my staying power. Maybe I don't have my staying power.

At six he leaves.

Night falls and the wind marks my face with its lashes of grass. The sunset is not bright in the drivers' faces because it's overcast now. They are going home to their dinners—the day satisfied or defeated. Can they see me here in the dusk? With their headlights on, will they stop giving? If there are any rules, I can't find them, and it doesn't matter.

I pack up at 6:30 on the dot. I'm tired too. It's cold. Light from no house, only headlights, streetlights. I trudge down to the car.

In the evening the slaves would sing. They knew work as white people simply do not know it, and the psyche of them in that way made a dense community. They sang on the cabin steps. They were more tired than I have ever been. But they sought art in the evening. They told old tales. So I spend a gift certificate on cat sand and a story after dark on film.

6 hours: $38.80. $6 an hour. If I had weeded that field would I have done better?

I get on my knees. I bow my head to the carpet. I pray for my sister's life. I pray for my daughter. For Dave. For Angelo. I like praying for Angelo. And for me.

18 March, Thursday

In the first car is an East Asian young man. He gives me coins and says, "It's all I've got." I like it when people say this, as they frequently do. It means that's all the change they have, or their income is limited, or their hearts are unlimited and they wish their purses were. It means they've given me all they have in their bucket at the moment. A Zen zero.

I have too much criticism in me. What I'll do instead is find things to like. Cars for instance. I turn my nose up at modern cars because for the most part they have no style. Looking at a low turquoise car, I realize that I love this car, not because it is loveable but because I feel love. I ask the driver what it is. "Dodge Stealth," he says. The license plate: "4TH DMN."

And then a SHOTGUN EXPRESS truck drives up and, because I like the funny name, I talk merrily to the driver.

I notice a big blue truck pulled off the freeway onto the grass below. For the past weeks, based in this truck, road workers have been working on—on what? I had dismissed them, but I now live in a world of professions carried out under the factory roof of the sky beneath which, like various beetles under a log, each bent to its own vocation, none interfering with the others, we work in sight of one another. I strike out toward the blue truck.

They're putting in an overhead electronic sign to tell motorists what traffic conditions prevail ahead, a gadget equal to the bankrupt Richmond School District's yearly budget.

Standing here thinking of God—what a privilege!

A man stops and asks if I'm hungry.

"Yes," I lie to get money with pity, never a good move and not one I often make. He says he'll feed me at McDonald's. "Thank you. I'm not hungry right now," I say. What conversation I would have had with him, where it would have led, I will never know.

"Where have you been? I been looking for you." a black woman shoots at me as though I have stood her up.

"I was offered some jobs and took them."

"I had money for you on payday, but you wuzn't here," she scolds. Later I realize I might have asked her when her next payday is so as to be sure to be on hand.

I feel such happiness, I don't know why. I know that for the first two hours I've only received a few bills, but I am in paradise. I can't contain it: I am always so surprised when people give me something, or smile, or wave, or are nice. Why is that? I've been doing this three months now, yet it's still fresh.

A black woman reaches a bag out with two huge Nation's hamburgers stone cold. "God bless you," I say. "God bless *you*," she says. I eat them looking at the traffic as it passes.

What is blessing? Where does it live in the frame? How is it that blessing is real when said, becomes true at that moment for both beggar and blessed, each equal? I don't understand how God allows this one word to penetrate every soul with immediate divinity. The blessing is inherent in the word. It doesn't come from the sayer, it comes from the words said.

I stand in the radiant sun and eat so everyone can see me, happy. Yesterday I feared if people see I have food, they will not give to me. But today there are no rules. While I eat a woman stops traffic to get out and give me coins. A black boy in the middle lane jumps out of the passenger seat and comes around to me with money. Cars stop so I can pick up fallen bills. A woman cheers when someone ahead of her gives.

But that's just my roadside stuff. What's God's stuff? I stand here on my own two feet, but how am I going to stand on my own two feet is the question my being here asks of my life. I want to put my soul to work, for we are here on Earth to sell our souls, that's what God wants, nothing less than our souls is worth selling.

A run-down couple in a tired gray van drives up. She has one tooth and he has two. They are not as old as liquor has made them. They ask if I have gone to Unemployment for work. "For months. There's nothing there."

"We do yard work, that's the only way we can make a few bucks," he says. The one-toothed woman looks suspiciously at him: he's a lying drunk. But still they make a bid for communion.

Another criticism: I don't like women with gray hair to wear it down.

Immediately, a *beautiful* woman with long, straight, gray hair worn to her shoulders stops, gives me money, and I fall in love with her and with her hair. Fast-food transformation!

The cars zip by, zip by.

Today, people ask what I do—but because they are zipping by I can't give an answer. One woman sitting there for a long time finally asks it. If people have work, why don't they just say so and ask if I can do it?

A beep behind—a man in a big old long yellow car beckons.

I look in and say, "Hi there, what can I do for you?"

"Get in." He has a ratchet voice.

I assume he wants to talk to me about a job.

He says he's just going to park across the street and that a church group has sent a bag of groceries in the trunk.

"I would like them," I say, "but unloading's the same here as over there."

He concurs and he gets out and opens the trunk and hands out a big bag.

"It's not much," he says, "but it'll get you through the day. Our group has seen you here a while."

"When you say 'group'. . . ?"

He hands me a card:

Christian Biker Outreach. Motorcycle Ministry
750-HELP
Hells Angels Who Have Found Jesus
"TODAY is the day of SALVATION" II Corinthians 6:2

I can well believe it. The card pinpoints them as the North Bay Congregation, which suggests many another. What sweethearts people are!

A pretty, young, blond woman stops her car in the middle of the waiting traffic, gets out, goes to her trunk, gets her wallet out, walks back to me and hands me a bill, and gets back in. What brilliant aplomb, knowing she could do it all and get back in before the light turned green!

A good-looking young man in a red Camaro gives and says good luck. He sits down there behind its appointments. He's much younger than I and of a world I do not belong to, a world in which computers provide direct employment. When I ask for work, he says he is going on Tuesday to just outside Houston to start a new job.

"What do you do?"

"Construction." He's happy and excited with his prospects. You don't have to be good-looking to be happy, but he's both. I wonder if I should try construction.

A man from yesterday asks, "Where's the other guy?" Another man asks me if Dave wasn't my son.

A pretty, blond, young woman in a gray Mazda stops and says she'll give me change. Later, because the money is folded, I learn that, for her, change means a five-dollar bill. She's friendly and comical, so we chat.

"What do you do for a living?" I ask her, wondering if it's something I might do.

"Clean houses," she says cheerfully.

"What sort of money can one earn doing that?"

"Fifty or sixty a house—about three hours work."

"How do you get that much?"

"Oh, I tell them I won't set the price until I'm done. So I do it and give an estimate. And then I come back and do it when they're not there when I can do it much faster, see. The difference is, I'm a foist-class housecleaner." Housecleaning—is that what I should be doing?

As the traffic moves through the last of the yellow light, a car honks dictatorially at the car in front. The car ahead staggers across the yellow light and away. But the honker still can't make the light. The driver's a vanilla-blond, pug-faced woman, who immediately screams at me, "Why don't you get a job!"

To mollify her I approach her.

"Don't you come near my car!"

"Aw, you're angry. Don't be angry."

"'Don't be angry!'" she mocks. "Get a job."

"That's why I'm here."

"Stay away from my car. Don't try to butter me up. If you dare come near my car I'll call the police."

"You were angry at that car," I say firmly, "and now you're angry with me."

"Don't give me that cheap shit. Get away from me, you bum!"

I withdraw. I don't have the wit to change her. Nor do I have the ability to come out feeling good.

A Hispanic woman waits for the light to change, aware of me next to her open window. She is nervous but she does not look at me. I put no pressure on her. As she drives away, "If you go to the Rescue Mission, they'll feed you," she says, but she doesn't say where the mission is.

"That's what I should be doing," says a young woman with a cigarette, "working for food or cash." She has an old car, and her way is the other-side-of-the-tracks way there's always been in this world. I like other-side-of-the-tracks.

At 6:15 I find myself exhausted. Bone-tired, I weave in the sunsetting light. I have stood seven hours in one spot and I'm almost too tired to think of God at all. My mind can't make a sustained effort in the matter.

"We got some trees gotta come down," says a man in a pruning truck. Maybe I'll become a tree surgeon! I give my number to him, but will he call?

When I get home, I explore the bag from the Motorcycle Ministry Hells Angels Who Have Found Jesus. 4 big oranges and 3 big green apples. 3 peanut butter sandwiches on very dark bread, good. Several containers of Marachan Instant Lunch chicken flavor noodle soup, one of which I have for supper. 4 fresh carrots. 1 can peaches. 2 cans pears. 2 cans Stagg chicken chili. 2 cans S&W sweet peas. Two bags almonds (them bikers know road food). A handful of cellophane-wrapped hard candy, and some pills: Double X Nutrilite, whatever that is, probably vitamins. And cards from Liberty Foursquare Christian Fellowship, Pastors Ray and Sharon Stark. Copiously generous.

I count one $10 bill, five $5 bills, the rest singles and change. Seven hours. $79.87. $11 per hour. I can replace the shocks that damaged the gas tank.

20 March, Saturday

I teach myself to change the gas tank in my car. I put a second one in. The first one didn't fit. When I told the the chucklehead in the junkyard he said, "Stuff rags in it." My good neighbor Jane ferries me around for this, God bless her. Soon I will be roadside again.

21 March, Sunday

Every day I call Briganti's answering machine, asking for the check for ninety-one dollars.

22 March, Monday

"I pass by here every day but I never had change. But today I do," says a pretty young woman and she hands it to me.

Although I am someone she does not know, she has a relationship with me—like all the people who have passed. I cannot hide out from them; I am not invisible. For years in the crowd of Manhattan I would walk as though invisible. I wanted to be world-famous and unknown. One day I saw a man standing in the nook of a 5th Avenue building, watching the people passing, hungry for it, and no one noticed him. He was invisible. It was Danny Kaye.

But all that time in New York, I, unbeknownst to myself, was in relation to every person who passed by me and saw me. Cutting myself off in the passion of thought, I disappeared while moving. Ridiculous. The ostrich is more noticeable when its head is in the sand.

In the middle lane a white van driven by a black woman, the rear filled with black children. A big black woman sitting next to the driver beckons me. It looks like they have collected money all around, but maybe not. I sense black people operate out of a community of aid. Yet these women give with a wonderful resentment, a duty handed through a chink in a wall of suspicion. White man, why aintcho wukin'?" they do not say. "I was the cricket," I do not say. "Someone had to be. I worked singing. And now it's winter."

Yesterday I saw a TV interview with Eastwood. He has turned out well. You wouldn't have thought it—a man too old to play the parts he plays of sex symbol and hero, his soul slain by their license and their violence. But it all seems to have washed off him. He's happy, God love him. His roles may have made him a bad icon, but he's ripened out of it. He says something so simple it stirs me: "I'm doing something I love."

Eastwood stands right over there, for I have summoned him and he is a compliant soul. Maybe he turned out well because he sought independence and strove to tell stories on his own. He had to fight maybe, maybe he still has to fight, I don't know. I don't know much about him, I simply see him. I'm not like him. I wish I were—not like him—but parallel. There's a piece in him that still reminds me of what I still may become, that's why he's here. He turned out well. It's painful. And yet, he did. I'm glad. I'm glad somebody did.

"Wanna cigarette?" a man says.

"No thanks, I don't smoke."

"I know how it is," he says, but he doesn't. He's a foul-weather friend. It's a sympathy-instead-of-money act.

The day is fair, the sun shines, I have on my straw hat.

"You had enough money to buy that hat," someone comments.

"No, I had it from before."

What I had before that paid for it was a job. Is it likely someone is going to give me a job, finding me here?

My soul hurts. I'm tired of what I am doing wrong that I don't know I am doing wrong. I land-mined my past, and now I have to walk over those fields whose defenses I thought would save me, and I can't remember where I laid the mines. My refuge was art. I have lived my whole life in devotion to it and could not have lived any other way, but is that devotion now killing me, killing me because the danger is over?—and does art brain me now, because the redoubt of art guards a strait no warship passes or will ever pass again?

I don't have the answer. Not having the answer is tiring and I want to sleep. I have never once taken time out from this work of standing here but if I may permit myself a break I will.

Behind the Doctors Office Building is a mown lawn. I go there and I lie down. I close my eyes. I feel the bumps under my back, the tickle of lawn on my neck, the want of a pillow on the back of my head where it rests on the sturdy earth, a mattress of planet. The plane is overhead. The traffic cellos on. Someone may come and harm me. No. No one will harm me. I usually nap twenty minutes. In a strange place will sleep come?

I wake before I open my eyes. Where am I? In my body. On my back. What's my head lying on? I strive to remember. What direction am I facing and how come what I am lying on is bumpy? Grass. But where? I open my eyes to find out. Now I remember where I am and what has happened to me.

I walk down to the exit ramp.

Orange poppies have come out as they do first thing in the spring. They eye passersby from the embankment. I want to put some in my garden right away. When I come in view of the turnoff, I see a man sitting in my place holding up a cardboard saying: "Please $."

I go up to him. I say, "Hi, how'rya doin'?"

"Makin' change for the road. Livin' on air."

He's a drunkard, not crazy, but a tobacco-stained life, a cantankerous society-is-at-fault type, his face a dissipation for which the world's abuses are its rationale. I condemn him as though condemnation were useful. But I also hunker down on the curb next to him. Got a dark ball-buster cowboy hat, the graying moustache of a man once able with women, and not much chin—a kind of Tabasco personality.

"You know something," I say, "I've been standing here every day for three months. Stood here this morning. I think you're in my place."

"Not today," he says.

"Went for a bathroom break."

"It's not a free country anymore," he says. This however is his resignation speech, and I do not question the logic of it. "How do you do here?" he says packing up.

"I get jobs here," I say, which is not what he meant. "Where ya headed?" I ask.

"Southern California. I has to get to Route 5 to do it, ya see."

"If you are going to LA you just take the first ride south, you don't go over to Route 5."

"There's probably someone at the other exits too." He gets up to go, depressed to give up his rights.

I reach in my pocket and take out a bill, which I check to see isn't a five.

"Nah, you keep it, you need it more than I do—or at least as much," he says.

"It's just money," I say. But he won't take it, and I, not overeager that he should, put the bill back. He goes across the freeway and hitchhikes north, the opposite direction from LA unless you're travelling via the poles.

A young woman drives by with a camera and snaps my picture. It's wounding to be photographed, without my permission. Immediately a second woman does the same. It's wounding. A boy opens his window and squirts me in the face with a pink plastic water pistol. One of my regulars stops and I tell what happened. It could have been a gun, though. No, it couldn't. But that boy's whole life is determined by this act. I don't want him to suffer any more than he has to. I forgive him. Do I? No.

The same black man in the silver Jaguar who has frequently stopped stops. He's small and handsome with a lady-killer moustache and perfect clothes. Again, I praise his beautiful car.

"It's another dependent."

"Well, it suits you," I say.

"Get your real estate license and I'll hire you," but he leaves without telling me his name.

An East Asian man, perhaps Vietnamese, offers me work tomorrow stapling walls. When I call him, the job's canceled.

Two women with kids lean out to tell me to try the Salvation Army Depot: "They have job listings."

I make conversation with everyone I can, networking for all I am worth.

And yet the Inner Brat runs the ship. If I rev up the engine and start for shore, I fall on fetid ports. The Inner Brat does not want me to work or even to network. If I do not honor what The Brat wants as legitimate, then all my good intentions of fair and decent voyages go nowhere.

And yet, how am I to honor you, Brat? What do you starve for? Maybe you have a wisdom I cannot guess at. Maybe you are the nurturer without whom I cannot move.

Meanwhile I am hamstrung.

I stand by the roadside because elsewhere I am nowhere.

I ask the truth to come in dreams, meditation, the chances of life, any way God may give them.

$20.53. 3 hours 20 minutes. $6 an hour.

23 March, Tuesday

I call Briganti's answering machine, always dreading him actually picking up the phone.

"Hello,"

I'm shocked. "Hello, this is the man who worked for you."

"What do you want?"

Are you kidding? "The check you said you sent hasn't come."

"What check?"

I pause. I hold my temper. I speak without irony. "The check was for ninety-one dollars."

"It hasn't come? Well I'll send the check today."

"You'll send the check today?"

"Yeah, I'll mail it today."

"When?"

"I don't know when: today."

"Today then."

"How much is it for?"

Am I hearing correctly? "Ninety-one dollars." I can't believe this. But I do believe, if not from anything he is saying, that I will be paid.

I start on Kate's garden.

24 March, Wednesday

The sun may be shining and my health may be sound, but I sense the irrevocability of my faulty character. I am bleak and mad. Mad as a wolverine is mad being unnecessarily vicious in its murders, mad as ground rats are mad, mad reproducing, mad gobbling up their young. Mad as nature. Fearful and faint-hearted, I still feel the wound of the director's persecution. I should not have put up with it for one minute because it is the sort of thing that does not go away. I could say I will never put up with such treatment again—but God knows I have so vowed before. But I do say I will never put up with it again. At the first sign of disrespectful behavior toward me or anyone I will speak out.

25 March, Thursday

My sister-in-law calls. I outline the prayer plan to her. She shoots it down incontrovertibly.

They're not going to listen to the likes of me.

So I call Kathy. She says that she didn't understand that it involved people sending money and disapprovingly declines.

They think they would be begging. But they don't know the good of begging. How could they.

As I drive up the Appian exit to work at Kate's, I think work will help me forget that I am impotent to help my sister live. I look toward my spot fondly. It is empty of me.

Then, I see a big woman in a red parka standing there holding a sign. She's not small, how come I missed her at first? The green light is on as I drive by, so I can't read her sign.

Later as I drive back I look to see if the woman is still there. No. But yes, there she is! Why do I have a hard time seeing her at first? After all, she's wearing a red parka!

Do I have to fight for my territory again? For this tit of corner is mine, this little gold mine of mine, this eggs-in-the-icebox is mine. The option of staying here forever depends on it being mine eternally. Like a job. Like a sinecure. Like a kingdom.

26 March, Friday

Roadside: $20. 3 hours. Forgot my notepaper. I stand there worthless. From forgetting the paper and from the firing and from the failure of my prayer plan.

Last night I prayed.

When Kathy became ill seven years ago I called one of those sects who would pray for a person—$5, I think it cost. Is this vulgar, is this corny, is this inelegant? Well, let me tell you something: I will do something undignified if it will work, I will do what makes me look like a jackass if it will save her.

So I raise my ass to heaven twice a day, and bow my brow to a none-too-clean carpet and pray for my sister's life. I pray with passion, I pray with tears. I have done so all this time and I say so now because she is not forgotten one day. Oh, she is forgotten, but she is not forgotten one day. I ask God to spare and save her, restore her to perfect health. If God does not do what I ask, I do not mean to disbelieve in Him or curse Him or be angry with Him. My prayers are angry, they are fueled by anger. In my prayers I weep, they are fueled by pain. And fear fuels them. And love fuels them. Don't give me any credit. What I'm interested in is success. I set my prayers down here because they are part of the record. I have prayed every day since I heard, sometimes twice a day. Sometimes I don't.

27 March, Saturday

As I drive to the roadside and turn on Appian, I look to see if the woman in red is there. No, thank God.

I leave the car on Poquito and make my way back down to the exit. Wait, there she is, oh God!

She's a tall, stout, buttery, Scandinavian type. The cold spring air is giddy and wet, yet her head is exposed, her long, bright yellow, once-permed curls bluster about futilely. Because she's a woman I'm careful approaching her; I don't start with an offensive, I don't put down my backpack or set up my signs to preempt her. Rather I keep my distance friendly-like. She doesn't look at me. She keeps facing the traffic with her sign: "Need $ 4 Rent."

"Hi, how are you?"

"Not so hot."

She does not turn to me when I talk to her.

"You know, this is my place."

She does not answer.

"I stand here every day."

Nothing.

"So I think maybe you should leave."

"I got to keep a roof over my kids' heads! I'm going to stand here until I goddamn get my rent."

She's lying, not about the kids, and not about the rent, but about the reason she is here, which her tone claims is tragic but which only has to do with drugs or liquor or men or all three.

"Look, it's my place," I say.

"Look, man, get out of my face," she raises her voice.

"No, you get out of—"

"Get away from me!" she screams. "I'm going to call the police. Get away from me! Get away from me!"

"No one's coming near you."

"Get away from me, don't you come near me!" she screams still facing the traffic and not looking at me.

She's weak but she has a weapon: making a scene. And with it she's won. Because she's a woman she can say a man was attacking her. It doesn't pay to get into a melee with a female, drivers-by would form a bad opinion of me. Unlike Dave, she's unpeaceable.

I leave. I'll see if she's here another day. But today I'm out of my livelihood. I may not get it back.

28 March, Sunday

Posterity if it looks back at all on me will look back not as it does on the Spanish poet Machado, as a person of fine character. "Not as self-serving as Jimenez," the translator Allan Trueblood tells us in *Selected Poems,* "Machado took a quiet course as a teacher of French language and then of Spanish literature, then took a masters in Philosophy under Ortega-y-Gasset." I hear he had no great enthusiasm for teaching and I wonder if teaching had solely economic motives. Since this usually does not serve the soul, I want to think he was not so noble after all and that he too lived the wrong life.

Although what difference does it make if, living in part a wrong life, he still had a fine character? We all in part live a wrong life.

The woman in red is not there.

The first car gives—a masculine, dark-haired, deep-voiced man in his thirties—can I believe what I see pressed into my hand: a $20 bill!

After that the money comes regularly. Mainly from men.

I stand here and feel drained. The sky is mixed clouds and blue. The air cool. I am strong, I do not have to wear a hat, but so what? I feel weak in my prayers to God. That is the way I am today. I stand here, helpless, infantile, a defective character, maybe a fraud, morally exhausted, exhausted in morale.

As I stand here, yes, yes, world, you see me. I stand here as I am. I am Bruce Moody. I have done many things. There have been articles in the *New York Daily News* and the *New York Times* about me and my work and I have also done things of which men would be ashamed and I too have been ashamed of them. This is my life such that this was its outcome and I stand here with it. Yet I feel strong as I stand here saying this, saying it over and over again. To every car going by. What you see is Bruce Moody. I have done all these things and here I am, naked. I stand here and I have a good figure, a slight paunch, a bald spot, a baker's face. I am without work and this has happened to me. I have lived my life like this and in no other way. And I am a man finding it hard to think of God today. Look, cars: I offer all that I am. Just as I would on the stage.

Amazing—suddenly I'm standing tall, inside myself.

I know! I'll offer to help my friends with a play they're putting on. I'm going to leave here right now and call.

I'm back.

They didn't need my services, but to have volunteered was good.

Three in the front seat of a truck. The driver male, two women, one of them sitting next to the window heavyset. This woman fetches through her bag—for me? No, she pulls out a black man's harp comb. She holds it upside down and grooms her long, frizzy auburn tresses cascading onto her broad bosom, grooming just the middle, without looking, with accustomed expertise. It is humorous to see the comb upside down and the odd, automatic passes of her combing. No money from that source, I warrant. The truck moves past quickly. Suddenly the driver holds out a bill.

Two stout black women stop, the passenger admonishing the driver not to give. But this same admonisher, when the driver opens the window, reaches over a card to me.

"Can you say, 'Lord Jesus is my savior'?" she scolds.

I knew it was coming. But I say courteously, "My spiritual life is my own business."

"Can you say, 'Lord Jesus is my savior'?" she demands still holding out the card.

"He is not my guru, but I believe in God and I know you have a kind heart, so I thank you, and God bless you." They soften. Their pitch dissolves. They smile. We are equal. A good exchange. I keep the card.

I wonder where in the Bible Jesus says to hit people over the head with it. For me Jesus is the grass the whole world has walked on since he was born. I'm not a churchgoer, but he's everybody's savior, isn't he? Everybody's, not just Christians'.

A brilliantly polished sedan stops, an older man and his wife in front. He opens the window with no hesitation and hands me money.

"Thank you, God bless you. Do you have any work I can do?"

"No, no," he says in the nicest way, "Your work is right there." Curious that he should so understand, for he is well kept—but also of a generation that knew its young manhood in the Great Depression. I feel moved by his attitude. He lowers the window again as he drives off and says, "Good luck."

When I'm done with the day, I feel good. The money was there, and I think I behaved well with people, and generally they with me. The dark's welcome cloak wraps itself around me. When I count it later I find a ten-dollar bill and a five. $57.01. $18-$19 an hour.

I feel lost without rehearsal to go to. I have no work.

29 March, Monday

The letter of rejection comes from acting school.

I should have been brilliant. Why wasn't I? Being fired from the play, being camera conscious, being poor at the Bay Auditions—are these signs to desist? Or are they signs to persist? Persist, I guess, because the letter says also what I already knew—that I have been accepted to summer school there. I must take out loans. I have less than $300 in that envelope.

I pray for Kathy, I pray for my sister that she may live, and I pray for her because I have been granted nothing else but prayer. My heart is bitter. But I pray. I am full of pride in this, pride in the passion with which I can invest prayer. But being imperfect does not prevent me from praying and I pray mightily.

30 March, Tuesday

Briganti of course won't answer.

"Hello," he says.

"This is Bruce Moody calling about the check."

"Huh?"

"The check for ninety-one dollars, the money you owe me, you promised to send it weeks ago."

"Oh yeah, yeah, sure, I sent it."

"You sent it?"

"Last week it was.

"When?"

"Thursday, I think. Thursday."

"Thursday. This is Tuesday. So it should be here by now." You lied before, you bastard, you're lying now. "All right, I'll see if it comes in the mail today. Goodbye."

If I want money I better get on the roadside. But I don't go. Instead I watch the Oscars. I accept mine, smiling beatifically, saying, "You're very, very welcome."

Afterwards, I light my candle and my incense that God may wholly occupy my atmosphere, that God may wholly be my light, and in the late dark I kneel down and bow my head to the floor and ask that she may live.

31 March, Wednesday

One reason I stand on the roadside is because I have plays and books to write and sell, and to do these things I need a roof over my head. I also had this acting career to start. But what am I standing here for now? Yes, for the rent, but I could drive a bus for that were I not too old for them to hire me. Yet I have no dreams for my life or my work. I go through the motions of practicing an art, sending writing to sell, but for many years now I have not dreamed of success. I deliberately stopped hoping so I would stop being disappointed. I perform success's gesture still, I stir it, I stir as though motion were animation.

I send in loan applications for the summer school tuition.

As I drive up to the roadside, I fear the woman in red is there, but no—is that true? Look again. Good. And once here I feel better. I set my things by the pole. I stand forth. I pray for one and all in their work and I pray for help finding work. Where are you mascot tree?—ah, there, my friend, in a deshabille of mist.

The roadside is every day a page of the weather to read what the heavens are doing: bumbling clouds of rain.

The highway is as always a scene of distant antelope and game, some rising off the vale below to canter to me, some to trot on, but all here passing by. The varying chances once again, the spin, the cast. This is the shore and the tide, and the driftwood rocking up on them, limitations and possibilities, things that are here and things that cannot be here, gulls that cannot fly east because the air is on fire. Water, spray, and the chances of spray—not apples falling in orchards—grit not ice. *This* is the kind of place it is, not *that*.

My thoughts and preoccupations, my moods, seedy, noble, or tedium-rent, my remembering God, my remembering I have forgotten God, my counting the seven eucalyptus trees, all these things breathe like a town I've lived in and taken for granted. The same green coat, the same blue sweater, the same wool shirt. The same cardboard signs as on the day I started, the same backpack propped up on the *Do Not Enter* sign, the same pale brown of the cardboard. The same windshield wiper kicked out of place from yesterday, the same pile of gravel constructed under my arch. All these are good, known, and familiar, part of my safety and home. Home is where you're fed.

My friends arrive in due course: Alvin Blum stops, looks sneakily at me, forces a smile through his bottleneck of supposition. He's in such difficulty. I have provided him with an opportunity too jammed to get through. But I don't feel bad. One must regard all contortionists with compassion lest one add the strangling kink.

And the woman flying by in the old brown Olds. She loves me in brawling laughter. She is beat-up, her car is beat-up, and she hails me as a brother also beat-up. And she's right!

A car pulls onto the dirt, down a bit. The driver beckons. A young man in his early thirties looks up at me from the window. He has a meadow face, a pleasing, browsing sort of face. I stand respectfully. The dark clouds plot noiselessly overhead. Such is our office.

"What sort of work do you do?" he asks.

As usual I don't know how to answer. "I've done a variety of things. I don't want to hold you up by listing them. Is there some particular work you had in mind?"

"No I was just wondering what sort of work you did." He has a nice sensible manner to him. "I mean what brought you here?"

"May I ask why you want to know?"

"I've seen you standing here for a while. You've been on my mind."

He's on the up-and-up, so I tell him all my jobs, my helping start and manage a small company, how I set up my life to write, the magazines my work appeared in, TV advertising in New York, my not being able to find a job, Brendan Moon.

We get along, and it's clear that something in our conversation satisfies him.

He needs someone to manage a coffee shop, he has already opened one in Orinda and is scouting locations.

"You know, I don't drink coffee, so I don't think I'd be a good salesman. I used to be addicted to it, now the smell of it makes me nauseous."

I ask him how he started out in life and so he tells me about his landscaping business. He got into it through his father who is thinking of selling the business but might could do with a good manager instead. It's gardening and it's outdoors. "Course that might take away from writing," he says. "Can I ask you something? How do you get the backing for a play once you've written it?"

"I send it to a friend, who sends it to a friend, and so on, so we hope."

As we talk he takes bills out of his wallet and hands them to me (It's $13, I find out later). The money is to pay me for the time I have spent occupied in his thoughts. "I thought you were an educated person," he says closing our conversation. "I'm usually a good judge of character."

"You're right, I am. Where did you go?"

"I never went. I'm a self-made man."

"So am I," I say.

He gives me his name, Paul Deere, and his father's card and drives away. We like one another.

Two cars roll up, side by side like chargers, each containing two teenage East Asian boys, and I can tell what their business is at once: each is out to maraud the steppe. The driver of the middle lane opens his window and talks to the one in my lane. They rev their steeds and let them back off, rev, back off. Their business is to be at the starting gate. It's unlikely they have money or work for me, and I turn my attention from them. The driver of the middle lane calls, "Wanna dollar?" and I say, "Yes, I certainly would," and hop over. "Thank you. God bless you."

In a black 4-wheel-drive a nice-looking, deep-voiced man in a beautiful pale purple corduroy shirt hands me money, and when I ask if he has any work, says, "I don't now, but I hope this helps you."

A man stops down the way. I approach cautiously. His window doesn't work so he opens his car door. He's inept, out of shape, a fish in a tree, but very alive. He hands me money through the open door.

An old, white Dodge van blasts its horn as a car veers over into my lane. From it a woman with white hair beckons me. She hands me a hot meat sandwich on a roll wrapped in cellophane. "It isn't much," she says.

"Oh, it's lovely. Thank you for your generosity."

I'm always surprised by the giving, and that surprise rejoices my heart. I pig the sandwich on the spot.

A woman hands out a box of Stone Ground Wheat Thins as she drives by. "They're the greatest," she throws back into the air.

A middle-aged man reaches out a bill and in contact and encouragement, squeezes my fingers as he hands it to me. My hand and heart reaches after him, but he's gone, the next car upon me.

In a pickup in the middle lane, a man with an orange face beckons me with a bill out his window and when I ask if he has any work says, "That's okay, at least you're trying."

A piercing tenor from a dirty, blue van in the far lane calls, "You dickhead motherfucker!" I raise my hand in peace. "You motherfucker!" he calls as he drives around the bend. I do not take it on.

"Here's for all the calls you made to Will in Sonoma," says a good-looking man I don't recognize. "I been thinking about you." He hands me $5.

"Oh, yes! Hello!" Will, the man who had trees to clear from his backyard. I had kept checking back because he had told me to. "What happened?"

"Got my cousin to help do it."

"Well, maybe next time."

Nice that he gave me money. But the astonishing and blessèd thing is that he takes upon himself the responsibility of a relationship with me. And many people are present in their relations with me here, for I am not a ship passed once in the night but one passed, over and over, in the day.

It begins to rain heavily. Wind blows up. The money stops fast, people close their windows, don't want to get their arms wet. I become The Other. But I stay; that's my job. The telephone may not be ringing, but I keep office hours.

"Keep yourself dry now," a woman says as she gives me coins.

And there!—the handsome guy in the fiery black truck waves back at me as he turns in the far lane as usual.

At 5:31 I sense there will be no more money, still I must stay till 6:31.

At 6:31 exactly a woman stops on Appian behind me and hands me a gift certificate to a supermarket, saying she has seen me here and hopes this helps. I leave, content in the wet dark.

When I get home I sort the money into the yellow envelopes. How am I going to make that tuition? I can barely make my rent. I had Grand Plans. Whether I can get to the roadside earlier and more often, I do not know.

My energy is heavy and dull. I've lost sight of something. But the roadside is the bright spot in my life, the one place I am happy. No. The roadside's the best place to think of God when I forget to, the place I have nothing to do but that.

1 April, Thursday

I call Paul Deere's father about managing his landscape business, but Paul has not told his father of me, and he doesn't know what I'm talking about.

I call Briganti.

Sahid, an East Indian man calls about my digging up his backyard. I make an appointment to do it.

The broad world I have no vision of. There's an antelope running around the Earth from continent to continent and I have no vision of its ebullience or of the Earth's roundness. When I sit here to record, I record nothing but the persons. I keep my bargain, but the story of the journey of my soul I do not take the time to map. I am afraid to know it.

Some days you can hold the sunshine on the redwood tree outside my window in the palm of your hand, a dry, pale green. The multifarious needles, the fly moving on the window glass two stories up, and beyond: the pale of the sky the same pale of the river.

The universe is a bowl I forget to drink from.

However, I like my concern for survival by the roadside. We're in winter still. I like the dry brown leaves of earning in my hands.

The woman in red, is she there? No, she's not there, but make sure, Bruce, look again, no, not there. Then, as I turn the corner and look back, goddamn it, there she is, standing there with her smashed hair, right where I was looking, why couldn't I see her?

I'm scared of another war with her—battlements red in the sunset, helmeted knights and soldiers gathered below. What'll I do? Well, maybe God means me to find another place.

I drive to Hilltop but I have to stand on the left for drivers to hand money to me and all the cars turn right. I try Appian north-bound. Brendan said north-bounds never work and he's right. Okay, try the Redwood turnoff in Sonoma, it has a light, it's southbound. But I'm scared. But because I am scared, I go.

I cross the river to a shady, narrow two-lane. At once a black man carrying a black sports bag walks down the exit ramp to the freeway and stops. Is he going to set up a sign here too? He doesn't. He waits. My body is filled with dread. Calm down, Bruce, invite God in. I'm jammed with disorder, I can't think of God.

On the first stop a woman gives me a dollar. But most of the cars turn right, not as many cars as Appian. I feel fear as physical pain, can hardly stand it, but I'm supposed to stay here until 6:30 because I said I would, the rent is due, I don't know if I'll make it, there-may-be-no-more-roof-over-my-head-tomorrow.

I wait an hour and a half. No money.

Eventually the friends of the black man pick him up.

Immediately a man stops before me. "How long have you been out of work?"

A police car pulls up behind him.

"Almost a year. Since April 4 last year."

He hands me bills, maybe five, the light changes and he drives off, and as the police car passes the policeman says, "Find another place."

"Can I talk to you?" I ask as he drives on.

"No," he says into his dust.

I walk back to my car. The castle is in ruins. Soldiers lie on their faces, awkward on the stones, awkward on the dead crenelations. I drive back to my old spot on Appian.

I don't see the woman in red. I park down below, walk to my exit. No, she's not there. And she's not going to be there either because if she'd taken a bathroom break she'd have been back by now.

I set up, relieved. Security is the familiarity of a place that feeds you. I like standing here. She will never come again. Why do I know that? The battlefield is green again, those battlements, chargers, as though they never were, red war never was.

Today is April Fools' Day and I have a notion of giving some passerby a dollar. A fine-looking woman hands me money. "How'rya doin'?" she says.

"Not so bad. How're you?"

"Well, I know what you're going through," she says. "A year ago my life was really bad also. I had no work, I was down to rock bottom. But now things are much better." She gives me her card, it says she does oil portraits.

We talk on. We like one another: she's commonsensical. As the cars start I ask for permission to call her, which she grants. Romance—who knows?

An older black man with his wife give me money. I say "Thank you. Do you have any work I can do?" And he says, "That's all right, as long as God blesses me." He's reminding me I haven't said "God bless you!" "Oh, I do bless you!" I say to apologize.

The Pinole police drive up, "Hi," he says. In this county the police don't move you on.

Alvin Blum drives up, same business: he nods self-consciously, a little embarrassed, a little angry. He thought his spare change would solve the problem of my whole life and I would have flown these mendicant shores.

A grand piano sized man calls, "Hey, ya wanna move a grand piano?"

Nobody wants to move a grand piano. "Sure. When?"

"But I gotta look for a friend first to see if it's happening. If I don't find him I'll come back for ya. I don't have much money for ya, though." He drives off. I hope he doesn't come back. Odd: I'd do it for a friend for free, but for money I am reluctant.

I wish everyone a happy April Fools' Day, though.

A woman with no teeth in a great big old gray Thunderbird, cries, "Here, here!" holds out bills, coins. Ordinarily, this is a face I would look away from, a lost face, yet I am equal with this face in its spry delight at being with me in this cause.

Four black boys bopping around inside a gray car. I never bopped around in a car as a teen. But these boys are okay and actually give me money! And keep on bopping.

Third car down. They're nineteen, she's in shorts, her bare feet on the dashboard, and she's as pretty as he is. They're not concerned with me, they're wrapped up in themselves, they're in love, full of the early juice of it. When alone they take one another's clothes off, delectable button by button, and eat one another like fresh-plucked plums. They give, naturally, two green apples.

In the drizzle that moves into and out of the winds that push the sun around, the traffic is easy. I feel the pitch of being here at the base of my lungs. There's a roadside place in me, near my diaphragm, which is this place. It has been here since the very day I started, the being-here-by-the-side-of-the-road.

A man down there holds money out his window. I run down to get it. Backing up to thank him and to keep other givers in sight, I see a woman over there waving money. I skedaddle through the cars and take it. "Yoo-hoo!" the woman in front of her. Ebullient gotta-be-quick larks of cars, "Hey," someone shouts, it's catching—the boy in that car reaching over his mother's lap. "Thank you, God bless you." "Hey over here!" the cars are starting. And as it passes, a woman from way down at the end of the line sweeps a bill into my hand as she takes the turn, one hand on the wheel, the other touching mine.

$7 in all. Six in one stop. What fun!

"Do you have a family?" asks the middle-aged woman in the white 4-wheel-drive.

"My family is grown and I'm divorced."

"Is that a smile of happiness?" she asks.

I give her my phone number for yard work.

I'm dog tired, why?—I've been standing here only two and a half hours. What to do? Taking a break would look bad, it's not proper to lounge on the job. But I can't stand up any more. I've got to sit. Either sit or leave, and it's not worth leaving and coming back. Try it. I sit on the curb.

Oh. Resting's not such a terrible thing. I thought it would be forbidden. But it takes only a moment to revive. I get up and stand comfortably the rest of the day.

Then I feel the need to pee. Being out in the sun and standing, the need to pee has never been imperative, and I have never before left to do that. I'm also inclined never to take a break. But actually it's unbusinesslike to stand here jumping out of my britches, it looks bad, so I leave. I come back to the roadside and clock in: 5:30. I will now just rest here standing.

Behind me on Appian Way, "Hellooo! Sirrr!"

I turn. I go to the car and look down in the passenger window. I see a wonderful baby sitting in its back seat carrier with Raggedy Andy orange hair. Neither parent has this hair-to-rule-the-world. A sweet young couple, they look poor, hold out a bag and some bills around a soda container. "We don't have any work for you," says the wife.

"Oh, that's all right. Thank you anyhow. I don't drink soda," I say, "so you can have that for yourselves, thank you so much."

As I stand here I notice that each time I say, "Thank you, God bless you," I do so because someone gave me something. But I resolve now to bless as distinct from receiving. Blessing's not a gift of deserving, it's a gift of God. Just as I am given money for no reason so also must I bless for no reason. Thus to give blessing for free. "Bless you" does not make me a priest and I do not have to be a priest to give blessing. And the one I give it to does not have to be in difficulty. Let blessings fall upon the joyous. Let them fall upon trees and stones. Let the air be blessed, the blue of the air.

Yes. When someone gives me money, the money has not caused the blessing, the money simply accompanies the blessing like two actors walking onto the stage together. Why is that? Bless You washes not just the feet of the poor; it washes the feet of everyone. Bless You washes the feet.

The unwitting reason we, the poor, give blessings is that blessings may always be given, and the poor are still not too poor to give the greatest gift in God's world: "God bless you."

I have learned to say "God bless you."

Yes, this is a strange good fortune, but there it is. I have learned to say "God Bless You," and I have learned that blessings are free. Alms is just a reminder that we live in the available midst of them.

Last night, a lively black beggar in Berkeley who I give money to, tells me the difference between being poor and being po'. Being "poor" means you have a job and food for the family and place to live, but you barely scrape by. Being "po'" means no roof, no income, no food. I have learned that being po' is the better place in that the po' are the ones who may say "God bless you" without appearing odd. We think we cannot say "God bless you" to the toll-taker, the checkout girl, the postman. What if I said it to everyone? The word "good-bye" is a run-together version of "God be with you."

"Thank you. God bless you"—I could say it to everyone, why not?

The sun goes down in the drivers' eyes and there is not much money. But I have been fortunate. Before I go, though, I want to give away an April Fools' dollar to a driver and time's almost up. Not a woman though—she might think I'm accosting her. Three minutes to go. A man stops in the middle lane with his window open. I hold out the bill, "Would you take it?" His face registers bafflement. "It's April Fools' Day and I want to give a dollar to a driver."

I toss it into his lap so he can't give it back. He laughs and accepts it and I laugh too.

The day is over. The cold night is smack on the backs of my hands, but the cold night is warm because I've earned enough to pay my way. I've stood here and done it, I haven't done nothing. I haven't done an odd job either and I haven't started up a career. But I've taken my survival into my own hands. The gorilla plucking tasty leaves is me plucking bills.

I drive down to the shopping center for staples. It's winter-black in the lot, bright over there in the supermarket. When I have done in the supermarket, I walk out into the cold, black air. I walk by the dim cemetery stones of the cars of the parking lot.

"Sir?" A voice behind me.

A young woman in a supermarket apron stands there. She's in her early twenties, short, dark. She has followed me out. I am a tall man with a good deal of presence, I am told, so I am sensible of the situation in which she finds herself.

"Are you buying food for your family?" She has a quiet manner.

"I beg your pardon?" I have to ask twice more before I can grasp her meaning. "Oh, I'm sorry, no, just for myself. My family is grown and gone, and I am divorced," which is a lot of information but I want to reassure her. "Why do you ask?"

"Because I've seen you on the road, and I want to give you some money."

"Oh, thank you."

She extracts a bill from a snap coin purse.

"Thank you. God bless you."

Having fulfilled her promise to herself, without a word further she turns and goes back into the supermarket.

In the cold lot I stand in the ink of human good. Good is black, as black as this night, as filled with strangeness. Good is unaccountable, taciturn. Good is cold. Her entire behavior with me was, from beginning to end, economical. She did not wait for thanks, she did not expect gratitude, she expected nothing. The dark is cold, it is inky as oil, impenetrable. It is black. It is good.

In the gas station the cashier also seems to recognize me. He mutters something.

"What did you say?"

"I didn't say anything."

But he did. When I come back and ask for a receipt he seems of the opinion that I am a fraud—that I should not own a car, even a thirty-year-old one. A fraud. Am I a fraud?

2¹/₂ hours. $61.37. $15 in the summer school envelope.

7 April, Wednesday

I finish Kate Piersanti's garden. Kate, blessèd lady, has paid me $15 an hour, better than the going rate, and says not a word about what she hopes I do with the money. What she's doing is giving me a boost over the wall. She's not going to have further chores, but she's paid me enough money to put an ad in the paper, if I want, to do gardening and odd jobs.

We wish one another well. "Kate, remember the time I left my red checkbook here by mistake? You know, when I got home, I found a ten-dollar bill tucked into it that I didn't remember putting there. Could that by chance have been you?"

She laughs and says no more.

8 April, Thursday

By now I was supposed to be famous.

Famous for what?

For my sorrow.

Oh, but there's so much competition, no wonder you couldn't make it.

Famous for my significance, then. Everything I wrote would have this aura.

What would be the subject?

Subject? I would just write. I didn't really care about things outside myself. I was the subject—unlike Tolstoy, that other Virgo. Actually I wrote about people I loved, because I wanted every one else to love them too. I didn't want to be Tolstoy. Tolstoy did that.

9 April, Good Friday

I place an ad in the *West County Times* to do yard work and odd jobs. It costs $90. I'm scared it'll be a waste of money and the piker in me hates to spend it. But work out-of-doors would be healthy, and would not conflict with my schooling.

I call to see when the loans will come through.

It is Good Friday. I remember sweet Easter hymns I used to sing as a boy. To start the day I sing them to myself as I stand on the roadside. "Welcome, happy morning, age to age shall say . . ."

At the end, a quarter to four, Easter is forgotten, and I think, "Well, there'll be just one more." It comes in the form of a bag held out of the window by an East Asian man. A big loaf of white bread, franks, margarine, and nice fat oranges. I expected money, but got this instead, good.

When people give, it is not lightly. Everyone goes through some kind of spiritual consultation with themselves beforehand, the benefit of which is that the spiritual energy of their prayer, long or short, comes right along their arm into the fingers holding the bill, and through that bill into mine.

I stay no longer than four. The lady in the beat-up old brown Olds, the man in the fiery truck, Alvin Blum—none of them came by today. It's a holiday. Good Friday! They're workday friends.

I walk up the hill satisfied. I turn right into Poquito, the three-house cul-de-sac where I park.

A black car drives in behind me, the man driving shouts, "So you have a car! I've been watching you! You've got a gimmick!" He circles me in the cul-de-sac. He's stalked me. He's elected himself my judge. And what does he mean, a "gimmick?" I'm frightened. I've got to change his mind. I don't know where to start.

"What do you mean, a 'gimmick?'" He still circles so I have to keep turning.

"A gimmick! I know your type!" He keeps circling me, he doesn't want to be cornered, he wants to circle me like hyena. I keep walking next to his circling car, but I don't know where to meet him, he's talking through his hat and he's also got an attitude and where can I meet him?

"You've got a gimmick!" he says. "You've got a car!"

"No one says I can't have a car."

"You say you're homeless. You're not homeless. I've got your number!"

"I'm not homeless, I'm destitute." I walk after him as he circles like a bull with a matador, but which of us is the bull, which the matador?

"Why aren't you on welfare?"

"Welfare is for unwed mothers."

"I'm going to report you!"

"Talk to me."

"Yeah, I see you: you've got a gimmick!"

"What gimmick? I don't know what you're talking about."

"Hah—you think you're smart!" Oh, he has the vigilante bead on me, all right. "I've seen you. I've kept my eyes on you. I'm going to report you to the police!"

It's exasperating to try for a meeting of the minds with someone who has made up his mind. Such people make themselves enemies all by themselves. I turn my back on him and walk to my car. "Fine. Do so."

He drives off meaningfully. I feel abused, beaten, and full of dread. All I can hope is that he will get over it, realize that talking to the police is only going to show his mean-spiritedness. As I will work for food or dollars and therefore am not a false advertiser, he may find out the police are not concerned with me. "I do not cheat anybody," I say to the police in my head as I drive down the freeway. "There are people poorer than I am, but how do you measure these things?"

I'm weltering in fantasy, which will not prepare me for an interrogation should one come.

Thus a satisfactory day ends in fear because of a bigoted busybody.

11 April, Easter Sunday

I wake at 4:15 full of dread. I do not pray or meditate. Instead I eat. To avoid it.

Now I stand on the roadside in great pain. I say my blessings to the widespread cars, I look at my mascot tree, but still I hurt. I have not known such pain since the first day I came here. I cannot breathe. Yes, I can, but with such pain. I cannot think, I'll think of God.

I cannot think of God.

My eyes wince closed. Why should I hurt?

Because I have avoided something I should do?

I don't know what to do. I've only been here a half an hour. I've never left before except that one time to see Brendan Moon.

But the pain has got to be a sign to leave. Isn't it? It's like wanting to go to the bathroom, a pain not necessary to endure, a pain that says, "Relieve me!" I am bent back in the sunlight with it. The drivers-by can see me in it. They can see my mouth open with it. They can see my eyes closed. I am in violation of the place. Being on this cross is not proper, not proper for the people passing by. Out of consideration for them I should go.

So I do.

Half an hour: 3:30—4:00. $0.

24 April, Saturday

The loans for summer acting school are denied. I withdraw my application.

25 April, Sunday

I call Kathy to see how she's doing; she's doing okay.

But it isn't enough just never to have abandoned her. I want her to have *proof* she's not abandoned. I write her a funny picture postcard every day but Sunday.

26 April, Monday

Two weeks since I have been on the roadside—and I must register it and that it may be that I am to be there no longer.

Because of the imagination of Kate Piersanti I got a grubstake and I do gardening now. Oh, I earned the money, Kate, I know, but I also know your generosity and the unstated motive behind it. She was larger than my situation. She saw me. My prejudice about Mormons drives off in BMWs. And so did my prejudice about BMWs, for I took careful tally, and six of them also gave.

So I'm making the rent and saving as before. I have had to work seven days a week to stay afloat, which makes me hard-pressed to write—but today I write all day, since a big hedge canceled.

I like earning my own living. It feels good and it's good for me. Gardening is hard work, but I am steady and reliable and I ask only $10 an hour, which is no more than a single person needs to live in the Bay Area. I also am willing to paint the fence, put up the trellis, fix the plumbing, clear out the attic. I have never done any of this before. I just case the job, figure it out, and do it. There may be people who can do it better, but here I am, and people are grateful. The daily fear of not making the rent is gone without a trace.

However, I fear old age in time may prevent me from gardening. Even now I'm too tired to write when day is done. And of course, there's no future in gardening, I am not going anywhere, which is of course the great virtue of it: I no longer have to live for that dreadful thing, the future.

27 April, Monday

"Maddy, a woman who saw me at the Bay Area Auditions called me to audition for *Harvey*. What should I do?"

"What I would do, Bruce, is get back on the horse that threw me."

I am reluctant.

I take *Harvey* out of the library. It's a very good play. I want the little role of the cabdriver at the end. But I am asked to read one of the leading roles, Doctor Chumley, and I am offered it. Against my better judgement I accept it. Again I want to be better than anyone, to be brilliant, new, different, electrifying, profound, in fact an artistic big shot.

I read in James Wyly's *The Phallic Quest* that the purpose of the god Priapus is to deflate the ego and make the male be impotent to reinflate it.

Humiliation, such as I have undergone in being fired, lies in the search for the authentic self. I have been brought down to hell by being fired, and I have been raised up from hell by the roadside, from which I also was fired. Humiliate is a word like exhume, humble, humus, all referring to the earth, the ground. To be humble is no more and no less than to be on the ground, and standing on the roadside I stood on the ground. But humility is not a sinecure: you don't earn it like a diploma, but like a salary, daily. I paraphrase Wyly: The phallos that has been split off from the psyche cannot succeed. At the point of failure, one simply tries another doomed cycle. Or one abandons the quest altogether. Submitting to humiliation is the price of liberation. Humiliation is to be turned to dirt. I had to be turned to dirt before I could stand on the ground. Humility is the highest state known to man. It is to be no more and no less than oneself.

I have not achieved it, but I had a glimpse of it on the roadside, and God will still force me down if I try to jump it. All my life I have feared the humble as humdrum. I lived in my princedom, but I was a prince who loved only some of his subjects. I am still that way.

So the issue in playing in *Harvey* is not my fabulous artistic career. What matters is always to be on the roadside. That I hear God means no more than that I hear God. It does not mean I will become renowned for it, rich, or holy. And the same is true of acting. Acting does not mean I will live forever in the glory of men's hearts. Ordinary men hear God. It is sane to hear God. It is normal. It is available to everyone. And I am like everyone in this.

I start acting again. God has sent me a gate.

1 May, Saturday

This evening, having cut down the two trees that last years' frost had killed, I stood outside. I counted the things I had done today: all promises kept.

And now in the evening I get down on the living room floor to learn Chumley. So why is acting worth it? Because in all this gathering of gear and calculating the slope and setting up for the unforeseen, there is a risk into life that is supreme.

5 May, Wednesday

I call Annie Hallatt regarding Briganti. "I'd like to set fire to his house, slash his tires."

"No," she says. "The only satisfaction is the money. Do you know the name of the people you worked for?"

"No, but I know where they live."

"Can you go out there and tell them the story? If he finds there are repercussions to his acts, he may cough up."

9 May, Sunday

I drive to the house in Moraga.

The door opens and I recognize the lady of the house, and the moment she opens it the man of the house appears around the side.

"I'm sorry to bother you. I don't know if you remember me, but I worked with Briganti on the retaining wall by your pool."

I tell them the whole story. "I wanted to tell you because, as a person on the side of the road, I don't have any recourse—"

"That has nothing to do with it," says the man quietly. "You should be paid. Do we have his number?"

"Yes," says his wife.

"We'll call him," he says.

"Thank you. I'm very grateful." My hand on my heart I bow to them.

18 May, Tuesday

I pick up the ringing phone.

"This is Briganti."

I stop breathing. "Oh?"

"So I owe you some money," he says, fear-courtesy in his voice.

"Yes."

"Okay, how much do I owe you?"

You insanely stupid jerk. "Ninety-one dollars," I say with the "insanely stupid jerk." left out.

"Okay, I have it for you."

"When?"

"Right now."

"How?"

"You can come over here and pick it up."

"Are you going to be there?"

"Yes."

"When?"

"I'll tack it to the door."

"Cash?"

"A check."

"If I leave now, I'll find it tacked to the door?"

"It'll be there."

"For ninety-one dollars?"

"*Yes!* You coming over?"

"Yes."

"When?"

"Is it going to be there?"

"Yeah, it's here. It's already made out."

"I'll be over."

Am I to believe him? I think I'll go later, just to spite him. But no. With this character, the money, as Annie says, is the only satisfaction.

He lives in a beat-up old stucco down an old ranch road. I park on the street below. I walk up through the trees. The place is threateningly quiet, no sign of life. Maybe he's got me over here to beat me up. Through the oversweet shade of the trees, I walk up onto the porch. One Sunday I drove over to get him to pay but there was no answer, so I already know his doorbell doesn't work. Nailed to the jamb is the envelope I gave him all that time ago. A check is in it, but not for ninety-one dollars. He has deducted withholding he is never going to pay to the IRS. I knock hard on the door. And again. Nothing. I'm sure he's in. No I'm not. His truck sits there. I slash the tires?—who me?—how could you suspect me of even imagining such a thing!

At night I finally reach him. He says withholding deductions for independent contractors is the law. A parakeet knows more about the law than he. I let it go. A thief is someone who must know he has cheated someone out of something.

22 May, Saturday

I drive to Moraga to thank the couple for calling Briganti. They never called him, they forgot. He must have sniffed it in the air.

25 May Tuesday

All these years, I had, through fear, tried to stand still. And when I got on the roadside and had to, I saw there is no such thing as standing still: one either integrates or disintegrates. I had disintegrated. For my notions kept me in place. Salvation comes in owning a little red pickup. Salvation comes in having a job that lasts. I learn salvation does not stand still. A job, love, a roof over my head? Only God holds out The Palm Of Salvation, and if I can align myself with God, I'll know what it is to rest in the hand of that sole security. And I have known it.

30 May, Sunday

I fall in love with Rumi and fall in love with myself. I hear Gieseking play and fall in love with myself. Gieseking touching keys touches Gieseking, and I am in love. To remember God is to fall in love with one's own life—Life—that annunciation. . . .

Harvey opens and I get good notices.

Arthur Miller's *Incident at Vichy* is casting. I get it from the library and know exactly how to play Prince Von Berg. When I arrive for the audition I am in costume, I speak with an Austrian accent from the time I walk in the door to the time I leave. They think I *am* an Austrian aristocrat.

I play Undershaft in *Major Barbara,* Hamm in *Endgame,* Polonius, Lady Bracknell. I appear in a one-man show, *The Education of Betty Grable,* which I write. I appear in Shakespeare festivals. I'm in movies, commercials. I play many parts, most of them large, some of them paying.

Over and over again Clint Eastwood appeared on the roadside—and why? Although I was too dumb to get it at the time, he was my guardian angel, my psychopomp, my guide out of hell, his very presence whispering in my ear: "Acting is a money-making proposition for you, bub: there's a living in it." He was the figure out of archetypical mind of which the Hagalaz rune spoke at the beginning. And why Clint Eastwood in particular? Because he is the highest paid movie star in the world and I needed income, and because he is an action hero, and action, a gate to move through, is what my soul had asked for. Take action, act, and you will get money. That still is his message.

We idolize movie stars because in real life there are no great men. Eastwood may have committed various so-called cultural crimes, but I have come to see something heroic in him. Not in his roles, nor as an actor, but as a human still trying. He is not perfect. Heroes are not perfect. Indeed they carry their defect before us. But they stand their ground and stick to their guns. Not stretching his instrument but exploring its limitations, he stood there all these years, steadfastly, and became an artist. This ripened him and ripened him and gave him the probity of long endurance. This perseverance standing in place by the bare roadside of his work makes him and makes him and makes him an actor, this imperfect artist whom greatness begins to surround and who holds up his sign and means it: "Will Work For Food Or $."

What has happened to me in relation to Eastwood? Just this: condemnation lifted. It is not that acting is not important enough to merit a severe sentence, it is rather that he himself chose a life sentence, so why should I condemn him; if I condemn him, he cannot get better, just as, if I condone him, he cannot get better. And neither can I.

As I place myself next to him, I see forty years of experience in him, and I'm too old to attain that and without that I may not ripen. On the other hand, art is a realm with its own pure laws—which is to say laws particular to the individual.

When I saw him standing next to me on the roadside, he never came to discourage me. But I still feel the force-field of an accomplishment standing next to no such possible accomplishment in myself. Of course, he has his skills, propensities, and defects, and I have mine. I know that for me as an actor I don't have a line of goods, as he does, and it's good for an actor to have one. There is no haven in art for me, there is only walking through the woods of it from inn to inn, night tree to tree. I have only the roles I walk toward. I don't know how to play any of them before I arrive at them, I only know I can. When I started, I did not realize that I set myself the task of challenging the intensity of my own limitations. Now, for me acting is no longer a question of fame or money or even excellence. I only know that now within me opens door after door after door.

Last night I dreamed Marlon Brando jumped from a window to his death.

Today I visit a psychic at a public forum and I recite my dream. The psychic asks what my relations to Brando are.

"He is the greatest actor of my time: The Holder Of The Truth. I have given up acting for a time to finish writing a book, which if I did not finish, I could not live with myself."

"In a dream, the great actor dies," concludes the psychic, "and you cannot live with yourself until you finish this book."

I fail to see the connection.

A man in the back calls out: "Maybe what has died is a standard for great acting outside yourself."

In November I go to Rochester with my daughter Amanda. I have not seen Kathy in many years. It's wonderful to feel in her presence that I love her in just the way I do, to remember how well suited, what good company we are to one another. She lies in a hospital bed at home, she is full of tubes, but I don't think she's going to die and neither does Amanda, and neither does she.

I sleep on a couch in an adjoining area and at three in the morning I rise and go to where she lies sleepless and I massage her in the dark, her feet, her thin shoulders. I caress her hands, her arms. For a long time. Standing behind her, I hold her head, my own head bowed, breathing. The hour of three is a terrible hour, the hour of death, and we both are awake to greet it. My hands are soothing to her, and she sleeps.

Once home, I write to Kathy's husband, Gerry LaMarsh, to offer him my friendship should he need anything. Each time I call I get good news from the girls and from Kathy about her progress. I set fear aside and become hopeful. I write her every day. I pray for her.

I left the roadside Easter Sunday. A year later, on Good Friday, which is also April Fools' Day, Kathy dies. The year has been given over to her. I go through all the vales and hills, or at least many of them, incurrent on a long and therefore one hopes not final illness. I have never passed through them before. I do not learn how wasted she is until the last two months. I have not seen her since November. I only had news of a wishful optimism, which I believed and which kept me going and kept us all going.

The spring after her death I am asked to tour in a play. I dedicate my performance to her, and it happens to close in Cincinnati, which is near Rochester, the day before her memorial service.

The church is not quite as big as a cathedral but it is large and it is full. At the end I stand reaching out my hand to hundreds of strangers, those who love Kathy's daughters and her husband and her. My hand is out very much as it was on the roadside. But this time, just as once it was given to, so it now gives. I learn there is no end to what it can give.

When I return to California, Gerry LaMarsh and I talk on the phone. He says, "They asked me whether it felt like this would go on forever," meaning taking care of Kathy, giving the injections, sitting by her bed, stroking the ringless hand remaining to her seventy-five-pound body. "I said to them, 'That would be wonderful. I'd be glad to do it forever.'"

And he meant it.

But it was not so ordained.

He behaved so beautifully toward my sister. They had a good marriage and they both knew it. She died, him watching her. He held her during all that long illness with care and calm and humor.

What an honorable man.

I go to Brendan Moon's woodland camp to find him. His things were still there but not he. A year and a half later, I pass him in the spot I first met him, I reach out of the car and shake his hand. I have to drive on but I'll stop when I have time to see what's become of him. Later the freeway's widening takes away his spot, and I come upon him on a traffic island. "Not so much money as there used to be," he tells me. I should tell him there needs to be a code for how long you stay. Not looking at the money you're given is good, but staying there too long is looking at the money you're given.

The life of the roadside taught me and still teaches me, though I have left it. I think it will teach me all my life. Whatever the reverse of progressive disease is, the roadside is to me. It is under my skin, in my cells. It is one of the good fortunes of my life that holds my soul. Its investiture is subtle, positive, regular, unaccountable.

What was the transaction?

Nameless. But what can be named I also may learn by. I mark many occasions where I attacked, rejected, banished hope. The virtue of that is the avoidance of inflation and collapse. But I see that, as is often the case with those who think they have taken care to stop hoping, I had set myself upon a quest and placed myself in a situation that would have been meaningless if hope were truly gone. For, if in its most still form, hope was there. I did not know what would happen, or if anything would. I knew nothing would if I did not persevere, and so, with no sense of hope, expectation, outcome, I proceeded as though something would, if only I were awake enough to notice it. Hope's a human quality. I shall not be prejudiced against it now any more than I would be prejudiced against sneezing.

Another aspect of my life that came to my notice there was the inner machinery of my greed, superstition, prejudice. As I have lived my life, before and since, I have opposed and fought all three. Yet on the roadside I found I was a vessel of all three. Prejudice, superstition, greed pre-existed in me and rose automatically in me. So I now allow them and such like a place in me. I fight prejudice on the one hand, and on the other prejudice resides inside me, I do not practice bigotry outwardly, I oppose it, but it is in me nonetheless. Such acceptance is a leading gift of the roadside. Would it be better if bigotry had left me entirely? No, it would not be better because it would not be real. It would not be better because what the roadside has given me, through accepting my bigotry, greed, and superstition, is a slightly wider breadth of acceptance of everything. I stood in one place but in the broad out of doors and opened myself to a thousand thousand. To accept what they had, what they did, the way they were, what I was.

The roadside is not a story with a happy ending; it is a record of a happy beginning.

Because of the roadside I now act on the stage and now seem to be in demand and could work without stop from one year end to the other, and sometimes do. I go from part to part; I earn a living at it.

As to acting itself, daring is not the issue, bravado is never in the heart. Courage is the issue. I need to exercise the courage to fight for my own life. And for me the fight consists of taking myself to the arena. And once there, to try for what I cannot promise.

As to *Catherine of Aragon,* I realize that, while I should not have been fired, my attack on the role was fatally conscientious, my research overloaded me. I spent more time reading about Wolsey than actually exploring his task in the play. Also, my attitude toward the play was contemptuous, and in future I hope I foil the temptation to work in plays I do not respect. Eventually, I am hired back by the very theater that fired me.

As to writing, I believe I will always write. I believe I will help save the trees. Everything that I would love to do I believe I will do in this lifetime. Being on the roadside has given me the chance to stand still and see that.

I have left the roadside forever. I will never go back. Or at least I don't think so. It was a bark that drifted where I stood and into which I stepped from a disappearing shore, which saved me for a time, and which I think has gone and will not come my way again.

Sometimes I think how I never said good-bye to it but left one day, not knowing it was my last. I think of standing there once more to see how my dear roadside looks, greet the mascot tree, the laughing lady in the old, brown Olds, Alvin Blum who couldn't give the second dollar, the guy in the fiery pickup.

But I won't.

I am not ashamed of it any more. I tell my daughter and others, and the more I tell it the less ashamed I grow. I learn to lay bricks, I clean someone's house, I garden, I learn something about horticulture. People usually want me back, but sometimes they don't. Gardening is good exercise. If not a calling, it's honorable work. And so was the roadside. I'll remember it always as a good time.

It was a time when, as never before, I thought of God and God came. God tickled my spirit. God washed me, and I knew this not viewing a waterfall but being under one. The gun of life was to my temple, and God smiled his sweetest smile on me.

People behaved impeccably toward me one after another until there were thousands. Those who gave, those who didn't, all who passed—they there, I here. If I needed in my life a time to correct a time when life treated me badly, the roadside was that time, a period to wash away grudges, resentments, longstanding blames, such that never could I say again that never in my life had people treated me well. People treated me impeccably.

And so, since that day and every day, I hope, for as long as I live, so as to remember those who were with me there, I say when I kneel, "And God bless Angelo," just as he asked me to.

Thank You

It was my original ambition to include in this book mention of everyone who gave, but it proved impossible. There was not the space, and I had not been able to record everyone. To those who gave to me, in your absence, you are thanked now, and remembered now. As is everyone who ever gave to a beggar from the beginning of time and forever more. A kind thought, a sawbuck, a wave. A "Good luck!", a chat, a job. A meal, a smile, a blessing. Thank you with all my heart.

Acknowledgments
Thank You
Dan Arnold, Bryan Boe, Ruth Blakeney, Robert Chapla,
Larry Distasi, Roxanne Dubay, Maddy Fluhr, Patricia Forman,
Ben Gleason, Jean Guillot, Robyn Heisey, Mary Holbrook,
Jan Johnson, Lucine Kasbarian, Gerry LaMarsh, Ned Leavitt,
Linda Lee, Amanda Moody, Jay Noller, Denise Piersanti,
Jill Rogers, Adele Slaughter, Britta Steiner